A SHOWER of STARS

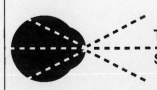

This Large Print Book carries the
Seal of Approval of N.A.V.H.

A
SHOWER
of STARS

The Medal of Honor
and the 27th Maine

John J. Pullen

G.K. Hall & Co. • Thorndike, Maine

Published in 1999 by arrangement with The Balkin Agency.

G.K. Hall Large Print American History Series.

The text of this Large Print edition is unabridged.
Other aspects of the book may vary from the original edition.

Set in 16 pt. Plantin by Minnie B. Raven.

Printed in the United States on permanent paper.

Library of Congress Cataloging-in-Publication Data

Pullen, John J.
    A shower of stars : the Medal of Honor and the 27th Maine /
by John J. Pullen.
        p. cm.
    Originally published: Philadelphia : Lippincott, 1966.
    Includes bibliographical references.
    ISBN 0-7838-8757-4 (lg. print : hc : alk. paper)
    1. Medal of Honor.   2. United States. Army. Maine Infantry
Regiment, 27th (1862–1863)   I. Title.
UB433.P8   1999
    355.1´342—dc21   99-41064

To Jean
1911–1982

Contents

Preface

The reader will keep in mind, I hope, that this book has been published as it was written just prior to 1966, and a few things were different then. You will read, for example, that a first class letter was mailed for five cents. The main purpose of this preface is to alert you to sections upon which the passage of thirty years has cast a new light. First, however, is an observation about Civil War literature in general.

When the centennial observances of the war were taking place in the 1960s, many people thought that interest in its literature would flare up during the commemorative period and then die. Instead, the interest seems to have continued and increased, particularly in the last quarter of this century. Ken Burns's nine-part television series *The Civil War*, along with the film *Gettysburg* and other such productions, has undoubtedly contributed much to this advance.

As a result, there has been a great outpouring of Civil War books, including unit histories written by survivors and reprinted, and those by modern authors. To the best of my knowledge, however, there is no book in print, except the one you are holding, about the youthful but heroic 32nd Maine Regiment, which fought itself out of existence, or the 27th Maine and its strange involvement in the history of the Medal of Honor. Therefore, this book really tells the story of the medal itself, from Civil War days to the present.

Now, as for some of the things that have changed, previous figures have been updated. On the first page of the text it is indicated that there were fewer than 300 living Medal of Honor recipients in 1966. I have since been informed by the Congressional Medal of Honor Society, the association of recipients, that as of August 23, 1996, the recipients numbered fewer than 200, or to be more precise, 174.

Also, as of August 23, 3,420 Medals of Honor had been awarded. Totals among the services are 2,355 to the Army, 745 to the Navy, 294 to the Marine Corps, 16 to the Air Force, and 1 to the Coast Guard. More than half of the awards since 1941 have been posthumous.

Another interesting change occurred in the story of Dr. Mary E. Walker. Since 1966 it has taken a strange twist. Dr. Walker was awarded a Medal of Honor in 1866 for her service in the Civil War as a contract surgeon. In 1916, however, her name was stricken from the Medal of Honor list by the review board (refer to Chapter Eight). Dr. Walker refused to return the medal and wore it every day until her death in 1919. In 1977, the Secretary of the Army, on recommendation of the Army Board of Correction of Military Records, reinstated her Medal of Honor, and in 1982 the United States Postal Service issued a stamp commemorating Dr. Walker.

On a different note, Elwin C. Tobey of Eliot, Maine, introduced in Chapter One as a veteran of severe World War II combat, died on March 5,1987. He and I corresponded until his death. I derived great enjoyment from his letters, and believe you will enjoy his presence in these pages.

Also in the first chapter, you will read about research difficulties I encountered in writing this book because in 1966 Maine had no central archives. Its records were scattered in haphazard repositories all over the state capital, Augusta. I remember looking at 27th Maine records in a barracks-like National Guard building a mile or so from the capitol.

Today, however, the state's records have been gathered and are readily available in a beautiful new building which also houses the Maine State Library and the Maine State Museum. Combining these three facilities has made the building a Civil War researcher's paradise. In the Maine State Archives, records have not only been gathered together, but they have been categorized and grouped in such a way that information, with the help of expert staff, is easy to find. In particular, the regimental records, in their completeness and organization, are unsurpassed in the nation. From the archives the researcher has to walk only a few steps to the museum to find an extensive collection of flags and other Civil War items. The museum is currently conducting a "Save Maine's Colors" campaign to restore the flags and banners that are now in fragile condition. The library, a few steps farther, makes available thousands of books and other nonarchival materials bearing upon the Civil War, as well as numerous other subjects.

Last among the changes, the Medal of Honor Grove mentioned in Chapter Nine has now become an impressive reality. It was planned in 1966 by the Freedoms Foundation at Valley Forge, Pennsylvania. The Medal of Honor Grove, located on fifty-two wooded acres, is equally divided among the fifty states, Puerto Rico, and the District of Columbia. The focal point of each area is a seven-foot obelisk modeled after the Washington Monument. The name, rank, and unit of each medal recipient, along with the place and date of the action that earned the award, is engraved on a marker placed beside a living tree.

Of special interest on the grounds of the Grove is the Henry Knox Building, which houses archives, photographs of several Medal of Honor recipients, and a display showing the evolution of the medal designs, dating from its original authorization by Congress in 1861 to the present. Added to the many historical attractions in the Valley Forge area, this unusual memorial grove is well worth a visit.

A Maine Mystery

Of all the medals issued by the United States Government there is one which has a somber glory all its own — a luster tinged with the shadow of death — for its recipients in most cases have confronted what a soldier once called the King of Terrors and have either survived or perished while exemplifying the word it bears upon its face, VALOR.

It is the Medal of Honor, sometimes called the Congressional Medal of Honor.

Since 1941 this decoration has been more often awarded to dead than to living men. Fewer than 300 men so honored are alive at this writing. And yet quite apart from the efforts and sacrifices of heroes, it is almost a miracle that the Medal of Honor has arrived at its present status as a sacred symbol of courage in action. During the more than 100 years of its existence its integrity has survived almost as many perils as have the men who wear it. And none of these adventures has been stranger or more shrouded in silence than the one which involved the 27th Regiment Infantry, Maine Volunteers.

While working on a previous book, *The Twentieth Maine*, the author of this narrative came across a peculiar bit of information according to which *several hundred* Medals of Honor had been issued to the men of just one regiment, the 27th Maine.

This provoked a certain amount of wonder. The men of the outstanding 20th Maine, which had saved the left of the Union line on the second day of Gettysburg and performed other feats of valor in the course of the war, received four of these decorations, which represented a remarkable achievement. Could there have been another Maine regiment that so far surpassed them in bravery as to earn *hundreds?* It didn't seem likely. On the other hand, if such a large award had been made for no substantial reason, would not so extensive a distribution have practically destroyed the meaning of the Medal of Honor?

According to the official Medal of Honor list covering the period from 1863, when the medal was first issued, to 1963 — during which time some 29,000,000 people served in the armed forces — there were only 3,170 awards, approximately. So it seemed certain that an issue of several hundred Medals of Honor to one regiment must have attracted a great deal of attention.

Yet the general literature of the Civil War revealed nothing on the subject of these medals and very little concerning the 27th Maine. There was a brief account of the regiment's service in the printed report of the Maine Adjutant General for the year 1863, written after the muster-out of the 27th Maine by its commander, Colonel Mark F. Wentworth.

There was another brief account in the report for the year 1866. Neither made any mention of Medals of Honor, and this was strange because Adjutant General John L. Hodsdon had stated that he wanted to afford the "due meed of praise for every person participating in it [the war], however humble his position."

The bestowal of a great number of Medals of Honor would certainly have been a meed of praise deserving of record. As for Colonel Wentworth, why hadn't he chosen to mention the medals in writing his report? Most commanding officers were quick to take all the credit coming to their regiments and in some instances a great deal more, with the result that *War of the Rebellion . . . Official Records of the Union and Confederate Armies* — that bible of Civil War students — needs to be read, in places, with the same understanding allowances that are made for the Deuteronomic historians who, in their after-action reports, trumpeted down the walls of Jericho and made the sun stand still during a battle.

Another fact which was apparent from the Maine Adjutant General's reports was that the 27th Maine, unlike many regiments which were recruited from widely separated localities, all came from one compact region of Maine. The 27th came from York County. At the southern-most tip of Maine, York is a county of beaches, ledges and numerous islands where it fronts the

15

breakers of the Atlantic, and of forests and rolling farmlands as it reaches inland. Vacationers know it as the county of Wells, Kennebunk, Ogunquit and other towns famous as summer resorts — readers of historical fiction as the country of Kenneth Roberts' *Arundel*. Several other eminent authors have also written about York County, so it does not lack for a literature of its own, and it did not seem possible that hundreds of Medals of Honor could have been dropped into this well-written-about little corner of Maine without creating a few ripples. Yet that is precisely what seemed to have happened. It was as though the medals had sunk into one of Maine's deep, pine-bordered coves, leaving not even a bubble on the surface.

It might be supposed that this mystery could have been cleared up by going to the official archives of Maine; but alas, Maine had no central archives when the search that will be recorded in these pages was under way. A few individual departments had kept certain historical records in order and available to researchers, but there was no central housing or control of archives. Happily, steps to remedy this deplorable lack are now being taken. A state archivist, authorized by the 1965 legislature, is at work and the voters are being asked (in November, 1966) to approve a bond issue for erecting a large building to house the state archives, museum, and library. But in the past the state's records have been stored in all sorts of out-of-the-way places — in sprawling warehouses, long-unused military barracks, an old powder magazine, even in an abandoned elevator shaft. The situation was one to discourage historical investigation; even if the searcher could get at the records, he might shuffle papers for years without coming across the desired information.

The question of the medals was put out of mind for five or six years, but like one of those senseless tunes or phrases that come back to iterate themselves endlessly in the middle of the night, it wouldn't stay out.

Quietude might also have been found in the thought that, at this late date, it would be impossible to unearth any significant facts since all the veterans of the 27th Maine as well as most of their children have long since departed this life. And yet after an extensive investigation involving another Maine regiment, the 20th, it was perfectly apparent that this argument was false. As if to compensate for the lack of a state repository over these many years, the people of Maine do maintain in their — it might be said — collective attic a record-keeping institution of considerable excellence. Part of the reason has to do with their saving disposition and part with architecture. Many Maine families are still living in large houses, with big attics, sheds and barns which provide for accumulated family belongings of generations. Elsewhere the passing of this commodious kind of living quarters — and their replacement by development-style houses where there is no room for books, let alone old papers — is making terrible inroads on the nation's historical resources. But Maine is still a great place for the pack rat, and in Maine the attic is still an institution which has only a few natural enemies such as leaky roofs, chimney fires and small boys who go up into the attic to play on rainy days. (Small boys have carried away, thrown away and beaten up more history than the Goths and the Vandals; they have within them almost all the instincts of pure barbarism, and civilization has suffered enormously from their not having been soundly thrashed at sufficiently frequent intervals and told to let things alone.)

In addition to that stored in the attic-archives there is also a great deal of information in the state which has been remembered and passed on from generation to generation. Maine is no Levittown, and there are in many communities descendants of families who have lived there for 100, 200 or even 300 years.

What is the best way to delve into this storehouse?

It is not to wander into a town and start asking questions. Using this method, you may discover that getting information out of Maine people is more difficult, even, than getting money out of them. And this is a matter not of parsimony but of prudence. The reasoning goes about like this: You can give a man a dollar and all he can do is spend that same dollar. But give him information, and God only knows what he will do with it;

one thing is sure — it will not be spent in the same shape and form as that in which he received it. So your Maine attic-archivist or informant will certainly want to know who you are and what you want the information *for*. Lacking this assurance, which is difficult to convey in a brief interview, he is likely to be an expert at politely not telling you what you wish to know. Then there is also the matter of mood. "If he feels like telling you he will, and if he don't he wun't," is the way one potential informant was described. The word "wun't" designates a particular sort of Maine stubbornness which sometimes goes away in a day or so. But if you don't happen to be there on the right day, you won't get the information you are looking for.

The best way to launch such an investigation is to write to people, explaining who you are, what you want to know and what you want to know *for*, enclosing a return envelope with a stamp on it. Most will reply, when they get around to it, out of natural courtesy, or because if a man has spent five cents to get a reply it is considered that he ought to have it.

Having learned this lesson with *The Twentieth Maine*, once the compiler of these notes decided to look into the affair of the 27th Maine — at least on a tentative basis — the letter-writing method was chosen. The object was to reach descendants of the 27th Maine soldiers and to determine what they knew about the medals. How is it possible to write to descendants of soldiers who have been dead for decades? Part of the answer is found in the previously mentioned series of records published by the Maine Adjutant General in Civil War days. These printed reports list — regiment by regiment — the name, age, rank, home town, marital status and the date of mustering in and out of every Maine man who served in the Civil War. The rest of the answer relates to the Maine postmaster or postmistress, who is an important source of intelligence in the smaller Maine towns and villages particularly. Proposals to close down the fourth-class post offices should properly be regarded with horror; they are important communications centers of which the mail is only a part; they are friendly meeting places not only in the community but as between the Federal Government and the people; and the lowering of their flags would be an unmitigated disaster. It is only one of the virtues of the Maine post office that the intelligence which may flow through it is not only current but historical, for the chances are that the holder of the post office would not be holding it unless his or her family had been living in the town long enough to establish a reputation for being reliable, which could be quite a while. Also, in nearly every Maine town there is someone, always known to the postmaster, who keeps track of things — not only things of the present, but of the past. And if certain residents have gone "outside" or "downriver" or "away," this central intelligence keeps track of where they have gone.

For Maine is not just a place on the map; it has more extensive boundaries in the geography of the heart. Thus, through the Maine postmaster and acquaintances there is often available an effective zip code into the past.

As a tentative first step into an investigation of the 27th Maine, the men on the Adjutant General's roster of the regiment were separated into groups according to the towns from which they had enlisted. These lists were then mailed to the postmasters of the indicated towns with a request to send, if they would, the names of any descendants still living in that vicinity or anywhere else that they knew of.

Soon, as expected, names and addresses of descendants of 27th Maine soldiers began to arrive, from postmasters or from people to whom they had handed the request.

The next step was to run off on a duplicating machine copies of a standard inquiry. This called attention to the Medals of Honor supposedly awarded to the men of the 27th Maine, explained that the object was historical research and asked if the recipient would kindly provide information of any letters, diaries or recollections that had descended to him. It also inquired as to the present whereabouts of the Medal of Honor which presumably someone in the family would possess. And of course stamped envelopes were enclosed.

This may seem like a naïve method of research, which indeed it is. The author has had no scholarly training as a historian and has been forced by want of wisdom to use what might be called the Bumblebee Method. This simply consists of starting somewhere (almost anywhere will do), letting one thing lead to another and thus bumbling about in ever-widening circles of understanding.

With some embarrassment the method was once described to Dr. Roy F. Nichols, a truly distinguished historical writer. Dr. Nichols, whether out of politeness or some similar experience, said that it was probably as good a method as any.

However, it does make for a lack of control that leads to many shocks and surprises.

People whom you have unknowingly energized fly off on unexpected tangents.

Once the process has been set in motion, the operator of the machine becomes its victim. He may wish to turn it off, but it can't be stopped. He may wish to escape — to forget about the whole thing. There is no escape. Dozens of people are now working with him, urging him on. These even include people, no longer alive, who have worked on the problem before and who have explored paths that cry to be followed further.

Also, characters from the past, such as in this case Buffalo Bill and Theodore Roosevelt, originally not suspected of having had any connection with the activities in question, come galloping out of the mist in a way that is often disconcerting.

And most surprising of all in the Bumblebee Method — what is at first believed to be the center of the whirling scrawl of delineation may in the end prove not to have been the center at all.

So it turned out in this case. For what happened to the 27th Maine medals was — to a very large degree — the story of the Congressional Medal of Honor itself from 1862 to 1966.

The story emerged slowly. After the first swarm of letters went out to descendants, old residents and so forth, nothing very satisfactory happened for a while. Letters came back, many of them written in quavery hands denoting the advanced ages of the authors, and these people were interested and provided all sorts of incidental information about the soldiers who were the subjects of the inquiry, even including the assertion that one had been born out of wedlock. But initially and for several weeks no one reported having a Medal of Honor or even having heard of its being awarded to the grandfather or great-grandfather in question. And this was completely astonishing, considering the number that had supposedly been issued. (It was also significant, although the significance could not be perceived at the time.)

As these early returns were studied, the thought kept recurring that the whole thing was a mistake and no such medals had ever been awarded. But within a couple of months letters began to arrive indicating that *some* of the 27th

Maine soldiers at least had received the medals, and their families still had them. And there was no question but that the medals were Medals of Honor; descriptions and sketches sent with the letters clearly identified them as Medals of Honor of the Civil War design.

This correspondence also began to reveal glimpses of some of the 27th Maine veterans. Margaret Soule of West Buxton wrote about her grandfather, Captain Joseph F. Warren, commander of Company C.:

As a child I went with my grandfather to the Grand Army memorial services at Buxton Lower Corner in which he always took part. The old soldiers formed a line and marched through the large cemetery decorating the graves of their dead. I remember that I was very proud of him so tall and straight. Grandfather died March 26, 1917. The last service we attended was May 30, 1916. I always kept the little program of that year. The poem on the back was as follows:

The little green tents where the soldiers sleep
And the sunbeams play and the women weep
Are covered with flowers today.
And between the tents walk the weary few
Who were young and stalwart in sixty-two
When they went to the war away . . .

And there were other stanzas in that sentimental vein, just the right sort of poem for that sadly beautiful day in May which was always important as long as veterans of the Civil War were alive. (Something must be said for the emotional impact of a war which, more than 50 years after the last shot, has whole communities turning out and marching in memory of their dead.)

Margaret Soule remembered that after the ceremonies were over, her mother always invited the veterans of the 27th Maine to come back home with Captain Warren and take lemonade on the lawn of the big old house in West Buxton. She also remembered that Captain Warren had one of the medals, but she didn't know what had become of it. He had, however, left a diary, and she would copy and send me portions of it. Further, she recalled that one of the old soldiers who was usually present at the lemonade lawn party was George H. Libby, who had served under Captain Warren in Company C. She believed that George Libby's medal was still in the possession of his son, R. J. Libby of Fredonia, New York. This proved to be the case. A letter from Mr. Libby disclosed that he not only had the medal, but a diary as well, which he, too, would copy for me. And he would also send some personal recollections, for he had attended reunions of the 27th Maine as a small boy.

A letter addressed to Alvin W. Curtiss, a grandson of William W. Keays of the 27th Maine, was not answered for several months. This was explained when the reply finally arrived:

I live in a big house which Mr. Keays built for himself in 1886. As neither he nor my mother ever threw anything away, you can imagine the collection of stuff in my attic. That is the reason I have taken so long to answer your letter. I have been looking through the accumulation to see what I could find that might be of interest to you.

The search was worth waiting for; he had found a war journal written by a company commander of the 27th Maine.

Apparently not only attics were explored, but that secondary repository in the big old Maine house, the bureau drawer, which is a sort of miniature attic, or in more abstract terms, a materialized human memory with some of the marks of a disordered mind. Typically, one of these might contain a tied bundle of Butterick Printed Dress Patterns, a bag of brightly colored wool left over from knitting an afghan, a box of .30-30 cartridges, a copy of *The Authentic Life of President McKinley*, a tangle of used ribbons from Christmas packages, a collection of dried wild flowers, a doorknob, a stereoscope view of Horticultural Hall at the Philadelphia Centennial Exposition of 1876, garments of babies who have long since grown up, a winding key to a clock that has ceased to tick and, down underneath it all somewhere, possibly a Medal of Honor in an old black morocco case or a letter from a soldier which might add a bit of needed information.

26

And so it went, with various people digging through attics and drawers and bits and pieces being added to a growing jigsaw puzzle pattern. To say that these people were kind and cooperative would be an understatement indeed. However, the most remarkable ally of all was enlisted in the following manner.

A lady in Kittery wrote advising me to get in touch with one E. C. Tobey who, she said, lived in the adjoining town of Eliot. Mr. Tobey was described as being keenly interested in history, genealogy and the like. I addressed an inquiry to Tobey and he replied with a cautious, short letter, which I promptly answered. A correspondence began. It developed that E. C. Tobey had been interested in the 27th Maine medals before — in fact, had been haunted by them; he had asked hundreds of questions about this affair, had lain awake at night thinking about it, and now he was delighted to discover someone with a kindred interest. Thus stimulated, he began his investigations anew, and it was soon apparent that in Tobey I had unleashed a whirlwind. Tobey was soon dispatching letters to me at the rate of one or two a week. Up until this point it would have been possible, and possibly prudent, to abandon the whole thing. But once Tobey was set loose, there was no turning back. His enthusiasm carried everything forward; his unwearying diligence sustained the whole project; to relinquish the pursuit after that would have seemed to be a deplorable breach of faith.

It is proper to state in passing that Tobey's reaction was exemplary of what was one of the most remarkable aspects of the investigation as it continued over a period of more than four years: the way in which people contributed time and energy with selfless motives, and the fascination which the Medal of Honor apparently has for so many. In fact, this medal seems to have about it an aura, a mystique, which transcends its official purpose as a military decoration. Perhaps in the workings of the subconscious there are still unbreakable threads which tie us to the days when the presence of heroes often meant the difference between life and death for the tribe, and accordingly so great a symbol of heroism is an object of affection and awe.

E. C. Tobey believed that the central figure in the mystery would turn out to be Mark F. Wentworth, colonel of the 27th Maine, who had lived in Kittery and practiced medicine there until his death in 1897. Other letters contained clues pointing in the same direction. One stated that at one time a shoebox full of medals had been found on the old Wentworth place; another said that this was a "pail full" of medals; and a third passed along a rumor to the effect that at one time Colonel Wentworth had had a barrel full of medals in his possession.

One of Tobey's first letters contained a sketch of the house where Wentworth had lived. Unfortunately, Wentworth had left practically no personal records behind, as far as could be discovered. It would be necessary to cast a wider net, and to piece many bits of information together. The letter enclosing the sketch was followed by one containing a map, putting the Wentworth house into relationship with several others. Other maps followed, radiating outward from the former home of Colonel Wentworth and indicating places where 27th Maine soldiers had lived — many marked as "only a cellar-hole now" — and graves where they were buried. For example, the map of the locality in which E. C. Tobey himself lived, Tobey's Corner in Eliot, had such detailed notations as "Sam Tobey built house in 1800 . . . Sam Dixon's house (fell in) . . . X marks spot where Edmund Dixon's brother killed by lightning . . ." and so on.

Mr. Tobey's technique was to begin his inquiries in the vicinity of the soldier's former home or his grave, using information from the headstone if any was available, and to forage outward in ever-widening circles. His reports were dispatched to me in hurried scrawls on sheets of blue-lined paper, writing-tablet size. He visited remote sections and traveled back-country roads where men of the 27th Maine had once lived. (*"Now everything silent. Bushes crowd out the fields. The old maple falling down. Only thing left a few memories."*) He found graves in out-of-the-way places. (*"— is buried under a juniper in a big field"* . . . *"I think I have discovered the grave of — in a pile of rocks near the old No. 1 School."*) Of places, and particularly of houses, he noted the smallest details. (*"One window trim is full of bird shot where someone fired at the second story window."*)

And sometimes his reports were seasoned with comments on characters he encountered. Thus, a wild man: *"Long white whiskers and lives in a camp so small half of him at a time lays down to sleep. I've only seen him once. He just fades into the woods."* A man to be watched: *"Any business dealings with him wind up with not enough of your shirt to flag a hand car with."* A suspiciously pious man: *"He sits up too straight in church to suit me."*

It is difficult to correspond with someone without forming a mental picture of him. I began to visualize E. C. Tobey as a small, wiry man of about 55 years of age, wearing a cap, steel-rimmed spectacles, and riding rapidly around York County on a bicycle, snapping up odd bits of information — an impression that later proved to be wholly erroneous. However, certain other impressions proved to be correct. For example, it appeared from the outset that Tobey was of a hypercritical turn of mind when it came to evaluating the information he obtained from certain local residents. But it further appeared that the Tobey family had been living in this corner of Maine for more than 300 years, so that if the grandfather of Informant X, say, had been a congenital liar, that deficiency would be known, as it would also be known if the hereditary weakness had been passed on to Informant X himself.

Before Mr. Tobey had been at work long, he

had found a very respectable number of letters and diaries written by soldiers of the 27th Maine. These he copied, sending a few hand-written sheets at a time.

Tobey had also begun to report the existence and locations of medals. One, he said, was in the hands of a lawyer in Kittery, Francis F. Neal. A letter was written to Mr. Neal. He replied, saying that this was a medal someone had given to him; the inscription on the back was *The Congress to George W. Wakefield, Co. 1, 27th Me. Vols.*; the decoration had been through a fire and had lost its ribbon and brooch; only the metal parts remained. However, the object had excited his curiosity. He had been on the lookout for other medals and had been wondering about them for 15 years. As our correspondence continued, it became apparent that Neal, too, was being drawn into the toils.

One morning early in the week, at about 6:30 a.m. the telephone rang and I stumbled out of bed to answer it. Someone was speaking in a Maine accent. It was Lawyer Neal, who, as I learned later (in fact I was learning it just then), often gets up and goes to his office early in order to have an untroubled hour or so of meditation. He had been thinking about this business of the medals, and one of the thoughts that had occurred to him was that perhaps I might like to come up to Kittery, where he and Tobey would introduce me around and show me the lay of the land.

Needing only the flimsiest of excuses for returning to my native state, I told him that I would be at his office in Kittery on Saturday morning at 9:30.

This was late in March. The temperature at the Philadelphia airport on Friday afternoon was 62 degrees. But as Maine goes, Philadelphia is often a semi-tropical city. At Boston the temperature stood at 41. The air freshened and got colder as the trip continued northward from Boston by bus. On the highway up through Massachusetts, the light faded and the sky in the west began to take on a luminous, salmon-pink glow. The signs along the roadway burst into a neon magnificence — green, saffron, lavender, ruby, indigo, other earthly and unearthly colors proclaiming Bottled Liquors, Pancake Houses, Plaid Stamps, Drive-in Banks, Lobster Pools, Pizza Palaces, Dunkin Doughnuts, Moccasins and Motels. In contrast, off to the right the sky deepened and darkened to the tone of thunder as though reflecting the presence of the rolling North Atlantic, which is never far away along this road; seemingly it might if it would surge in at any time and quench the illuminations that man the great doughnut maker has set too close to its shores.

The remnants of daylight disappeared; so did the neon lights as the bus entered upon the turnpike passing through wooded country where the trees, even by their silhouettes against a sprinkling of stars, could be seen to be lower, sharper and more angular than those left behind on the thick, rich soil of Pennsylvania.

Obliging relatives near Portsmouth, New Hampshire, provided lodgings for the night and a supper which included clam chowder made as God-fearing people make it, with milk, potatoes and onions — a satisfying reminder of being now safely beyond the reach of criminal restaurateurs to the southward who put tomatoes and carrots in a clam chowder, to the further damnation of their already irretrievably lost souls.

The next morning found me in a borrowed car driving through Portsmouth and out upon the old Memorial Bridge leading across the Piscataqua River to Kittery and Maine. (The river marks the boundary here.) The crossing of this river is always a splendid moment. In imagination if not in fact the salt-marsh sea smell begins and a man starts to think of what he will have for lunch: another chowder perhaps, or a cold boiled lobster topped off with a hot Indian pudding. On this particular morning the harbor was at low tide, and sea gulls were cruising and crying along the shores. Off to the right across Portsmouth Harbor the buildings of the Portsmouth Naval Base loomed above the water, and it must be noted in passing that this base is not in New Hampshire, as its name might indicate. Calling it the Portsmouth Naval Base was considered to be a high-handed outrage by the people of Maine; its island foundations are within the geographical limits of Kittery and Maine, and to this day certain Maine newspapers make a point of referring to it as the Kittery Navy Yard, three altogether different words.

Yet although it sits beside this great harbor — as I was reminded when I arrived and parked in front of Lawyer Neal's office — Kittery has an old, sea-weathered individuality all its own. Rather than a port village, it resembles the downtown section of many coastal towns in Maine, with a post office, town hall, library, a few stores and office buildings. Although the authorities in the state capital would deny this, Maine tends to think of Kittery as attached to New Hampshire because of its proximity to and involvement with the naval base. New Hampshire, on the other hand, thinks of it as part of Maine. Kittery, in psychological terms at least, is thus left as a sort of principality, and as I was to learn later in the day, Mark F. Wentworth, former colonel of the 27th Maine, had at one time been one of its princely rulers.

Francis F. Neal, who presently appeared, proved to be a man in his early 40's, clad in a Navy jacket for Saturday dress, about six feet three inches in height, with the build, quick energy and something of the features of an amiable football tackle. We conversed in his office a few minutes, and he showed me the Medal of Honor which had come into his possession. He thought that someone had once tossed it into a wastebasket and thus it had gone through an incinerator.

We then drove together to East Eliot and into the yard of E. C. Tobey's house, but Tobey did not appear to be around. While Neal was searching for him back of the house and elsewhere, I sat in the car and surveyed the premises. As I looked around I reflected that I may have been mistaken about the mode of transportation I had imagined for Tobey. There was no bicycle parked in the yard; instead there was a bulldozer, a truck, and an old Buick, and beyond the house a small fire engine. The explanation for the engine was not discovered that day, since there is no conversation in the world that can tactfully be brought around to the question: "What is that fire engine doing in your back yard?" I was privately advised by Mr. Neal later on that the fire department was located in South Eliot, the people in East Eliot complained of lack of protection, Tobey got mixed up in the dispute, and when the town would do nothing about it, Tobey bought his own fire truck.

I turned my attention to some papers and letters bearing upon the 27th Maine which I had on the seat of the car, and while I was studying these it seemed as though a twig had snapped, although there were no twigs around to snap. There had actually been no sound whatever, but when I looked up a man was standing about five feet from the car. He was a tall, muscular man, about Neal's age or a little younger, clad in the fashion of Maine men who are out of doors a good deal, in a red-and-black checkered woodsman's jacket, flannel shirt, work trousers and high boots. He had close-cropped hair, a ruddy wind-burned face and eyes that looked upon the world with a disposition to be friendly combined with considerable wariness.

Since this rugged character did not fit my image of a genealogist or historical researcher (where were his glasses?) I was moved to speak inquiringly:

"Tobey?"

That's who it was.

Tobey was reserved, though friendly, as he had been in his original correspondence. Not on that day or the next, but over the ensuing several months I was able to glean bits of information about him which served to explain his driving interest in the 27th Maine Medals of Honor.

Tobey had seen rough service in World War II. He had entered the Army in 1943 and had served with Troop F, 7th Cavalry Regiment, 1st Cavalry Division in the Pacific. Troop F, in other days, had been one of the five troops of the 7th Cavalry that had been massacred with Custer at the Little Big Horn, and it must have appeared to Tobey that this murderous tradition continued in World War II. At the age of 19 he was in a landing craft going in for the first wave of the attack on Leyte. He once said, "How many are left from that boat would be hard to find out. I know some without eyes, without arms and without legs. Now and then I get a letter from a buddy written with his left hand. His right didn't come home with him. Another had both eyes shot out. I went out to New York State to see him. When he asked about the rest, I could hardly tell him."

In the course of the fighting on Leyte he had been trapped under fire in the jungle with a small group of men. Frank Neal attributes his escape to the fact that Tobey had spent or misspent much of his youth in Maine prowling around in the woods with a rifle, so that he was half Indian by the time he joined the Army. Tobey recalled that of the men who went into the New Guinea campaign with Troop F, only a few came out whole at the end of the war.

Later, also, I was to realize that Tobey is that odd mixture, which you will often find in this country, of the veteran who realizes with wry acceptance that the hardships and sacrifices of the combat soldier are rarely comprehended and soon forgotten but whose patriotism has somehow grown deeper and stronger because of his war experiences. On Memorial Day he toured the cemeteries to make sure that all soldiers' graves were marked with flags — much in the same way, it may be imagined, as members of the G.A.R. used to do. He raised an angry protest when a community "name board" listing people who had served in World War II fell over and was thrown into a garage. (The years and the weather are now having their effect on these wooden structures erected in so many New England towns and villages during and after World War II, and very few, it is safe to say, will ever be replaced with the sort of stone monuments which were erected on innumerable village greens as an aftermath of the Great Rebellion. The author, whose own name is on one of these boards in a small Maine town, must confess to an envy of the Civil War veterans. As for our generation, alas! Our names are writ in cellulose.)

The foregoing does much to explain Tobey's interest in the Medal of Honor. Anything that concerned veterans would be likely to concern him; they were his buddies no matter what war they had been in. And then, too, he was a historian — not in any academic sense, but as one who felt and saw the traces of history around him every day.

This part of Maine is surpassed in antiquity by very few places in the United States. Kittery was incorporated in 1647, but English people were exploring, trading and fishing up and down the coast of Maine long before that. One Maine settlement under English government antedated the landing of the Pilgrims at Plymouth Rock by 13 years. As for wars, men of York County had fought in five of them prior to the Revolution when the Indians and French were perpetrating their deviltries. These now-peaceful fields and woods have been in the distant past the scenes of enough bloodshed and violence to supply TV producers for a century if the Old West should ever run dry as a source of these entertainments.

And all this was very close to Tobey. It was not

on a page of a history book but "over back of Dad's barn" where the Indians had captured So-and-so and carried him off to Canada. As we drove about later in the day he would be saying, "See that grove? That's where some of my folks got killed." Or "See that house? It was being moved on the day Lincoln was shot. When the movers heard the news they unhooked the horses and left the house right in the road. Out of reverence for Lincoln . . ."

Tobey, as was the case with a great many people in the vicinity, worked "on the Yard," and when not doing that he worked as a logger and millman. (This explained some of the equipment around his house.) At that time the future of the Navy Yard was a matter of concern. Founded in 1800, the Navy Yard — where the *Kearsarge* and other famous ships were built — had been the chief economic mainstay of the region as well as adjacent parts of New Hampshire for more than a century and a half. It was currently reported to be employing 7,500 persons with an annual payroll of around $60,000,000. The closing of the Yard over a period of ten years would be announced by the Defense Department in November, 1964, and although this announcement was still in the future already there were premonitions that the Yard was going down, and one of Tobey's comments was significant: "If Wentworth was alive, he'd never let this happen." Wentworth had been gone for 65 years, and yet echoes of his influence still remained in York County.

Since Wentworth appeared to be a key figure in the story of the 27th Maine, it became important to learn as much as possible about him. Gathering the various pieces of information was not, of course, all accomplished on the first visit; the process was to take several months, but many of the bits and fragments which spoke of his life — the newspaper clippings, personal memories, pages of books, old pictures and so on — seem best assembled as a collage against the background of that early spring day in Kittery.

The bare facts of the record are impressive. Wentworth came of the oldest colonial stock; he was a lineal descendant of Elder William Wentworth, who had come to this country in 1640. Born on a farm in Kittery in 1820, young Mark at the age of 12 saw his prospects for an education blighted when his father died. But he pushed forward resolutely, working on the farm in summer, going to the local school and academy in winter, "toughing it out," as the saying goes in Maine. On the same pattern, scratching a living out of the rocky soil in the warm weather and teaching school in the cold, he worked for five years until he had laid up enough money to study medicine — first with a doctor in southern Maine, then at Dartmouth and later at the University of Pennsylvania, where he obtained his diploma.

There was, however, a four-year period,

1845–49, when Wentworth suspended his studies to serve as chief clerk to the keeper of naval stores at the Kittery Yard. Later, in 1861, he was appointed naval storekeeper, and he performed the work of this office, interwoven with his medical and military careers, for several years — an experience which did much to explain his lifelong interest in the Navy Yard.

After his war service, brevetted a brigadier general, Wentworth returned to Kittery to practice medicine there the rest of his life, and it was as a doctor that the older residents remembered him.

We visited the house on Wentworth Street where he had lived and practiced. It was a large, square, white-clapboarded, green-shuttered building of the type so often seen in New England villages, and it was being used for offices by another physician, Dr. Paul E. Taylor.

Frank Neal showed me a picture postcard view of the house as it had been at some time in the past when Dr. Wentworth lived and practiced medicine there. This view showed parts of the house that are no longer there, including a front porch and a small one-story attachment which the Doctor used as a waiting room or office. Neal explained that the lot once had been much larger, taking up most of the land within a rectangle formed by four streets. It was what might be called an "estate." But land had been sold after his death, and now other dwellings and a commercial building had edged in, leaving only a lot of average size for Dr. Taylor.

On the north side of the lot, however, these encroachments had been brought to a halt — as though they had run upon a fortress — by a low granite structure half covered with sod. This was Mark Wentworth's tomb, its solidly locked stone door bearing this inscription:

GEN. MARK F. WENTWORTH
Died July 12, 1897
Aged 77 yrs. 3 mos.

ELIZA J. his wife
Died Feb. 25, 1883
Aged 63 yrs. 7 mos.

ANNIE E. Died Dec. 11, 1862
Aged 15 yrs. 11 mos.

Besides Annie, Mark and Eliza had two other daughters, who grew up and married, Frank Neal pointed out. He also called attention to something I had noticed in correspondence with Tobey — that in this part of the state there are graves in back yards, in fields, and almost everywhere else. In fact, Tobey had once written me, during one of his searches for a veteran of the 27th Maine, "I expect I'll find him buried under somebody's door step."

I asked Tobey why this was, and he said he didn't know. The only explanation for back-yard burials he could think of was that upon one occasion the Indians, following the burial of someone of whom they particularly disapproved, dug his body up and hung it on a stake, a spectacle that may have distressed the early settlers to the point of causing them to locate graves where they could keep an eye on them; and this is how the custom might have started.

Advisable as this practice may have been in the 1600's, the results here were somewhat dismal as viewed among the dry weeds and bare branches of late March and against a winter's accumulation of trash in the neighboring back yards.

It had been quite a different scene in the 1880's and 1890's, as seen through the memories of a granddaughter, Jessie Hobbs Dunshee. Peach and apple trees grew on a knoll behind the tomb; on a June day the scent of their blossoms filled the air. Green lawns, smooth graveled walks and a profusion of flowers surrounded the buildings, which then included a stable and a carriage house. Her grandfather she remembered as a giant of a man, very tall and straight as a ramrod. In fact, the General was so large he couldn't wear "boughten" shirts; he had to have them specially made.

"Brusque but gentle" are the words Jessie Dunshee used to describe him. And, she added, he was a bit absent-minded at times. One of the family stories was that he had once, as a disciplinary measure, ordered Jessie's mother, then a child, to climb into a chair and remain. Three hours later he was conscience-stricken when his wife came into the room and said, "Mark, that child is still sitting there!"

He was fond of children, and also of animals. The household included canaries; a white poodle, Pompey, who could pray; a shepherd, Pedro, who could climb ladders; and a fox terrier, name forgotten, who rode about with Dr. Wentworth in his carriage making calls. And there was also a parrot, Polly, who once yelled at the minister when he bowed his head for grace at the table: "Do ya want yer head scratched?"

At this same table there were often famous guests, including Thomas B. Reed, renowned Speaker of the House, who liked gravy on his bread . . . Hannibal Hamlin, Lincoln's first vice-president, whom Wentworth had served as chief of staff when Hamlin was Governor of Maine . . . Stephen A. Douglas, for whom a household cat, in no disrespect, was named . . . and others high in the political constellations of the nation.

Wentworth was an enthusiastic Republican from the time of the organization of the party; he was personally acquainted with many of the founders; and he had been one of the delegates to the national convention which nominated Lincoln and Hamlin in 1860. Through his work on town, county and state committees, he became the acknowledged leader of the Republican Party in the southern end of the First Maine Congressional District, which is to say the southern end of Maine — a man not without power in the land.

It was widely remembered also that when Wentworth came back from the war, he brought with him a colored child, Tom Murray. Tom, as one of the officers of the 27th Maine recalled, had appeared in camp from nowhere one winter day — a smart little fellow no bigger than a pepperbox — and he had attached himself devotedly to the colonel. In Wentworth's home in Kittery, the greatest scientific marvel in the eyes of the little colored boy was the doorknob. Coming from wherever he had come from, and then living in tents with the 27th Maine, he had never seen such a thing. Every now and then Wentworth's wife, Eliza, sitting in a room by herself, would see the knob of a closed door moving to and fro for minutes at a time; and that would be the little boy on the other side, working the doorknob and contemplating the wonder of it. As Dr. Wentworth drove about Kittery with his dashing team, Major and General — sorrel horses with silver manes and tails — Tom was often seen sitting on the seat of the carriage beside him. After going to a Kittery school — the only colored boy in attendance — Tom grew up and went to work on the Boston and Maine Railroad as a roundhouse hand and Pullman porter; and he came to be well regarded in his community.

Wentworth appears to have had a strong sense of responsibility for the people with whom he was concerned, and also for his animals. When the horses grew old, he took care of them to the end. Major and General — along with another horse, Dolly — the dogs Pompey and Pedro and the other animals and birds were buried on the estate, up back of the orchard. Looking to his own interment, Wentworth once said that when his funeral was held, "If anyone has a red dress or hat, wear it." He loved the color red — red roses and carnations, the red candied cherries he gave to children, the flash of a distant flag against the summer sky.

On the occasion of this first visit to Kittery, Frank Neal also took me to see Richard Rogers, said to be the town's oldest resident. Mr. Rogers, who was 96, remembered everything that had gone on in Kittery for nearly a century, Frank said, and he would probably remember something about Mark Wentworth and the 27th Maine. We drove through the town northward and knocked on the door of a small white house on Rogers Road. Mr. Rogers himself came to the door. He bore a remarkable resemblance to the late Robert Frost. We were conducted into the living room and, once seated, began to speak with him — not immediately of what we had come to speak about — but as is the custom in Maine, of this and that. It developed that Mr. Rogers was in the seventh generation of the Rogers family living on that same land. His ancestors had come here in the 1600's. His great-grandfather had been a captain in Washington's army; Mr. Rogers showed us his commission. As for the veterans of the 27th Maine who had enlisted from Kittery, he appeared to have known almost every one of them. When one of their names was mentioned without the middle initial, he would instantly supply it. He remembered Mark F. Wentworth well. It appeared that in a sense Wentworth's colonelcy had continued long after the war. "He always liked to have a crew of men around him," was one of Mr. Rogers' recollections.

The subject of the medals was introduced, and while Mr. Rogers admitted to having heard rumors, he dismissed them as something of which he had no personal knowledge. In his otherwise encyclopedic knowledge, this represented a gap that was later to strike us as significant.

The conversation returned to Wentworth, and Mr. Rogers dwelt at some length upon the Doctor's influence and power in the town and in the affairs of the Navy Yard. It would have been easy to gain the impression that Wentworth's political skill lay at the base of this power, but apparently such was not the case. It was rather his imposing size and personality, his quick perception and ability to convince others of what was the right thing to do and his readiness to take action and responsibility that made him an effective leader. And usually, it appeared, his influence was exerted quietly, from behind the scenes.

After an hour or so we took our leave, Mr. Rogers conducting us to the door, calling our attention to a grandfather clock of great antiquity that stood in the hall and saying with a twinkle, "I'll be 97 in May." (He was, too.)

We drove back down through the village, passing on the way a building with a balcony where General Wentworth always stood on Memorial Day to take the salutes of the G.A.R. parade. The next call was on Kittery Point, where a great-granddaughter of Wentworth, Mrs. Marion Billings, awaited us. She and her husband received us most hospitably and we sat for an hour or so in their living room overlooking the outer reaches of Portsmouth Harbor and the dark green Atlantic beyond. Mrs. Billings knew nothing of the medals, but she did further our acquaintance with General Wentworth by bringing down from upstairs a portrait of him that had been painted by an unknown artist. The painting had originally been done in roseate hues of some sort but it had darkened, and Mark Wentworth gazed out at us as from a room illuminated only by the glow of dying red embers in a fireplace. Deep-set eyes, a firm nose, a wide moustache, a wiry beard. Between moustache and beard a line that could have come only from the most resolute of mouths underneath. This was the face of a man who could — as he often did — whip the cloth off a dining room table in a patient's home, cover it with a clean sheet and perform an emergency operation right then and there. (Once, by quick action, he had saved a premature baby so small that its wrist would pass through his wedding ring.) One would warrant, after seeing this face, that Wentworth's patients, the Republican Party in York County, the Navy Yard and the 27th Maine had all in their turn been in good hands.

As for the 27th Maine, its picture also began to emerge from several attics in the form of letters, diaries and other records. In fact, personal records of this sort were eventually accumulated to cover practically every day of the regiment's nine months of service, which was no small tribute to the archival virtues of the Maine attic. With his singular persistence, E. C. Tobey dug out many of these, including a number written to his grandfather by soldier-friends in the 27th Maine. Others were made available through the kindness of many Maine people.

Worth mentioning as typical of one of these letter-finding expeditions was a call made the next day. The destination was the home of Gladys Paul, about five miles north of Kittery, whence had come indications that there might be letters of a 27th Maine veteran on the premises. To get there I drove northward along Route 236. Once back from the ocean, the broken and rocky ground of the coastland quickly gave way to rolling farmlands and pine forest. The weather had turned sunny and unusually hot for this time of year. The balsam scent of the pines was as pervasive as it might have been in July. The Paul residence proved to be a big old square white house on a hill — and one that could be quickly spotted as a natural archives establishment. (Big old house: everything

49

saved. Small new house: no papers inside.) It was also typical of many of the big old houses in Maine where it is difficult to tell whether the front door is the real door or not, the front door in some houses being used only for special occasions. The visitor to one of these houses and the occupant of it sometimes circle one another, one on the outside of the house and one on the inside, knocking and shouting for as much as five minutes.

There was the beginning of this noisy maneuver here, but Gladys Paul, a most pleasant lady who is also quick of foot, intercepted me at the front door, which proved to be the real door after all, and soon I was seated in the living room while Gladys Paul went "up attic" to see if she could find the letters that Elbridge Paul had written home from the war, and his medal.

The letters were found — a good-sized bundle — and also the medal. Elbridge hadn't lived long enough after his return to wear his medal, so it was like new, the first one I had seen in this state of preservation. The black case was perfect, and on its inside cover the name *Wm. Wilson & Son, Manufacturers of Silver Ware, S.W. cor. Fifth & Cherry Sts., Philad. Established 1812* was black and clear. The bronze was in mint condition.

This of course was not today's Army Medal of Honor (the Army changed the design in 1904) but the original, consisting of a red-white-and-blue ribbon from which is suspended a bronze star bearing in bas-relief the dramatic scene, so

50

expressive of the Civil War, of Minerva Repulsing Discord — Minerva a noble goddess holding a shield against which a half-naked ruffian launches fork-tongued serpents.

The decoration lay on the table where I was copying Elbridge Paul's letters. A slanting ray of March sunlight shone through the window upon it, and from the red stripes of the ribbon leaped a glow of color not unlike that of a candied cherry.

It was easy to believe that Mark Wentworth might have taken a great fancy to this old-style Medal of Honor.

The 27th Maine

Since the yeomen of York County who served in the 27th Maine were to figure so prominently in the history of the Medal of Honor, it may be instructive to contemplate through the various windows opened by E. C. Tobey and others how the war came upon them and what they did in it.

For Mark F. Wentworth — doctor, Republican leader and naval storekeeper — these years of conflict would provide still another role, that of military commander. This was not a vain trumpeting and showing forth in armor, as was the case with so many political leaders turned colonels or generals. There was a strong military tradition in the Wentworth family; for a century and a half Wentworths had been at war, off and on, with Indians, French and British. Mark Wentworth's great-grandfather had fought in the battle of Quebec and had been, so he came back to relate, one of the officers who carried the wounded General Wolfe to the spot where he expired. A grandfather and two great-uncles served in the Revolution.

So Wentworth had been born with a little gunpowder in his blood. His physical size alone made people look to him as a leader; his education further qualified him to be an officer. Even before the war seemed imminent, as though he had already sniffed the smoke of coming battles, he had helped to organize and train a company of militia known as the Kittery Artillery, which came to be regarded as one of Maine's best militia units. When hostilities began in April of 1861 the men of the Kittery Artillery were fairly steaming with patriotism; they hissed out of the hall one orderly sergeant who asked to be excused from a meeting. The Maine authorities anticipated that an attack by rebel privateers might be made upon the Navy Yard, and so they ordered the Kittery Artillery to garrison Fort McClary, which guarded the approaches to the naval installation (even in the order being careful to refer to it as the Kittery Navy Yard, not the Portsmouth Naval Base). Wentworth had just had his artillerymen outfitted in dashing new uniforms: blue jackets trimmed with red, State of Maine buttons and gray trousers with stripes down the seams. But Fort McClary was far from being ready. The barracks were rotten, leaky and dirty. The fort had no guns. If a rebel raider headed into Portsmouth Harbor, about all the Kittery Artillery could do was scowl at it.

Wentworth, as was his habit, promptly took the initiative.

Through his Navy Yard connections he borrowed four unmounted 32-pounders and had his men make carriages for them. He borrowed ammunition for the cannon. He bought lumber, two secondhand cook stoves and some cotton cloth and straw for making mattresses, trusting he'd get his money back from the state. Along with the work of putting the fort into shape he instituted strict military discipline, with drill four hours a day. Soon Fort McClary was comfortable — and operational.

But as the summer of 1861 wore away, Wentworth became more and more restless. The big bearded Republican was finding Fort McClary too tame a place. In August he was writing to the Adjutant General of Maine urging that he be allowed to raise a company of infantry for the 8th Maine and go off to war with it. Wentworth was then 41, which is a little ripe for soldiering; he was a leading physician in Kittery and as such might have deserved exemption. Or he might have joined the military service as a surgeon; but what Wentworth wanted to do was crack heads, not patch them up; he wanted to go with the infantry. He wrote the Adjutant General, "I for one am willing to forego personal comfort, home and everything else for the sake of serving my country in any capacity in which I may be of most use to it, at whatever cost."

The 8th Maine proposition was not accepted, but Wentworth kept on badgering the Adjutant General and the Governor for an assignment in the field. He advanced the idea that there ought to be a regiment of infantry from York County, and used every political and military argument for it that he could think of. He offered to raise the regiment and command it, or help raise it and take a lower place on the field and staff.

For those who were destined to become enlisted men — most of them farmers, mechanics, fishermen and seamen, although there was a scattering of business and professional men among them — the war was far from being such an urgent matter as it was for Wentworth. Busy with their work, they were as a whole slower to grasp the significance of national events; for most of them blue skies gave way only gradually to threats of summer thunder.

The rumbling and darkening of the coming storm were reflected in some of the letters that Charles H. Tucker, then 17 or 18 years of age and employed in a woodworking shop in South Berwick, was writing to a friend in Eliot, Martin Parry Tobey. In March of 1861:

Now winter is most gone and I am very glad of it. The warm sun begins to shine and the birds begin to sing their sweet songs about our doors. I love to hear them. We have plenty of work this time of year. The old water wheel goes nice now.

But in the same letter there were less tranquil notes, phrases obviously foreign to Charlie's vocabulary, lifted bodily from a newspaper or magazine: "Strife and agitation rife in the land" . . . "low deep mutterings of disunion" . . . "this mighty republic being shaken from center to circumference" . . . and so on. Another letter dated

55

June 6, 1861, came closer and more personally to the issue:

Parry, what do you think of the war. I think it is bad to have our country in such a fix. I think it is bad to have the Stars & Stripes trampled on in the manner they are, don't you.

I feel like fighting for them a bit, don't you . . . I saw another regiment of one thousand stought harty men pass over the Boston & Maine Rail R. bound for Washington & thence to the battlefield. They was a jolly set of fellows, I tell you. Some went from here to the junction to see them . . . One fellow told me that while standing there one of them hailed him from a car window & made this re-mark. I say old friend look er here. We are the boys. We are after Jef Davis and dam him we are going to have his old scalp too. I hope he will don't you Parry. I say may good luck & prosperity go with that fellow and also may god go with him.

And on July 22, 1861:

How do you get along down to Old Eliot with your haying . . . I see in the papers this afternoon they are having a great fight in bulls run. It says the federal troops are retreating fast. Where is your company? Is it ready for action? . . . Presume you get purty well drilled

56

some days when you swing the scythe all day.

In December, Charlie had brought himself so far abreast of the war that he felt free to comment on its international aspects:

About Mason & Slidell Parry I don't know how that will be. The folks up here is waiting to hear the results of Old England. I say let her come don't you Parry. We will take our old fowling pieces & start them anyway. Old England can't whip America & I tell you the reason why. The Yank boys will make them sing root hog or die . . . You must excuse bad writing and spelling. Rote in a hurry by lamplight.

There was in this letter an echo of an illusion that many people had inherited from the Revolution. Should there be a threat to the nation, it was felt by many people that all that was needful was for the citizenry to take their muskets down from the mantels and sally forth to fight the enemy on the village green. For this and other reasons — as was the case in other states — the organized militia had been allowed to languish until it had become merely a paper organization — a list of men of the ages 18 to 45 who were liable for military service.

However, the list did provide the names of people who could be drafted if necessary, and it was the threat of this draft that led to the raising of the 27th Maine. During the summer of 1862 there were, in theory, two systems for raising troops. One was the system of voluntary enlistment in the "volunteer regiments" provided for by Congress. The other was the draft upon the militia. In practice the two systems got all mixed up.

Only July 2, 1862, President Lincoln called for 300,000 men to volunteer; this was responded to in Maine by the raising of five three years' volunteer regiments: the 16th, 17th, 18th, 19th and 20th Regiments Infantry, Maine Volunteers. Enlistment for these regiments was encouraged by bounties from the state and from towns and cities; if this encouragement had failed the law provided for a special draft upon the militia to make up the state's quota.

But before the organization of these volunteer regiments had been completed, there was another and more direct call upon the militia. On August 4 the President ordered 300,000 militia troops drafted to serve for nine months. Maine's share amounted to eight regiments — the 21st through the 28th Maine. The raising of the 27th was assigned to York County, and this gave Mark Wentworth the opportunity to go to war with the regiment of York men he had been asking for.

However, this was not a matter of sitting back and waiting for his regiment to be drafted. Although the draft was an equitable way of assigning military service to the able-bodied male population, equity was not what the majority of the population wanted. Men with families and men of property and responsibility could produce several reasons why the privilege of following the flag should be assigned to others who were less encumbered; the draft was a sort of dangerous Russian Roulette which had no place in a well-ordered community. Also, many local politicians were against it; a draft might hurt the Republican candidates in the next election. Therefore, when the draft upon the militia became imminent most towns and cities offered generous bounties to turn this, too, into a "volunteer" method of raising troops, and these sums were augmented by private contributions from draftable men who didn't want a draft to take place. For example, Tobey's home town, Eliot, appointed Edmund A. Dixon recruiting officer, voting him $150 for each man he obtained and giving $20 to each recruit. Dixon paid each man the entire $170, and private contributions increased this amount to $200. Federal and state bounties increased the amounts further; the total might be around $300 in some towns or as much as $500 in others.

The next step was up to the recruiting officers, who hoped to become commissioned officers in the companies they raised. These were usually prominent men in occupations wholly unrelated to military experience. Perhaps the most extreme example in the 27th Maine was that of the Reverend Henry F. Snow of Cornish, who had a fiery disposition and whose leanings were apparently more toward the Old Testament than the New; he was so stirred up by the war that he went around enlisting men while carrying his dinner with him to save time, and thus he eventually became the Reverend Captain Snow, commanding Company H. Military competence was not the essential qualification in becoming the captain of a militia company; a man had to be first enough of a salesman to enlist his soldiers, and second enough of a politician to make sure they would vote for him. (When a militia regiment was organized, the men elected the company officers, and the company officers elected the regimental commander and other officers of the field and staff — all of these later being commissioned by the Governor of the state.)

So the successful raising of such a regiment called for a mixture of patriotism, ambition, finance and politics; it was just the sort of enterprise that Mark Wentworth could manage, or help manage, very well. The 27th Maine was raised without recourse to the draft. The regiment assembled at Camp Abraham Lincoln near Portland, where Wentworth was elected lieutenant colonel, with the command of the regiment going to Rufus P. Tapley, a popular and prominent attorney and politician. And every man in the regiment was a "volunteer."

The Maine Adjutant General observed that the state's militia quota, as well as the earlier quota for volunteer regiments, had been filled with the assistance of large bounties, and as the season wore on and men got scarcer, the nine months' militia men received even bigger bounties than the three years' volunteers, which annoyed him because it didn't make sense. In his 1862 report he grumpily classified the 27th and other regiments of its kind as "Maine Militia," but in the 1863 edition he relented, and these regiments were designated as "Maine Volunteers."

But even if the Adjutant General was irked by the bounties, everybody else seemed to be pleased. Those who had evaded the draft were elated; in one York County town they stayed up until midnight cheering and firing guns on the day their quota was completed through voluntary enlistment. The volunteers were also delighted; they had pocketed a good deal of extra cash for going to a war to which they would sometime probably have to go anyway, and they were suffused with a heroic spirit of pride and self-congratulation which was a good thing for morale. On August 30 Charlie Tucker wrote:

Berwick is doing nobly towards putting down the rebellion. She now has sixty-nine enlisted under the call of the President, and I can proudly say that I am one of that number, who shall sacrifice our lives for our country. It must and shall be restored to peas again. The Stars and Stripes shall float to the brezes over every Capitol throughout the United States or we will leave our bones upon the southern soil. We are going to show them the best company ever shouldered a musket, from this little one horse town.

A better fighting spirit could hardly be asked for, and there is no reason to suppose that Charlie did not mean every word of it. There was good stuff in the 27th; its basic material was probably as good as that of most of the Maine volunteer regiments; and it was borne off to war on the same wave of public enthusiasm and emotion that was prevalent in the autumn of 1862. A lady even wrote and inscribed a poem to the regiment in the rhythm of "The Battle Hymn of the Republic"; her name was not Julia Ward Howe, but it was based on much the same sentiments, full of references to God, freedom and lifted banners, and it was inspired by the passing of a regiment en route to the South.

The 27th Maine departed from Portland on October 20, 1862, and the soldier's typically quick descent from illusion to reality is nowhere better traced than in the entries that Sergeant Joseph Doe made in his diary as the southward journey proceeded:

We arrived at the Depot in Portland about ½ past seven, where we staid about one hour bidding adieu to many friends and connexions, then started on our way to Boston. Nothing of importance occurred until we arrived at South Berwick Junction, where we had to stop almost an hour to see a great many friends and many connexions and bid a last adieu to them. . . . We arrived in Boston about 3 o'clock p.m. and marched through the city to the Boston & Providence Depot, where we looked around about one hour and saw a number of Ladies who bid us goodbye and God Speed. We left the Depot about six o'clock and arrived at Stonington to take the Splendid Steamer Commonwealth about midnight and found her a splendid craft with good quarters.

Tuesday, Oct. 21, 1862: At daylight we went on deck and saw some fine scenes such as Forts and handsome buildings. . . . We arrived at Jersey City about 6 o'clock a.m. where we got some soup and hot coffee. We saw quite a number of old women trying to sell things to the regiment and the soldiers were each presented with a testament by the Bible Society. We then took the cars for Philadelphia, and as we passed the Cities & Towns in New Jersey we saw many people bidding us adieu and God Speed. We arrived in Philadelphia about six o'clock p.m. where we had the benefit of the Cooper Shop Refreshment Saloon, and got a very good supper then formed a line again and marched through the principal street with a great number of Ladies following, to say a last goodbye.

In common with hundreds of thousands of

Union soldiers who passed through Philadelphia, the men of the 27th couldn't say enough about the hospitality they received there — a hospitality which must have contributed immeasurably to the image of friendliness which the veterans took home to widespread regions and which the city enjoys to the present day. As one Maine man remarked, "They never thought to inquire of a soldier, or of a regiment of soldiers, as to what state they were from; it was enough for them to know that they were soldiers in the service of the Republic, and all their wants were supplied with a most generous hand." Captain Seth E. Bryant of the 27th noted that as men of the regiment passed through Philadelphia after their meal at the Refreshment Saloon, they were greeted with a warmth and sincerity hardly to be expected from strangers; the streets were so crowded with people that they were difficult to pass in places, and at the depot the crowd was the largest of all — a satisfying share of it composed of females who were extremely sociable with the soldiers.

But from Philadelphia on, it was more like a traditional Army trip. At the depot there was a jarring come-down when they were loaded into cattle cars, which set off for Baltimore. Once during the night the train stopped and ran backward at a furious rate for 12 or 15 miles to avoid, as they heard later, a collision with an oncoming train which happened to be on the same track. Sergeant Doe's diary continues:

Wednesday, Oct. 22, 1862. We arrived in Baltimore at an early hour, and formed a line and marched through the principal streets and saw the place where the gallant Sixth Mass. were mobbed. We marched along to the Depot of the Baltimore and Ohio Railroad where we got some breakfast and saw a number of prisoners. We stopped in Baltimore until noon, when we started again in some very poor cattle cars for Washington, worse than any we had before and some of the Regiment made pretty large holes in the sides of the old cars . . .

Having thus so quickly been introduced to the horrors of war, they arrived in Washington that afternoon. Here they were issued old-fashioned flint-locks, altered for percussion and carrying a charge of one round ball and two buckshot — these not to be replaced until many weeks later by Enfields. On October 26, a wet day, they marched across the bridge to Arlington Heights, where the land belonging to Robert E. Lee was now being used as a camp ground and assembly point, with the once-beautiful forest growths cut and slashed in every direction and the fields rutted and trampled — a dismal sight in the drizzling rain. Soon afterward Charlie Tucker wrote home that they were "on the Rebel General Lee's property near his house." Then he added dryly: "He is not here now."

But although General Lee was not there, it was

the imminent possibility that he might return which dictated the role that the 27th Maine was to play for the rest of the year and the first half of 1863. A couple of months before the arrival of the regiment, in the second battle of Bull Run, Lee had driven the men of Pope's army back into the defenses of Washington, smiting the hindmost of them within cannon sound of the city.

Then, in September, Lee had crossed the Potomac, driving north to bring on the Antietam campaign and posing another threat to the capital. In his conduct of this campaign the Union general McClellan was considerably hampered, as Meade was to be later in the move to Gettysburg, by a stream of precautionary messages from General-in-Chief Halleck, urging the Union commander to watch out lest the slippery Confederate leader, by some trick, should manage to turn his flank and get between the Army of the Potomac and Washington. The result of these alarms and constant fears for the safety of the capital was that between 80 and 100 regiments and batteries were deployed in the defenses of Washington in the early winter of 1862–63 — enough troops to have fought a large-scale battle.

When Lee retired below the Rappahannock in the autumn of 1862, where he was to maul and claw his attackers in the battles of Fredericksburg and Chancellorsville, there was also need for rear-echelon troops for the purpose of guarding every mile of the supply and reinforcement routes leading south to the Union army. Meanwhile the over-all problem of guarding the capital and the communications with the army had been made even more severe by the development, on the part of the Confederates, of an extremely effective form of guerrilla warfare. It was described thus by its most famous exponent, Colonel John S. Mosby:

My purpose was to weaken the armies invading Virginia by harassing their rear. As a line is only as strong as its weakest point, it was necessary for it to be stronger than I was at every point, in order to resist my attacks. It is easy, therefore, to see the great results that may be accomplished by a small body of cavalry moving rapidly from point to point on the communications of an army. To destroy supply trains, to break up the means of conveying intelligence, and thus isolating an army from its base, as well as its different corps from each other, to confuse their plans by capturing dispatches, are the objects of partisan war. It is just as legitimate to fight an enemy in the rear as in front. The only difference is in the danger. Now, to prevent all these things from being done, heavy detachments must be made to guard against them. The military value of a partisan's work is not measured by the amount of property destroyed, or the number of men killed or captured, but by the number he keeps watching.

Every soldier withdrawn from the front to guard the rear of an army is so much taken from its fighting strength.

I endeavored, as far as I was able, to diminish this aggressive power of the Army of the Potomac, by compelling it to keep a large force on the defensive. I assailed its rear, for there was its most vulnerable point. My men had no camps. If they had gone into camps, they would soon have all been captured. They would scatter for safety, and gather at my call, like the Children of the Mist. A blow would be struck at a weak or unguarded point, and then a quick retreat. The alarm would spread through the sleeping camp, the long roll would be beaten or the bugles would sound to horse, there would be mounting in hot haste and a rapid pursuit. But the partisans generally got off with their prey. Their pursuers were striking at an invisible foe. I have often sent small squads at night to attack and run in the pickets along a line of several miles. Of course, these alarms were very annoying, for no human being knows how sweet sleep is but a soldier.

Mosby might have been writing a textbook for the Viet Cong. It was his contention that he could compel the enemy to guard a hundred points, while he could select any one of them for attack, and alarms often occurred in camps he was nowhere near. A lesson of warfare which

Mosby demonstrated, and which sometimes has to be learned all over again, is that when any force undertakes the security of an entire region against skillful and determined bands of guerrillas, it had better be prepared to outnumber its roving foe by at least ten to one.

As part of the defense plan against Mosby's "Children of the Mist" as well as more substantial forces, Washington was encircled by forts, earthworks, strong points of several kinds and, at a greater distance, by a long necklace of picket lines supplied and supported by temporary camps. In late October the 27th Maine moved to Camp Seward, about half a mile south of Arlington Heights, and in early December to a camp south of Hunting Creek, Virginia, where it held a portion of a picket line extending from the Potomac near Mount Vernon to the Orange and Alexandria Railroad.

Companies moved out to the line on rotation, each remaining for a period of four days. Picket details usually stood "two hours on and four hours off" during the four-day period. Many of the men made little shanties of pine boughs as shelters against the changeable weather.

Private Elbridge Paul wrote home that he liked this duty first rate, giving a description of a night on the picket line:

The moon was about as brite as day and we had a nice time. One of the boys in Co. K shot one rebel spy through the thigh. They could hear him holler about two miles when the buck shot struck him and we tuck five more prisoners. They gave us the name of being the best pickets that they have had on this line since the war has begun.

In early December they observed the gathering of forces for Burnside's ill-fated assault upon Fredericksburg. One soldier wrote, "There goes along here days artillery, batteries, cavalry, infantry. There are great movements about this time. We can find out but little where they are going." As an aftermath of the Union defeat at Fredericksburg, they began to pick up Union stragglers, deserters who brought alarming reports with them. Nervousness grew along the picket line. On the night of December 21–22 one soldier reported seeing five rebels who turned out to be five pine trees. A couple of nights later a man fired at his own shadow, causing a widespread alarm. There was a great deal of indiscriminate musketry. On December 28, Sergeant Doe wrote in his diary:

Great excitement about some Rebel cavalry driving in our cavalry. Our pickets were drawn up in line of battle and were quite excited. The 27th Regiment ordered to sleep on their arms and be ready to march at a moment's notice. They loaded their guns and folded their blankets ready for a march.

Their slumbers were being disturbed in exactly the manner visualized by John Mosby.

However, that winter the men of the 27th Maine were seldom in any danger of sudden physical harm, except for the chance of being stunned by some of the bad whisky that itinerant vendors might purvey to a cold and thirsty picket. The greatest hazard, as it was for the Army generally — a much greater danger than that of bullets — was disease. Sanitary precautions were few because at that time neither Army doctors nor anyone else had an adequate understanding of what needs to be done to keep disease and contagion in check. The weather also had much to do with health; it was bad enough for a regiment that went into well-constructed winter quarters as was the case with many troops; but when the men of a regiment had to go out on picket duty and live in the open through a Virginia winter, it was a sure thing that many of them were going to die. Virginia came as a surprise to men of the 27th Maine who had had visions of the "Sunny South." Snow fell in early November, and there was snow off and on until the fourth of April according to diaries. In between these dates — unlike Maine where the ground froze and stayed frozen, where the cold was fairly constant and other conditions were such that the human system could become accustomed to them — Virginia could give a man a dose of nearly everything within a week or so: frozen ground thawing to mud in a rainstorm,

71

deep snow coming down on top of the mud, a hot day drying everything up, wind filling the air with dust, another freeze and so on. In camp, living in tents heated by smoky wood-burning stoves and sleeping on sacks of straw, the soldiers could find some comfort, but even here the wind and cold penetrated and men sometimes woke up covered with snow that had sifted in during the night. Out on the picket line, where the only shelter was usually a "dog tent" or a little hut made of boughs, corn stalks or whatever material was available, a man could be miserably wet and cold much of the time. Racking coughs, colds, sore throats and fevers were prevalent. In early December, Elbridge Paul was writing home, "One of our boys died last Tuesday night. Typhoid fever. He had got most over the fever and Dyptherea set in. We have sent him home to Kittery. . . . There are six or seven died."

The toll continued. Almost every week a body would be escorted to Alexandria, where it would be embalmed and sent home. On January 14 Captain Joseph Warren wrote in his diary, "Lt. Came is *very sick*. Orderly Milliken and I sit up with him tonight. It does not seem he can live very long." And two days later, "Sad intelligence has greeted us today. Lt. Came has died. He has ended his military career. The rich and poor, high and low must die."

As a result of Lieutenant John H. Came's death something that was not uncommon in the

Civil War happened. Captain Warren wrote to Came's sister, she replied, the correspondence continued and the grief they shared turned into another emotion. After the war he would go to call on her and they were married.

Along with the more serious ailments went another malady, which soldiers were never so unmanly as to describe but which they hinted at. One wrote, "We have seen comparatively easy times as yet, but we have had enough to make us realize the value of home." And homesickness was even more strongly indicated in a letter a boy wrote to his mother: "I want to know how the dog gets along, and how many cats you keep now."

The sadness of families separated often became acute sorrow, as was the case with Mark Wentworth. In mid-December he received news of the death of his daughter, Annie, 15. He went back to Maine for the funeral and returned to the regiment in a grim and sober state of mind, anxious to get on with the war. He would soon have a chance to make his influence felt. On January 23 he replaced Colonel Rufus Tapley as commander of the 27th Maine and was promoted to colonel shortly afterward.

Immediately discipline and training were stepped up, with company drill every forenoon and battalion drill every afternoon. "Wentworth," as one punster put it, "is drilling us up to the Mark." Some noncommissioned officers were reduced to ranks; certain privates were promoted. Breaches of good order were punished by sentences of hard labor or knapsack drill. Inspections of arms were frequent.

One of the young soldiers who started coming into his own about this time was Calvin L. Hayes, age 20, the sergeant major of the regiment, who had left his classes at Bowdoin College to go off to the war. Hayes had previously served with Wentworth in the Kittery Artillery; he would serve with him in still another regiment after the 27th Maine had run its course; and he would be a devoted friend of the older man all the rest of his life.

With the assistance of young noncoms and officers such as Hayes, who were beginning to prove themselves as the incompetents or those in poor health were weeded out, Wentworth whipped the 27th Maine into shape. When it was mustered for pay at the end of February, a staff officer from division headquarters gave the regiment a high rating.

It was well that this was so. In March, Colonel John S. Mosby went on a rampage which was a triumph of boldness. Like many great commanders, Mosby had no lack of confidence in himself. For example, he once related:

One day I rode down on a scout in sight of the dome of the Capitol, when a wagon came along, going to Washington, which was driven by the wife of a Union man who had left his home in Virginia and taken refuge there. I stopped it, and, after some conversation with the driver, told her who I was. With a pair of scissors she had I cut off a lock of my hair and sent it to Mr. Lincoln, with a message that I was coming to get one of his soon. A few days after this, I saw in the *Star* that it had been delivered to him, and that the President enjoyed the joke.

What Mosby was doing in Fairfax County in March of 1863 was, however, no joke. One night at 2 a.m. he boldly entered the town of Fairfax Court House and captured a visiting Union general along with a number of men and horses, with the colonel commanding the post only escaping "in a nude state by accident." In a midday attack at Herndon Station he drove a body of cavalry into a saw-mill, threatened to set the mill on fire and took 25 prisoners with all their horses, arms and equipment. In another action, when pursued by a strong Union cavalry force along the Little River Turnpike, Mosby waited until his pursuers were well strung out by the chase, then turned and countercharged; one of his tactics was to forego the saber and dash in among his foe opening a deadly fire with revolvers; it worked so well on this occasion that he killed or wounded ten of his pursuers, captured 35 and put the rest to flight.

Through these and other blows, delivered with a small, rapidly moving force in the vicinity of Washington, Mosby created the impression that the Union lines in front of the capital were in an extremely shaky and vulnerable condition. It was to help strengthen the ring of defense and prevent a repetition of such depredations that the 27th Maine, now considered fit for dangerous duty, was sent along toward the end of March to the outermost lines of infantry. Brigaded with the 25th Maine, the regiment marched out along the Little River Turnpike and took position at Chantilly, 25 miles west of Washington. This had been the scene of a brief but bloody battle during the retreat from the second battle of Bull Run, with a thunderstorm raging and Phil Kearny, the great Union cavalry leader, killed in one of the confusing charges. Now the new grass of another spring was effacing the scars of battle, although the men noted plenty of bullet holes in trees and fences and occasionally stumbled across the bones of soldiers who had been left unburied on the field.

The Little River Turnpike, a macadamized road, stretched off to the west like a shining spear passing through gaps in the Bull Run and Blue Ridge Mountains to the valley of the Shenandoah — that great thoroughfare of armies during much of the war. However, its likeness was to a spear that could be quickly reversed, for a good road is a convenience to anyone who wants to use it, and along the smooth surface of the turnpike, debouching from the Aldie gap, an enemy force could make a dash at Washington at any moment.

The glint of danger shining through the spring-time blossoms seems to have been very stimulating. Private Elbridge Paul wrote:

> We have to drill about five hours in a day. We have to go on picket once in five days. The rebels are thicker than hell. I expect they will come in some night. If they do, we have got some pills for them that will make them spit blood.

Another man reported that with the proximity to scenes of battle, the boys "took great interest in skirmish drill." There were sessions of target practice. Officers studied Casey's *Infantry Tactics* with intense diligence. But disappointingly nothing much happened at Chantilly. A distant vedette may have flung a faint curse at the Maine men down the wind, or an old lady may have shaken her umbrella at them, but on the whole there was no action worthy of the name and the adrenaline in their veins gradually subsided.

Meanwhile, they assumed, their time was running out. The expectation was that they would be ordered out of service on June 10. This was nine months from the date of the draft they had prevented by volunteering, and someone had told them that this would be the date of their release. Muster and payrolls were made up, and on June 8 the paymaster came into camp, paying off the regiment for March and April. But June 10 came and went with no word from the War Department, and the days continued to go by without orders. It was rumored that the Department understood their date of discharge to be June 30, that being nine months from the date of their being mustered into Federal service; and at this there was, as the Bible says, murmuring in the tents.

Meanwhile, Robert E. Lee had launched another great blow at the North, and they were soon to be almost engulfed by the swirl of action that followed Lee's invading army. Looking south, the men of the 27th Maine saw clouds of dust on the roads, and out of the dust appeared hard-marching columns of the Army of the Potomac. There was some bewilderment as to the purpose of these movements. Captain Warren wrote, "What the object is, we do not know . . . it is reported that all of Hooker's force is falling back."

What was happening was that all of these marching people were heading for a crossroads village the name of which most of them had never heard — Gettysburg — with Lee moving northward behind the Blue Ridge and Hooker following, maneuvering to stay between Lee and Washington. Union troops were passing through Chantilly and on both sides of it, among them several Maine regiments.

Warren was visited by an old friend, a Lieutenant Stevens of the 5th Maine, marching with the Sixth Corps. The regiment, he noted, had been in ten engagements, and its number had been reduced to between 200 and 300, but Lieutenant Stevens "looked rugged and in good spirits." There was other visiting back and forth between men of the 27th and Maine friends in the passing regiments under Hooker. Much of the excitement and spirit of the great army was communicated to the 27th Maine. There was stirring news of a fight June 17 at Aldie, where Stuart was driven back and the 1st Maine Cavalry in a victorious charge lost its colonel but added another shining battle name to its colors.

The brigade comprising the 25th and 27th Maine was now transferred to the Army of the Potomac and assigned to Slocum's Twelfth Corps. On June 24 the brigade received orders to join the northward march on the following morning. "We are all ready to move and in good spirits," Warren wrote. Seven days more, and the 27th Maine would have been standing on Culp's Hill at Gettysburg.

But that night higher headquarters discovered that these were nine months' regiments whose terms were about to expire. The march order was countermanded and the two Maine regiments were told to move back to Arlington Heights for transportation home and discharge from the service.

At Arlington they camped once again on the hill by the Lee mansion with its great columned portico, even then a sad place, full of memories and shadows. Off to the west and northwest where the dust of marching armies was turning

79

the sunsets red, they knew that some mysterious engagement was probably in the offing. But whatever it was, it was no longer their responsibility.

Thus did Destiny brush the soldiers of the 27th Maine lightly with her shining robes and pass them by.

But Honor would stop and visit with them awhile — and she would not find them inhospitable.

Athena Americana

The symbol of Honor that awaited the 27th Maine, through circumstances that will presently be revealed, had been available, in June of 1863, about four months. But the need for it had been apparent ever since the war began — war being an activity with which the natural instinct of self-preservation does not harmonize.

A Civil War company commander once roared at a soldier who was taking, he thought, unheroic measures for defense against flying bullets, "Come out from behind that tree, you baby!"

The soldier yelled in plaintive reply, "I wish I *was* a baby! And a girl baby, at that!"

Another soldier, caught deserting, declared that his motto was, "Home or die!" Something of that same spirit had prevailed in the aftermath of the first battle of Bull Run in July of 1861. In fact, if there had been some miraculous way to interpose the enemy between the desperately northward bound Union troops and their homes, the Confederacy might have been overrun and crushed on the spot.

Actually, these fugitives from Bull Run were not inordinately lacking in bravery. They had fought remarkably well before the rout started. It was simply that they were unaccustomed to war and entirely unprepared for its being so hard on the nerves. Before they were gathered into the great armies of Antietam, Gettysburg and other battles that were to prove for all time the valor of American fighting men, both Northern and Southern, they would need a great deal of training, direction and inspiring example. And of these conditioners, example was perhaps the most important. It was not "Do as I say," but "Do as I do" that provided the most effective leadership for the breed of man that had been raised on this continent.

The power of example was, of course, no less important for Union sailors, and this was something that was very much in the mind of the Secretary of the Navy, Gideon Welles of Connecticut, as he sat in his office on the next-to-the-last day of the first depressing year of the war. An imposing man with thoughtful, resolute eyes and a fine suit of fluffy whiskers, Welles was a somewhat unlikely person to be holding the office of Secretary of the Navy. In a jocular mood, Lincoln sometimes referred to him as "Neptune," but actually he looked like the standard New England country squire as portrayed in some of the illustrated periodicals of the time. And he was far from being a seafaring man. One reason for his appointment was that Lincoln wanted a New Englander in his cabinet; but additionally the President may have supposed that anyone coming from a coastal state would have some familiarity with the sea and ships. Instead, Welles had been nothing saltier than a newspaperman and public official.

Nevertheless, Welles was turning out to be a surprisingly good Secretary of the Navy. He was a good manager, with all the knowledge of people and skill in human engineering that this implies. And a fact that was overwhelmingly apparent to Welles as he reviewed the events of 1861 was that something more than the ordinary qualities of human resolution were going to be necessary in pressing the war to a successful conclusion. He had been disappointed in several of his officers, one of whom he later described as being "timid, but patriotic when there was no danger, for he was not endowed with great moral or physical courage, yet believed himself possessed of both, and was no doubt really anxious to do something without encountering enemies . . ." And a couple of others he characterized as being "intelligent officers and in their specialties among the first of their respective professions, but neither of them was endowed with the fighting qualities of Farragut or Sheridan. . . . They were prudent, cautious men, careful to avoid danger, and provide the means to escape from it."

When victory and defeat hang in delicate balance, with decks flying up in splinters and bloody pieces of people hanging in the rigging, this was not the instinct that tips the scales, as Welles saw it. This was not the spirit of "Don't give up the ship!" or "I have not yet begun to fight!"

And these thoughts were far from being exclusive with Gideon Welles. Now that it had become apparent that the North was not going to crush the South, or the South the North, in a summer's excursion of arms, leaders on both sides were thinking seriously of the resources and qualities necessary to win a war. Factories . . . railroads . . . ships . . . arms and munitions . . . supplies of tents, food and clothing . . . all these were important. But it had also become evident that there was something quite simple, though mysterious, which could turn the tide of battle as a sudden shift in the wind turns a grass fire. And that something was personal courage on the part of a few men or even of one man. Therefore it became important to recognize courage in a conspicuous way.

And so the old idea of military medals came back into view. It is spoken of here as an old idea because in this country, before the Civil War, the military decoration was considered to be a European vanity. There was no established standard medal for either officers or enlisted men, although several medals had been struck by order of Congress for individual awards to distinguished generals and other prominent Americans. (There had also been the Purple Heart, created by George Washington in 1782, as a decoration for "singular meritorious action," but only three men had received this award, as far as the records show.)

Early in 1861 E. D. Townsend, the Assistant

Adjutant General, proposed an Army medal to General Winfield Scott and others in high office. The desire to recognize and encourage gallantry was only one of Townsend's motives. He also thought that a medal might help prevent further cheapening of the brevet commission, which had frequently been bestowed as an honor through political influence, all too often without much military justification. The medal idea was not accepted. It was particularly offensive to Scott, who had been brought up in the earliest and purest traditions of Americanism and who didn't want to see his men tricked up with such foreign frippery and foolishness. However, Scott's was an age that was fading fast; in October of that year, worn down by an accumulation of years and ailments, the old general resigned and the medal proposition was again introduced. But in the meantime Gideon Welles and the Navy had got ahead of the Army. In December Congress passed and the President approved a Medal of Honor for the Navy. On December 30, 1861, Gideon Welles dictated a letter to the U.S. Mint, asking the director of the Mint to provide an appropriate design and suggest an engraver. With the sending of this message began the many adventures of the Medal of Honor and the many difficulties over which it was eventually to triumph.

Within a day or so the letter arrived at the U.S. Mint in Philadelphia, an imposingly pillared and marbled Greek revival building standing at Juniper and Chestnut Streets, where it was often mistaken for a church. This impression was not entirely discordant with the man who presided within, James Pollock, who had strong ideas about right and wrong and who was an enemy of cards and liquor. A Princeton graduate and formerly a lawyer, Congressman, judge and Governor of Pennsylvania, Pollock had only recently been appointed by Lincoln to the directorship of the Mint. He was finding it a new experience in a number of ways, one of which had to do with inscriptions and designs. Even as the letter from Welles arrived, he was struggling with one of these assignments: a request from Secretary of the Treasury Salmon P. Chase to put something about God on the coins. The Civil War had stimulated a surge of religious fervor, and a number of people had written to Chase suggesting that a reference to the Deity be placed on U.S. coinage — something that would indicate the faith of the people. Pollock was working on this, and he had got as far as "God Our Trust." Later this would develop into "God and Our Country," and it would take another two years or so before "In God We Trust" would be arrived at.

Pollock was discovering that it is one thing to have a great idea or concept, but quite another thing to give it a simple and memorable expression — words being in many respects like the keys of a piano, offering endless dissonant combinations that may be struck before one pleasing and appropriate chord is sounded. This is one of the oldest of fundamental creative difficulties, applying not only to words but to lines, colors, shapes and forms; but when the Secretary of the Navy's letter arrived requesting a design for a Medal of Honor, Pollock apparently failed to realize that he had the same sort of problem, only worse; Welles hadn't even given him an idea to start with.

Pollock answered Welles promptly, saying that he would have the design ready by the following week! He was not counting on the normal difficulties of artistic creation when channeled to a purpose and blocked by a deadline, or on the unusually difficult and delicate nature of this particular assignment. The three designs which he sent the Secretary of the Navy on January 14 were simply terrible. So were three more he sent on April 17. Welles, with an exercise of good judgment and taste for which posterity should thank him, rejected all of them. In the meantime legislation authorizing an Army medal had been introduced in Congress, and Pollock went after that order, sending a design to Secretary of War Edwin M. Stanton. There is no record that Stanton even replied, and Pollock's discouragement at this point may be imagined. He had struck out in every turn at bat.

One of the difficulties which the designer or designers had run into was the problem of portraying America as a figure on the medal — something that he or they had quite properly felt impelled to do. The dominant figure used on most U.S. coinage had been the Goddess of Liberty. Sometimes the head of the Goddess was shown with a turban bearing the word LIBERTY. Sometimes she was shown with a liberty cap, derived from the floppy, conical cap worn by Roman freedmen and later adopted as a symbol both by the French revolutionists and the youthful United States, and sometimes as a seated figure bearing the word LIBERTY.

However, the Goddess of Liberty was not appropriate for these times. Not for a military medal. Liberty in its sense of liberation from the U.S. Federal Government was what the rebelling Southern states were fighting for. And this sort of Liberty was what Northerners were fighting against; yet there was a famous document which declared that Liberty was one of man's unalienable rights; that to secure such rights "Governments are instituted among Men, deriving their just powers from the consent of the governed"; and that "whenever any Form of Government becomes destructive of these ends, it is the Right of the People to alter or abolish it, and to institute new Government . . ."

It was not the first time that the Medal of Honor would be found in the middle of such a conflict of principles; perhaps because the word "honor" itself is an aspiring abstraction, the medal would always have an almost magnetic power to attract to itself moral dilemmas. But in 1862 one thing was clear. To be in accord with the emotional climate of the North, the design of the medal had to partake of the mystic sense of great human importance that was beginning to attach itself to the words "The Union." In 1787 John Jay had predicted that "whenever the dissolution of the Union arrives, America will have reason to exclaim, in the words of the poet: 'Farewell! A long farewell to all my greatness!' " And now another poet had written:

Thou, too, sail on, O Ship of State!
Sail on, O Union, strong and great!
Humanity with all its fears,
With all the hopes of future years,
Is hanging breathless on thy fate!

It was James Pollock who put the design-concept into words. He wrote, "The medal proposed to be struck should bear devices emblematic of the nature of the contest in which the Government of the United States is now engaged, for the preservation of the Constitution and the integrity of the Union."

All well and good. But when it came to expressing this concept on a piece of metal there was little or nothing in the traditions of American medallic art to serve as a guide. It was true that Congress had authorized many national medals before this time, beginning with one for George Washington, but these were nearly always commemorative of individuals or events, and they provided little in the way of satisfactory precedent for the heroic representation of America that was now being sought. The best medals had been the very earliest ones, done by French engravers and distinguished for their good taste and numismatic style. One good example was a medal which Ben Franklin, who always did things properly, had executed in Paris under his own supervision in commemoration of the surrenders of Burgoyne and Cornwallis. On this medal America is depicted as the infant Hercules strangling two serpents while France as a classical female wards off a leopard (England) with spear and shield.

On several other medals a prominent French engraver had represented America as an Indian queen — a couple of times with an alligator at her feet. This was of little help. Following Pocahontas, Indian female royalty had gone out of style very rapidly. As for alligators, they were Southerners and repulsive ones at that. Also it might be argued that the whole Indian queen idea had been conceived by foreigners who were looking down their fine French noses at the United States.

There was little beyond these attempts to represent the new country on medals, and the general quality of medallic imagery in the United States left much to be desired. When American designers and engravers took over from the French, as they did after the Revolution, the classical style began to recede and stark realism gradually took its place. Thus, a typical medal might show in bas-relief on the obverse the head of a naval hero complete to the warts on his chin, or as near to life as the engraver could come, with a battle at sea portrayed in equally realistic detail on the reverse. Whatever may be said for classical mythology, it is a fountain of useful and beautiful symbolism having some currency in human understanding, and when this fountain dried up in the 1800's, the consequences in U.S. medal design were in many cases regrettable.

It was in this perilous artistic climate that the Medal of Honor was trying to get born, and it might have turned out to be a clinker. But someone — and this is another remarkable thing about the Medal of Honor — was always bursting out of a closet with drawn sword or coming over the hill with bugle sounding to rescue, protect and preserve it.

In Philadelphia, on the southwest corner of Fifth and Cherry Streets, there was an establishment of silversmiths which had been in business since 1812. It was the firm of Wm. Wilson & Son, and the Wilsons, apparently independently of the Mint, had been thinking about a design for the Medal of Honor as early as January, 1862. At some point they got together with the Mint, and there is evidence that they "furnished" the design for the medal that was finally accepted. The actual creation of the design has been credited to Christian Schussele, a talented immigrant from Alsace who had studied painting in Paris, where one of his instructors had been the well-known historical painter, Paul Delaroche.

The successful design consisted of a star suspended from an anchor, this in turn hanging from a ribbon. On the face of the star were symbolic figures which James Pollock described as follows in a letter accompanying the design when it was sent to Washington on May 6, 1862:

Obverse. The foul spirit of Secession & Rebellion is represented by a male figure in crouching attitude holding in his hands, serpents, which with forked tongues are striking at a large female figure, representing the Union or Genius of our Country, who holds in her right hand a shield, and in her left, the fasces. Around these figures, are thirty-four stars, indicating the number of states composing the Union. At the top of the medal or star, is the holder, in the form of an anchor around which a cable is entwined, indicating the naval service.

This little scene told a dramatic and easily understood story — and told it in a style of classical imagery which was a happy reversion to the forms of earlier years. The "large female figure" which the designer chose to represent the Union was the goddess Minerva, as she was known in Rome, or Athena in Greece, goddess of civic strength and wisdom, bestower of victory and patroness of certain professions, arts and crafts — to mention only a few of her virtuous attributes.

However, the artist made a slight modification. In what is perhaps her most familiar classical presentation, Athena wears a deep-bowled helmet surmounted by a graceful crest. If the viewer of the original Medal of Honor will look at it closely, using a magnifying glass if necessary, it will be seen that something remarkable has been done to Athena's helmet.

In place of the crest the designer has placed upon it an American Eagle with outstretched wings!

At first glance this seems to be an outrage perpetrated upon classical mythology. But as a matter of record, in her manner of dress Athena was an exceedingly adaptable goddess. According to the region of her worshipers and the locations of her shrines she wore various styles of helmets. One might have a crest upon it, another a war horse and chariot, another a figure of the Sphinx, and so on. Thus, for example, Athena Parthenos of Athens would wear a different helmet from, say, Athena Chalinitis of Corinth.

So in clapping a flap-winged eagle upon her head and converting her to Athena Americana, the designer was only doing what came naturally.

The figure of Athena (Minerva) thus rendered lacks the graceful, lithe exuberance and joyful fluidity of line that a Greek sculptor might have given her, but after all, the Greeks worshiped her, and there is nothing like worship to translate itself into beauty in art. Perhaps the designer of the Medal of Honor may even have been inhibited by feelings of resistance to idolatry, for the figure on the medal has a certain earthbound and respectable solidity. However, this excellent and virtuous goddess holding the fasces (ax bound in staves of wood) — symbol of unified authority — was wholly appropriate.

Upon her attacker, crouching at left and launching his forked-tongued serpents at her shield, the designer managed to cast a remarkable degree of reprobation. Small as the figure is, villainy stands out all over him; he is just the sort of rascal who *ought* to be thrashed. The scene in bas-relief has come to be known as "Minerva Repulsing Discord," and it was, of course, emblematic of the Civil War. But it would be equally appropriate for any war, enemies being *ipso facto* villains and the Medal of Honor destined to be exclusively a war medal.

Gideon Welles' reaction to this design was one of instant approval and the welcome inquiry, "How much?" Offered prices for gold, silver and bronze, he chose to have the medal executed in the least expensive, bronze. The Navy received 175 medals in December for $823.75.

Meanwhile, on July 12, 1862, Lincoln's approval of a joint resolution of Congress had finally authorized the manufacture of 2000 Medals of Honor for the Army. Pollock promptly wrote to Secretary of War Stanton suggesting that the medallic star already engraved for the Navy be adapted for Army use. It would be a simple matter, Pollock pointed out, to replace the Navy's anchor at the top of the star with an eagle or some other emblem appropriate to the Army.

Unlike Welles, who had shown great interest in the Medal of Honor and who seems to have attended personally to many details of its procurement, Stanton was dilatory in his attention to the matter. For all his virtues, and they were many, in the story of the Medal of Honor Stanton must appear as a somewhat sinister influence. A thickset man, with a bull neck, massive head, a thatch of black curling hair and a bushy crop of coarse whiskers, Stanton was as irascible as he looked — a man of snap decisions and summary judgments. Whereas Welles thought of the medal as a reward for action, later events were to prove that Stanton considered it also as an inducement — a badge to be widely distributed among soldiers who were being called on for extra effort. In the early autumn of 1862, however, standards for awards had not become a problem. The problem was how to get Stanton to approve some sort of design for the Army.

On October 10 he complained to Senator Henry Wilson of Massachusetts that he had examined several designs, but none of them were any good and they were all too expensive (this in spite of the fact that the proposed use of dies prepared for the Navy medal would save considerable money) and he wondered if the Senator would undertake the selection and commissioning of an artist to get the job done. Nothing came of this grumbling. Early in November of

1862 Stanton was finally persuaded by a representative of Wm. Wilson & Son to approve a design and sign a contract for 2000 medals, to be manufactured jointly by Wm. Wilson & Son and the Mint.

This design did turn out to be an adaptation of the Navy medal. Its main element is the same bronze star with its scene of Minerva Repulsing Discord. Suspending the star, instead of the Navy anchor, is a very substantial eagle, standing astride crossed cannon and a hefty pile of cannon balls; the heavier mass of this attachment, replacing the light and graceful anchor, tends to make the medal look a bit top-heavy, but the eagle is a noble bird with both muscle and spirit. The ribbon — consisting of a blue field above 13 alternating red and white vertical stripes — is attached to the wing tips of the eagle, leaving his head free to strike a fierce and defiant attitude. The brooch bar at the top of the ribbon employs a balanced design: a U.S. shield in the center with a cornucopia on either side. Concerning the cornucopias, Charles P. Hey, a devoted student of U.S. medals, once made this remark:

Signifying peace and prosperity, they spill beneficences exemplified in the fruits of bountiful crops. Yet on more than a score of fields, Bull Run to Fredericksburg, before any of these medals had been bestowed, death had reaped grim harvests. The brooch bar de-

Army Medal of Honor, 1862

Navy Medal of Honor, 1862

sign is certainly not without grace and balance; it was carefully executed and, in the design of the U.S. shield there is evidence of a knowing regard for the translation of heraldic tinctures in line. . . . But the design is reminiscent of a wood-cut heading in an Old Farmer's Almanac. Just a not-unbeautiful blooper for an army at war.

So the Medal of Honor that was thus fashioned for the Army, mostly by accident, was not a perfect decoration, but it caught in some peculiar way both the beguiling innocence and the awful grandeur of a youthful America going into its first big war.

Far less perfect was the legislation that was being framed in 1862 and 1863 to govern the awards of the Army Medal of Honor.

The joint resolution of Congress approved July 12, 1862, which authorized the decoration, bore a title that very clearly stated its purpose:

A Resolution to provide for the Presentation of "Medals of Honor" to the Enlisted Men of the Army and Volunteer Forces who have distinguished, or may distinguish, themselves in Battle during the present Rebellion.

An award for gallantry in combat action was manifestly intended, as indicated not only by this title but by an amendment a few months later. But what was promised in the title of the joint resolution was taken away in the text. The verbal weakness in this legislation, which was to prove nearly fatal to the worth of the medal, is indicated by author's capitalization in the following:

Resolved by the Senate and House of Representatives of the United States in Congress assembled, That the President of the United States be, and he is hereby, authorized to cause two thousand "Medals of Honor" to be prepared with suitable emblematic devices, and to direct that the same be presented, in the name of Congress, to such non-commissioned officers and privates as shall most distinguish themselves by their gallantry in action, AND OTHER SOLDIER-LIKE QUALITIES, during the present insurrection. And that the sum of ten thousand dollars be, and the same is hereby, appropriated out of any money in the treasury not otherwise appropriated, for the purpose of carrying this resolution into effect.

It soon became obvious to the Congress that this 1862 legislation was not completely satisfactory. It was too narrow, in that it limited the awards to noncommissioned officers and privates. What about commissioned officers, on whose part a certain boldness might often be required? Also, it limited the awards to the "present insurrection." What about future wars or men who had distinguished themselves in the past? Shouldn't the Medal of Honor have a permanent value comparable to that of Great Britain's Victoria Cross?

But in another sense the legislation was too broad. Besides providing for soldiers who distinguished themselves by their gallantry in action, it would award medals to those who displayed "other soldier-like qualities." This could stand for a whole host of noncombat virtues. Shouldn't the Medal of Honor — intended to be the nation's highest military decoration — be specifically limited to those who had earned it in action?

An act of Congress having to do with appropriations, approved March 3, 1863, included a section which read as follows:

Sec. 6. *And be it further enacted,* That the President cause to be struck from the dies recently prepared at the United States Mint for that purpose, "Medals of Honor" additional to those authorized by the act (Resolution) of July twelfth, eighteen hundred and sixty-two, and present the same to such officers, noncommissioned officers and privates as have most distinguished or who may hereafter most distinguish themselves in action; and the sum of twenty thousand dollars is hereby appropriated out of any monies in the treasury not otherwise appropriated, to defray the expenses of the same.

It will be noted that the phrase "and other soldier-like qualities" is conspicuously absent, and if this 1863 law could have been the guiding legislation from that point onward, the integrity of the Medal of Honor would have been assured. However, the previous law, the joint resolution of 1862, was not formally repealed; the two pieces of legislation were considered by the Army to be complementary. Together they were quoted in matters pertaining to the medal, and together they formed the legal basis of awards until the year 1897, when a Presidential directive and Army Regulations made the 1862, or "other soldier-like qualities," law inoperative in actual Army practice.

It may be wondered why this loose legal framework was allowed to continue. It is not usually difficult for the Army, particularly in time of war, to obtain the exact legislation it desires upon a matter so closely concerned with military affairs. It does not seem possible that Secretary of War Stanton had only a casual understanding of the legislation behind the Medal of Honor or of the real intent of Congress as indicated by the title of the 1862 joint resolution and the pertinent section of the act of 1863. Stanton had made his reputation in the law.

One can only wonder if it did not better suit the purposes of the Secretary to have both laws continue on the books, so that he could enjoy much greater discretion when it came to awarding Medals of Honor for whatever purposes might seem to be expedient.

However that may be, one thing is certain. The phrase "and other soldier-like qualities" left a big hole in the legal defenses of the Medal of Honor. And it was into this breach that the 27th Maine innocently marched, through the personal invitation, it must be added, of Secretary Stanton.

Two Paces Forward

As the thunderclouds rolled on toward Gettysburg in late June of 1863, the 25th and 27th Maine Regiments escaped the vortex of the gathering storm. But as the Army of the Potomac marched past Washington northward to its fateful encounter, it gathered into itself and took along many units which had up until then been assigned to the defenses of the city. As a result Washington began to feel naked; clerks and other normally noncombative people were armed and assigned to patrolling and guard duty; and the city was in somewhat the same condition it would be in a year later when — with the Army of the Potomac far away at Petersburg — the Confederate Jubal Early made a northward dash and rang his spear upon the gates of the capital.

In this nervous situation, President Lincoln and Secretary of War Stanton took thought of what extra troops might be available to them for defense, and thus the 25th and 27th Maine came to their attention. Here were two big strong regiments which ought to be extremely useful if only they could be persuaded to stay in service. The persuasive agent chosen was Daniel E. Somes, a Representative from Maine in the 36th Congress who had remained in Washington to practice law, and Stanton wrote the following letter:

WAR DEPARTMENT
Washington City
June 28, 1863

Hon. D. E. Somes:
Dear Sir:

I am directed by the President to say that he very much desires the Maine Regiments whose term of service is about expiring to remain in the service a short time until the present emergency passes over.

They will render aid of great importance to the Union which will properly be acknowledged by the Government.

You are authorized & requested to present the matter to the regiments in hope that their patriotic feelings will induce them to remain a short time.

Yours truly
Edwin M. Stanton
Secretary of War

Apparently Somes first visited the headquarters of the 25th Maine, commanded by Colonel Francis Fessenden. No one could ever question Fessenden's courage or say that he was not eager for action. He had been wounded at Shiloh before joining the 25th Maine, and after the 25th was disbanded he was to go back to the war with still another Maine regiment to lose his right leg in battle.

Colonel Fessenden soon discovered, however, that he was not going to see any further service with the 25th Maine. The request for extra duty was refused by the men.

This was not pusillanimous or as unpatriotic as it may sound. Many of the officers and men would return to the war in other units, as Fessenden did. But they had made many personal and business plans for the summer of 1863 based on the expected expiration of their term.

True, the Government said it was an emergency, but there had been an emergency the summer before when Lee invaded Maryland, and in another month probably there would be another emergency; war could hardly be thought of as anything else but a series of these unpleasant events.

What was happening here was simply a repetition of the classic blunder the Government had been making in wartime ever since the days of the Revolution — the mustering in of militia for short terms of service. By the time a nine months' regiment had been trained to any worthwhile degree of combat readiness its term ran out; meanwhile, it had cost as much to maintain in the field as a regiment of veterans. Worst of all, these short terms always seemed to be running out on the eve of an important battle. General Washington had been up against this problem over and over again in the Revolution.

In May of 1847 the army of General Scott, facing a campaign in the interior of Mexico, had been depleted by almost one-half when a militia term of 12 months expired. In the early days of the Civil War General Patterson had seen his Army of the Shenandoah nearly demoralized by the we-want-to-go-home clamor of the three months' men. On the day of the first battle of Bull Run a regiment of infantry and a battery of artillery with terms expiring — although appealed to by their commanding general and the Secretary of War — had begun their homeward march with the sound of the enemy cannon booming behind them.

So this sort of thing was almost traditional in America, and it was brought about not so much by a lack of warlike spirit on the part of the men as by simple considerations of equity and law. If a man served his agreed-upon time, he was entitled to go home. If not, of what use were agreements? And with other units going home, why was not this particular one, or that particular one, entitled to go also? Of the eight nine months' regiments from Maine, all went home in the summer of 1862. At least one very distinguished volunteer regiment, the 2nd Maine, had twice mutinied because of disagreements with the Government about dates of discharge, and no one could say that the 2nd Maine was not a fighting regiment; it had smitten the Confederates hip and thigh on a great many battlefields, and on one occasion, having been issued an over-generous ration of rum, it had even whaled the daylights out of a couple of Union regiments with its fists.

So this matter of staying in service or going home was not quite so simple or reflective of courage as it might seem today.

Having failed in his approach to the 25th Maine, D. E. Somes appeared at about 10 o'clock on the evening of June 29 at the headquarters of the 27th, and it must be imagined that he was in a state of some discouragement. What happened here, however, gave him cause for cheer. Colonel Wentworth promptly called a conference of his company commanders; and the captains of the 27th were all in favor of remaining in service; they also expressed the opinion that the men would be willing to stay.

There then ensued a tremendous hubbub in the regiment, with, it seemed, several hundred arguments all going on at once. Some men were trying to persuade others to stay, while some were attempting to convince comrades that they ought to go home. One extremely weighty question: what might happen to them if they remained in the defenses of Washington? If Lee's army evaded or defeated the Army of the Potomac and struck at the capital, the Army would live to fight another day and the politicians would probably make their get-away to another capital. But defeat for the thin line of defenders left round the city could mean only death or imprisonment.

There was also the question of what would happen to their families and property at home. Haying time was coming on in Maine, and the imminence of this particular season seems to have been one of the most important considerations affecting the decision of many of the soldiers. As far as labor-saving machinery was concerned, the family farm had advanced very little since the days of Washington's farmer-militiamen, and the farmer's reason for wanting to go home when he had planned to was exactly the same — specifically, if the hard physical work necessary for his family's survival was going to get done, he had to be home to do much of it himself. A woman or a child couldn't swing a scythe all day, and hired men would be too expensive even if one could be found. Moreover, it was haying time more than any other time that made this problem most severe, for then the weather was both friend and mercurial enemy. The sky might be bright as a diamond, but get a field of hay cut and curing and one edge of doomsday would come up over the horizon. Panting and exhausted people and horses might, if they were lucky, have most of the hay under-cover when the rain descended from the black, thunder-racked and lightning-ripped sky, but the whole business of haying was very much like war itself, and its urgency weighed upon the minds of the embattled farmers of the 27th Maine in a way that could not be fully appreciated today.

On June 30, while loud and agonized discussions of these and related matters were going on, Colonel Wentworth called the regiment out and formed it in a hollow square. Standing in the center, he read the orders for discharge and transportation home and then announced the request of the President and the Secretary of War. He said that he himself intended to remain and invited those officers and men who wished to do likewise to take two paces forward upon command.

In preparation for this order, the hollow square was unfolded and the regiment was formed in line. It was a solemn affair — a little like a revival meeting wherein those wishing to be saved are invited to "come forward," only it was possible destruction and not salvation that Wentworth was offering.

"Two paces forward — MARCH!"

The blue lines stirred and shifted. When they had rearranged themselves, a surprisingly large number of men were seen to have advanced. Captain Seth E. Bryant recalled that there were 176 by actual count.

But this was not the end of it. The arguments, the persuasions, the general to-do continued. Company commanders held additional call-outs and counts. The talking and arguing, which was growing very tiresome to everyone, continued until the middle of the evening, when those who had decided to go home — more than 550 — were allowed to depart. They marched off toward Washington and the railway depot under the command of Major John D. Hill, who had apparently volunteered to remain but who had been detailed to take charge of the departing troops. They went without band or colors and the camp was soon quiet again.

Meanwhile, the total of volunteers had increased to somewhere in the neighborhood of 300. And in the meantime, as recorded by Captain Bryant in his journal, Colonel Wentworth had made a trip into Washington, where he had visited the War Department and offered the service of an estimated 250 to 300 men. Bryant also noted that the Secretary of War had requested the names of the volunteers, saying that they were all going to get Medals of Honor.

Whether this talk of Medals of Honor took place after Wentworth had returned from Washington, or whether it was part of the message brought by Somes and so was also involved in the persuasions earlier in the day, does not appear to be of record. But there is no question about the source of the promise. Wentworth was later to state, "I was informed at that time by Mr. Stanton that Medals of Honor would be given to that portion of the Reg't that volunteered to remain." Under the law providing medals for gallantry in action *and other soldier-like qualities,* Stanton had a perfect right to award the decoration to the volunteers of the 27th Maine.

Yet to a man who would hand it out on this scale, the medal was obviously no great emblem of honor. And it apparently had small weight as an inducement with the men of the 27th Maine who remained in service. As one of the officers was to put it years later, "We thought little of it at the time as we considered that we were merely doing our duty." Others would refer to it rather vaguely as a "badge." The Medal of Honor had not been long established, and its meaning to the men in ranks was insignificant compared to what it might be today.

No one, of course, realized that what Stanton had done was to deal the Medal of Honor a staggering blow; it was now on the way to becoming a sort of good-conduct medal. And this was not all he had done. On the day following that on which Stanton wrote the letter to Somes, there was made by his direction as Secretary of War still another official promise that was to haunt and harass War Department officials for decades. Here is the form in which it appeared:

GENERAL ORDERS
No. 195

WAR DEPARTMENT
ADJUTANT GENERAL'S OFFICE
Washington, June 29, 1863

The Adjutant General will provide an appropriate Medal of Honor for the troops who, after the expiration of their term, have offered their services to the Government in the present emergency; and also for the Volunteer troops from other States that have volunteered their temporary service in the States of Pennsylvania and Maryland.

> by order of the Secretary of War:
> E. D. Townsend
> Assistant Adjutant General

The predicament that Army administrators had to face years later, and the threat to the Medal of Honor which this order raised, revolved around two questions:

First, was the "appropriate Medal of Honor" mentioned in this order the same medal as that authorized by Congress in its acts of 1862 and 1863?

Second, was it the same medal as that promised and later issued to the 27th Maine?

If the answer to both questions was yes, then a dangerous procedure had not only been ordered, it had also been executed and given precedent in the promise to the 27th Maine; and the precedent was a potential disaster, for it was later estimated that as many as 50,000 men would have been qualified under the broad provisions of General Orders No. 195. Congress had appropriated only $30,000 for Medals of Honor, which would have hardly been enough for such extensive distribution; moreover, Congress had indicated, in its act approved in 1863 at least, that this was a decoration intended to reward distinguished service in combat — not something that might have been as widely distributed as a G.A.R. badge.

For the moment it is enough to record the birth and existence of General Orders No. 195 and to leave it ticking away like an infernal machine; it would tick for a great many years, and it will be returned to later in this narrative.

A much more immediate threat to the future of the Medal of Honor had been posed by Stanton's improvident promise to the 27th Maine and by the taking of two paces forward by a portion of that regiment. And yet that short march itself would awaken the guardian spirits who were eventually to fend off its effects upon the Medal of Honor.

In the Army there is an old saying born of long experience and deep wisdom: "Never by word, deed or *bright look* ever volunteer for *anything*."

People sometimes do volunteer in the Army, and when this happens everybody is delighted, but by its very nature the Army is organized on the assumption that men are going to be ordered to do what they do and therefore its procedures can be predictable. Most of its forms, rules and regulations are based on this assumption of predictable, dependable behavior.

By innocently violating the system, approximately 300 men of the 27th Maine plunged the Medal of Honor into the most dreadful difficulty of its history. But the violation itself was what eventually did much to save the integrity of the

113

medal; it gave rise to a magnificent snarl-up in the administrative process which followed and to Olympian clouds of protective confusion beneficial to the Medal of Honor.

Historians have frequently observed that the Civil War was the first truly "modern" war because it made use of the railroad, the telegraph, aerial reconnaissance, and so forth. It might be added that the Union army also made use of paperwork on a massive modern scale.

At one time or another during the year — daily, monthly, quarterly, annually or on special occasions — a company commander had to deal with forms for around 20 rolls, returns, requisitions, reports, certificates and so on. There was even a quarterly Return of Blanks on which he was supposed to account for the books, forms and blanks he had on hand.

One of these which would be familiar to the company officer of today was the morning report, which the company sent to regimental headquarters daily. (There was also a consolidated morning report for regiments.) The purpose of the morning report was to show the number of officers and men the company had present for duty and to explain what those who were not "for duty" were doing, also to show the numbers the company had lost or gained. On it a man's name might be recorded if he were not "for duty"; then it was necessary to record that So-and-so was sick or absent without leave or in confinement or whatever. But the morning report was not intended to be a list of names; it was primarily a numerical status report.

Much more difficult to prepare were the reports that did list every individual by name. These included the descriptive book, in which was recorded a great deal of information about the individual; the descriptive list or roll which was sent with a single man or detachments of men when transferred and which included clothing accounts, pay information and many other items of information; and the muster roll which was prepared when men were mustered in, paid or mustered out.

Making out a muster roll was an ordeal which a new company clerk often approached in a state of panic, and the sergeant major of a regiment sometimes choked in purple rage upon receiving a roll sent in by an inexperienced man. The company clerk's manual was careful to point out that "The Muster Rolls are much the most important papers to make out, as well as the most difficult to execute. Companies are frequently kept without their pay for months, owing to the inability of the officers to make out the Muster and Pay Rolls . . ."

The muster roll was much more than a list of names. Once a man's name had been written down (which seemed simple enough, but wasn't if it was to be written correctly) a long string of facts and figures had to be attached to it. When did the man enlist? Where? Who enlisted him? Who paid him last? To what date? How much bounty had he been paid? How much was due? Was he entitled to extra pay? Had he been promoted — if so when and by what order? Any stoppages of pay, fines, sentences? Any wounds? Absences? What was the number of miles traveled to place of rendezvous . . . how many miles had he to go from place of discharge? What was the state of his clothing account? Value of arms lost and destroyed? And so on — there were many questions to be answered by appropriate entries on a muster-out roll. What the clerk had to deal with was a bag of bees — a swarm of names, figures, dates, order numbers and endless other details.

To handle this sort of thing well takes an extremely conscientious person; to do it perfectly takes the determination of a fanatic. The actual quality of record-keeping that generally resulted was a matter of considerable anguish for John L. Hodsdon, the Adjutant General of Maine, for he realized that in the near future these documents would provide the basis for widows' pensions, claims for bounties in arrears and other matters of vital importance to many people. Hodsdon found that muster-out rolls of certain regiments lacked so many names he knew should be there or were so marred by other obvious errors that to correct them he had to consult all sorts of collateral records down to the original enlistment contracts, even sending his chief clerk to Washington to check on payrolls and other records filed there from units in the field.

In the 27th Maine the company commanders and clerks evidently had planned to work on the muster-out rolls when they reached Maine, where they would take several days to complete these massive documents. (They actually took about ten days when they did arrive.)

But then on June 30 came the bomb that bewildered the clerks and shattered all their plans — the sudden schism of the regiment taking place all in one day, with some men going home and some staying. Which part was supposed to contain the headquarters of record — that going home or that staying? Which part, in fact, *was* the regiment? Anyway, there was obviously no time to make a separate muster or descriptive roll for the men who were departing; that would have been a complete impossibility in the turmoil of that single day, with the nonvolunteers packing up and leaving that very evening.

The officers of the volunteer section apparently assumed that when the nonvolunteers reached Maine a separate muster-out roll would be made for them and they would be discharged on that basis. Then, when the volunteers got home, another muster-out roll would be made. But the volunteers remained at Arlington Heights only until July 4; the outcome of the battle of Gettysburg then being made known, they started for Maine. If, during the period June 30–July 4, any official record of their names was made, nobody was ever able to find it.

In Portland the regiment was reunited, and the

clerks must have heaved a mighty sigh of relief; the 27th Maine could now be mustered out all in one piece. A single, unified muster-out roll was prepared and filed with the state and Federal governments. And as far as the official records were concerned, this left unanswered a certain question which was to arise and become the subject of great controversy years later: *What were the names of the officers and men who had remained to serve in the defenses of Washington and how many were there?*

Captain Joseph Warren had written in his diary on June 30, 1863, "296 men have volunteered to stop a while for the protection of the Capitol."

Colonel Wentworth early in 1865 reported to the Governor of Maine that "315 men & officers of the 27th Reg't volunteered to remain and the balance with the 25 came home." (He meant came home with the 25th Maine.)

Sergeant Major Calvin Hayes was later to state that "around 300" volunteered to remain.

In 1895 the survivors of the regiment published a small history listing the names of 312 officers and men who "volunteered to remain and did remain."

In 1898 a War Department official stated that, according to the consolidated morning report for July 1, 1863, the officers and men present at Arlington Heights numbered 301.

At the time of the event the matter of who had stayed and who had not was apparently of no great moment. By remaining four extra days the volunteers did not feel that they had accomplished anything of heroic importance. In fact, they tried to minimize their contribution, as shown by a letter from the New England Soldiers' Relief Association of 194 Broadway, New York, sent to the Governor of Maine on July 7, 1863:

The patriotic three hundred members of the 27th Maine Regiment arrived here on Sunday evening about 11 o'clock. A public reception here was offered them by the Sons of Maine, resident here — which was declined. A meeting of the Officers was held at the rooms of our Association, when the dispatches from his Hon. the Mayor of Portland were read to them, tendering and urging them to accept a public reception in Portland today. But as the officers are anxious to return to the Army and take as many of their old men with them as possible, they declined the reception at present, it would create bad feeling among the balance of the command who have preceded them home. They left last night by the Stonington line.

So ended the medal-winning service of the 27th Maine, but this did not represent the last attempt made by Edwin M. Stanton to effect a wholesale distribution of Medals of Honor. A little more than a year later the following telegram came to the office of the Secretary of War:

PADUCAH, SEPTEMBER 1, 1864
(RECEIVED 9:15 P.M.)
HON. E.M. STANTON
THERE ARE FIVE REG'TS OF ONE HUNDRED DAYS MEN IN MY COMMAND, TIME EXPIRES THE SEVENTH, EIGHTH AND TENTH OF THIS MONTH. IF TWO REGIMENTS WILL REMAIN TEN DAYS OVER THEIR TIME TO ASSIST ME WILL THEY BE PAID FOR THE EXTRA TIME?
E. A. PAINE
BRIGADIER GENERAL

The reply was prompt:

WAR DEPARTMENT, WASHINGTON, D.C.
SEPTEMBER 1, 1864, 8:40 A.M.
BRIGADIER GENERAL PAINE, PADUCAH
ANY REGIMENTS THAT MAY REMAIN OVER THEIR TIME TO ASSIST YOU WILL BE PAID FOR THE EXTRA TIME, RECEIVE THE THANKS OF THE DEPARTMENT, AND A MEDAL OF HONOR.
EDWIN M. STANTON
SECRETARY OF WAR

There is no doubt that *the* Medal of Honor was intended, for it was the only Army medal in existence. The special medal Stanton had authorized through General Orders No. 195 in 1863 (if it was a special medal — a decoration other than the one established by Congress) had never been manufactured and never would be, nor would any money ever be appropriated for it.

Fortunately, the large-scale award to General Paine's men was never made, and so the Medal of Honor escaped what would have been another terrific blow. The exchange of messages with General Paine was chiefly significant in that it provided additional evidence of what Stanton's attitude toward the medal was. It also may have prompted the Secretary of War to remember that he had made a certain promise to Mark Wentworth of the 27th Maine, and he took steps to make good on the promise. But once again there descended a benevolent administrative fog that was eventually to help guard the Medal of Honor from harm.

Soon after Stanton's exchange of messages with Paine took place, E. D. Townsend, the Assistant Adjutant General, sent the following message to John Potts, chief clerk of the War Department:

The enclosed list is sent to you by direction of the Secretary of War with a view, as I understand, of having medals prepared for the men in consideration of their having remained in service after their time had expired about the time of the battle of Gettysburg. The regiment was the 27th Maine, Col. Mark F. Wentworth.

The list was the entire muster-out roll of the 27th Maine, containing the names of 864 men!

In September of 1864 Edwin Stanton had a great many things on his mind. General Grant, after having subjected the army to immense slaughters during the spring and summer, was piled up in front of Petersburg. The public was shocked by the heavy losses. A presidential election was coming on. And there were many other large matters concerned with running a war that must have had the Secretary, normally an excitable man, in a dither much of the time. (Artemus Ward, the popular comic of the day, advised President Lincoln to "tell E. Stanton that his boldness, honesty and vigger merits all praise, but to keep his undergarments on. E. Stanton has apeerently only one weakness, which it is, he can't allus keep his undergarments from flying up over his hed.") It is easy to imagine that one day Stanton might have said, "By the way, I just remembered . . . those fellows in the 27th Maine are supposed to get Medals of Honor. See to it at once."

And the Assistant Adjutant General, without looking into the matter further, sent for the 27th Maine muster roll, which would have been filed with his office upon the regiment's discharge, and caused to be made from it a list of all the names on the roll.

Clerk John Potts, receiving this list, dutifully sent it to Wm. Wilson & Son in Philadelphia.

And the Wilsons set about the considerable task of engraving inscriptions on the backs of 864 medals, afterward placing each one in a neat morocco case.

This job would last for the remainder of the year. Then the bulk shipment of about 200 pounds of medals would go to Maine. And eventually Mark F. Wentworth would receive the assignment of making distribution.

Thus, although perhaps not realizing it, Wentworth would find himself on the spot at a critical moment in the history of the Medal of Honor.

At this time the medal had no long-established meaning. It was simply a bit of bronze and bright ribbon worth about $2.50. (The price had gone up since Gideon Welles bought the first lot.) Wentworth might have reasoned that a thing of this kind is whatever you want to make of it. For example, Secretary Stanton apparently didn't hold the decoration in too high a regard. He could have meant its award as a sort of unit citation for the 27th Maine. Perhaps that is what Stanton really intended.

As for handing it out, it would be a lot easier if Wentworth simply gave it to all members of the regiment, whose names were engraved on the reverses. Easier and more advantageous in the strengthening of Wentworth's political influence in York County.

There would be only one thing troublesome and that was the name of the confounded thing. It included the word "honor."

Wentworth's understanding of that word — which was already more than adequate — was to be further enlarged before he came to his fateful assignment.

"They Never Failed to Understand"

The expiration of a Maine regiment's term of service did not necessarily mean a cessation of hostilities on the part of all its members. Many took a discharge from one regiment only to serve with another, some going off to war for the third time. In the late fall of 1863 the inducements for veteran enlisted men were particularly strong; a veteran reenlisting could collect at least $700 in bounties. The Adjutant General pointed out that this was a sum sufficient "to lay the foundation for independence and place him beyond the reach of want" — a somewhat optimistic estimate with flour selling at $12 a barrel and a pair of shoes at $18.

For officers there were opportunities for new commands or promotions. But quite apart from this there was a whole complex of emotions driving men back to the conflict. The mixture might include feelings of duty and patriotism, a desire for comradeship and excitement and a certain discomfort at being seen hanging around home while others were away in the Army. But almost certain to be one of the ingredients was the realization that something big was going on, and a man felt he ought to be there and continue to be a part of it, or he could not say that he had lived one of the great experiences of his generation.

This feeling was particularly acute for Mark F. Wentworth. With the 27th Maine he had bought his ticket and got into the circus tent — he had even heard the music of the band — but it couldn't be said that he had seen the show.

Wentworth began writing to the Governor and Adjutant General asking that he be given another command. One of his requests was even supported by a letter to Governor Abner Coburn from Vice President Hannibal Hamlin who said, in effect, "You will recall that this is the fellow who kept his troops in the defenses of Washington when others went home, and you ought to do something for him."

However, there were not many opportunities for a major assignment in the remainder of 1863. There was a battery of artillery being raised, but this was not a sufficiently large command for a colonel. There was also a regiment of cavalry, but cavalry was apparently not considered to be Wentworth's dish. That left only two regiments being raised in 1863, the 29th and 30th Infantry, but two other colonels were ahead of him. George L. Beal, who had recovered from severe wounds received at Antietam, took the 29th, and Francis Fessenden took the 30th, going off to give a leg for his country.

Things began looking up early in 1864. Two additional three years' regiments of infantry were authorized, the 31st and the 32nd, and Wentworth received command of the 32nd.

If Wentworth had not seen enough action to suit him with the 27th Maine, he would see plenty with the 32nd. In some ways this was the most remarkable Maine regiment to participate in the war. It was the last fully organized infantry regiment to be raised in the state; it was made up of boys to a greater than normal extent; and it was destined to fight itself completely out of existence in Grant's campaign of 1864.

At that stage of the war, even in the North, it was not easy to get a regiment together, so drained and depleted was the able-bodied male population. While the term "volunteer regiment" continued to be used, there were powerful spurs toward volunteering. The draft was no longer an instrument of the states and the old militia laws; it was now being put into effect under a national conscription act, so that more than ever it was a case of volunteering or else being drafted. High bounties were added inducements, as were the sums that well-to-do men, when drafted, might pay substitutes for going to war in their places.

The order authorizing the 32nd Maine indicated a desire that two-thirds of the officers should have had previous experience as commissioned officers in active service. This proved to be not completely possible; two-thirds of those obtained did have previous experience, but not all of these had been officers. For his adjutant Wentworth procured a commission for Calvin Hayes, who had proved his worth as sergeant major of the 27th Maine. (The quartermaster was also a former noncom of the 27th Maine, and several of the company officers had served with the 27th. A couple of these had previously been officers, but the others including one of the company commanders, Captain Horace H. Burbank, had entered the 27th as enlisted men.)

For a regiment assembled at this late date in the war, the 32nd Maine had fairly good officer material. For the enlisted men it had to dip into the lower age bracket to a degree that might be considered pathetic. The historian of the regiment, as it turned out, would be Henry Houston of Company C, but Henry did not get around to publishing his history until 1903, which put a strain on his memory and drove him to consult a great many collateral but not particularly pertinent sources. What tells as much about the regiment as anything is Houston's own photograph taken at the time of his enlistment; it is that of a small boy who is trying to look fierce and who is clad in a Union overcoat many sizes too large, the open collar yawning so wide that by a slight movement Henry would have been able to sink down and withdraw his head, tilted forage cap and all, completely out of sight.

The legal military age was 18 to 45, so on enlistment papers the age had to be represented as at least 18. In going over the muster rolls, Houston noted that about one out of three enlisted men was recorded as being 18, which meant that many of them had "borrowed" time in order to arrive at even that tender age. Writing about it almost 40 years later, Houston was frank to admit that he himself had borrowed almost a year and a half in order to pass muster and had tried to enlist twice before he got past the examining surgeons and into the 32nd Maine. Even so, he was far from the youngest boy in Wentworth's regiment. There was a private named Edwin C. Millikin in Company H who was said to be 14. He and his father, Benjamin F. Millikin, had signed up for the 32nd Maine together. The old man made corporal and thus was able to maintain his position of parental authority. Both survived the war.

It is to be hoped that no regiment ever went off to any war with less preparation than the 32nd Maine.

Their place of rendezvous and encampment in that winter of 1864 was the flat top of a hill on the west side of Augusta known as Camp Keyes. This would have been an excellent site in summer, but often as not in the winter it was swept by gales and buried under the snow. Here, in long rows of rough wooden barracks heated by smoking stoves, with triple tiers of bunks running lengthwise down the interiors, Wentworth assembled his men and tried to make them into a regiment of infantry. The deep snow often made it impossible to drill on the field, and the limited space inside the barracks would not accommodate the instruction of even small squads. As late as April there was a tempestuous storm of three days' duration which piled added drifts about the camp.

Colonel Wentworth figured that when spring came they could get out and do some training. But even while the snows of April were deep upon Camp Keyes, a short, cigar-chewing Union general hundreds of miles to the south was making plans that would deny Wentworth's men even the most rudimentary instruction. Ulysses S. Grant wanted to get the war over with, and the surest, fastest way he knew of was to bring to bear a continuous, grinding superiority of sheer manpower. This meant putting in every soldier available. At some point the author of such a policy has to disregard excuses, inconveniences and even impracticalities.

And so it was that Wentworth's regiment, without having even learned the manual of arms satisfactorily, in fact without being completely organized, was ordered south to participate in the Wilderness Campaign, the most brutal and destructive action which the war had yet brought to pass. On April 20 the companies that happened to be organized, A through F, left Camp Keyes designated as the first battalion. They traveled a route familiar to the former members of the 27th Maine who were among them: by rail to Boston and thence to Fall River, and from there on a steamer to Amboy, New Jersey, where cattle cars awaited them, "and by no means clean ones at that," as one of the men remembered. The 27th Maine veterans among them must have been amused at the indignation which these miserable conveyances called forth; it was just the reaction that *they* had displayed when they were rattling southward in the autumn of 1862. They must also have reflected upon this as an index of the Civil War's increasing incivility; in the 27th Maine they hadn't encountered this humiliating come-down until they reached Philadelphia; now the cattle cars were picking them up in Jersey.

There was another and more somber difference the 27th Maine veterans noticed. When they had passed over this same route a year and a half previously, there had been ovations all along the way: people had gathered at railway stations to wave, cheer and wish them luck. Now these same stations were silent and seemingly deserted by comparison. The glory had departed; people had become so accustomed to seeing large bodies of troops passing along this route that the spectacle had lost all its novelty.

And the silence was symbolic, too, of the sort of war the youngsters of the 32nd Maine were going to; it had passed from its exciting spring and summer into the dusty boredom of a late afternoon in September, and the light that illumined it was tinged with weariness and an accumulation of endless griefs. Yet among those who had been schoolboys when the conflict began, the sense of anticipation and adventure could not be dimmed. They were off to a theater of war that was already passing into legend,

131

where their older brothers and friends had given names like Malvern Hill, Manassas, Antietam, Fredericksburg and Gettysburg a storybook sound.

At Arlington Heights, that rendezvous of so many Union regiments, the 32nd Maine became part of the 2nd Brigade, 2nd Division, Ninth Corps. The 2nd Brigade at that time consisted of four battle-worn regiments, to which were added, along with the first battalion of the 32nd Maine, the 31st Maine and a regiment from Vermont. This brought the total strength to around 2,700 men, but with the old regiments so reduced by previous service, the new men made up the greater part of the brigade. The veterans resented having their identity overwhelmed in this manner, and so on the first march they undertook to show the recruits who was who in the 2nd Brigade, striking out into a long, swinging route step which they kept up mile after mile without letup. Wentworth's youngsters had had no previous conditioning; they had been cooped up in barracks, a boat and cattle cars; they had come suddenly from a cold climate into weather of unaccustomed warmth; and they were borne down by equipment they were not used to. Yet in contradistinction to the history of almost every other unit on its first day of extended marching, the first battalion of the 32nd Maine pulled into Fairfax Court House that night with very few missing after a march of 16 miles.

Next day the temperature was even higher and

the pace faster. Henry Houston recalled:

It was rather an eager, breathless race than an ordinary march, but we felt as if the honor of the Pine Tree State depended on our exertions. And if we suffered, we had the keen satisfaction of knowing that our persecutors of the day before were being punished quite as much as ourselves. So we kept up a killing pace throughout the second day, and went into Bristoe Station wearied and worn out, but with few vacancies, comparatively speaking, in our ranks. . . . The hint that we thus gave was good-naturedly accepted by the veterans of the brigade, and a proper appreciation of our abilities in the direction of marching was always subsequently manifested by them.

At Bristoe Station the battalion underwent about a week of training including, for the first time, firing. Even though they had come from a state where familiarity with firearms was somewhat traditional, there were those among them who needed the practice. One, a sailor, failed to observe that his piece was misfiring and kept cramming charges into the bore until he had inserted three or four. The next time his file was to fire, a more effective cap than the others he had been using ignited the whole train of charges. There was a terrific explosion. The barrel of his musket was split like a peeled banana. Several soldiers were powder-blackened, and the whole platoon was scared almost out of its wits, but fortunately there were no casualties.

A few days later they were in the Wilderness.

Grant had begun a drive toward Richmond that was to result in 50,000 Union casualties in a little more than a month's time. It proceeded somewhat in the manner of a high school football play which begins as a plunge through center and then, as the defense proves too strong for penetration, verges into an off-tackle play and finally into an end run. The armies would collide and entrench; the Union forces would make fruitless and costly assaults against Lee's field fortifications; and then Grant would order another turning movement around Lee's right flank — a move the Southerners always seemed to anticipate by being somewhat ahead of the Union flankers, in position, and ready for the next attack.

For the Union infantryman this often meant a hard fight immediately followed by a long and desperately hurried march. Distances of 25 to 30 miles a day were not uncommon. The soldiers of the 32nd Maine were doing their best, but Wentworth must have felt more than a twinge of compassion at seeing boys among them, perhaps not much older than children he had known back in Kittery, bearing their muskets on thin and tired shoulders.

Late in May they began to recognize their proximity to places they had read about, such as Gaines' Mills, Fair Oaks and the White Oak

Swamp. And there was a river called the Chicka-hominy. Henry Houston wrote:

> For several days past we had been tra-versing historic ground, for the old Army of the Potomac was once more on the soil of the peninsula. . . . And even for us, who were younger and less experienced soldiers, who had donned the uniform since those events had transpired, there was an inspiration and incentive in the very names of the localities amid which we found ourselves.

They were presently to know another name which would be remembered as about the blood-iest of all — Cold Harbor, in the vicinity of which between June 1 and June 12 the Union army lost more than 12,000 men and where the 32nd Maine had its share of casualties. It is doubtful if anyone found much inspiration in the area after that. There was a brief spell of trench warfare around Cold Harbor during which the war began to look and smell and feel very unro-mantic indeed. It was so bad that the medical di-rector of the army addressed a letter to General Meade which said in part:

> The army has been marching and fighting thirty-two consecutive days, in which time no vegetable rations have been issued, and has now reached a region of country notoriously miasmatic and unhealthy. The water now

used by the troops is entirely derived from surface drainage and is saturated with organic matter derived from decaying vegetable tissues. The ground around many camps is strewn with dead and decomposing horses and mules, and with the hides and offal of slaughtered beef-cattle. Very few regiments provided sinks for the men, and their excreta are deposited upon hill sides to be washed from thence into the streams, thus furnishing an additional source of contamination to the water. As is to be expected, under such circumstances, sickness is increasing in the army . . .

On June 7 there was an attempt to police the area; a two-hour truce was arranged with the Confederates, and rescue and burial parties went out between the lines. There were few soldiers to rescue; most had died of their wounds, exposure, hunger and thirst. The dead were in most cases so bad off as to be unrecognizable, and they were buried where they lay.

Even though the four remaining companies of the 32nd had arrived from Maine on May 25, bringing the regiment up to the requisite number of companies, the condition of the regiment following Cold Harbor corresponded to that of a veteran regiment that might have been fighting for a couple of years. On June 10 Colonel Wentworth wrote to Governor Samuel Cony of Maine, "We have lost heavily from our very best men & the remainder are nearly tired out. Our Regt now numbers only about three hundred and fifty muskets." On the same day his adjutant, Calvin Hayes, recorded in his diary that they had lost about 125 killed and wounded. Sickness, exhaustion and other subtractions had done the rest. The untrained regiment had been in action a little more than a month and already had the Wilderness, Spotsylvania Court House, the North Anna and Cold Harbor behind it. Worse was yet to come.

In the middle of June, Grant became dissatisfied with his position, which was unhealthy in more ways than one. He gave up the idea of a direct assault upon Richmond and took the army on still another flanking movement — this one exceedingly far-flung — which was to take it across the James River to Petersburg, almost directly south of Richmond. Petersburg was an important communications center between Richmond and the rest of the South; roads and rail lines ran through it to the Confederate capital; if Petersburg could be captured by a surprise attack, Richmond would fall as a matter of course.

How fast Grant moved was something that the 32nd Maine remembered in the soles of its feet. On June 14 the regiment marched 35 miles in 27 hours — not a record by any means, but an exhausting exercise considering that the air was hot and sultry, the dust was suffocating and they only rested one hour on the way. The romantic adventure which they had pictured had turned into the sort of laborious and agonizing dream from which one tries in vain to awake but which can hardly be remembered once it has gone. Men plodded on in a daze, with the march taking a steady toll. Many who were exhausted by the long campaign simply walked to one side and fell down; and many of these vanished, some dying by the roadside to be buried in graves that were soon overgrown by weeds and forgotten, some picked up by Confederate patrols and taken away to prisons where they died without record.

The fantasy of the march continued; on the evening of June 15 they passed across a vast expanse of water, walking a few inches above its surface; it was the James River and someone said the pontoon bridge they were on was 2,000 feet long. On the night of June 16–17 they moved into an attack position in front of one of the outer lines of Petersburg, and there followed another weird experience. Under the cover of darkness, with other troops of their division, they moved silently into a ravine leading to the enemy earthworks. Orders were to keep dippers and canteens in haversacks to prevent rattling, with no talking, no shots to be fired during the attack. When the first light of dawn gleamed on their fixed bayonets, there was a stealthy and savage rush over the fortifications, and around 500 Confederates were captured before they knew what had happened.

But this and other breaks in the Confederate

lines were not exploited. Grant had made his move to Petersburg with brilliant secrecy and swiftness; breaches in the outer lines were made; but then there were mix-ups and delays, and by the time the whole army had arrived and arranged itself, the defenders had pulled back into shorter and stronger lines, more fortifications had been thrown up, and Lee had moved some of his best troops down from Richmond to the support of the beleaguered city.

The 32nd Maine, which had been in the forefront of the successful dawn attack on June 17, participated in more inconclusive fighting during the next two days, then dug in. The men tore the earth with knives and bayonets, throwing it up with hands and dippers for temporary cover. These entrenchments, deepened and elaborated, became their permanent fortifications for the next several weeks.

The war around Petersburg then became something new and strange, with men digging deep holes in the ground and burrowing about like moles. The regiment settled down to the deadly routine of siege warfare — digging trenches that zigzagged this way and that, constructing underground shelters, building bomb proofs and dodging death that came straight down out of the sky in mortar shells or suddenly from nowhere in the *thwack* of a sniper's bullet.

The Maine men were still in the Ninth Corps commanded by General Ambrose E. Burnside, whose singular lack of good luck would soon involve them in the most bizarre and fatal adventure of the war.

This was the notorious battle of the Crater. The Union and Confederate lines on the Ninth Corps sector of the front were fairly close together. A regiment of Pennsylvania miners in the corps conceived the idea of digging a 500-foot tunnel to a point underneath a Confederate fort, placing four tons of gunpowder under it, laying a long fuse and blowing the fort sky-high. Burnside approved the scheme and made certain dispositions of troops, including Negro soldiers, who were to rush through the gap made by the giant mine and seize a hill dominating the defenses of the city.

The 32nd Maine, or what was left of it by then, was included in the assault force.

As the work progressed, rumors of the gunpowder plot were widespread and even reached the Confederates, who either dismissed them as scare stories or were unable to determine exactly where the explosives were placed. One of the rumors even carried all the way back home to southern Maine where, on July 30, readers of the *Portsmouth Journal* read a story that had been picked up from the *Richmond Whig*, written by a prophet without honor in his own country, a man named Browne who predicted that Petersburg was going to be destroyed as by a tremendous blast from the infernal regions and who wrote, "I tremble to think of it. Perhaps a few hours will bring the dreadful realization."

The timing of the story was right on target as

far as the Maine readers were concerned. The tunnel had been dug without detection and on that very morning the explosion had come off shortly before 5 o'clock, and while Petersburg itself was not blown up, it must have seemed that it had been to observers because the uproar was tremendous.

One soldier-historian described it thus:

> . . . There was a deep rumble and the earth in the neighborhood trembled as with an earthquake, and then with a tremendous explosion a conical mountain, seemingly half an acre in extent, rose in the air, carrying with it stones, timbers, caissons, bodies and limbs of men, and some of the heavy guns of the fort. Remaining poised for a moment, the black earth in the center streaked and serried with lightning, surrounded by white smoke which still came pouring out of the volcano, the mass settled back to earth.
>
> Of the two hundred Confederates in the fort, many still asleep, none escaped. . . . The Confederate troops in the works for nearly a quarter of a mile on both sides of the exploded fort left their positions, fleeing in terror from the wholly unexpected sight so much resembling the Day of Judgment. A great gateway to Cemetery Ridge and Petersburg was opened up . . .

But it was a gateway that was soon to close. As

was the case with so many of Burnside's misfortunes, what happened next was not altogether the whiskered general's fault. The Union attack started, but it had been badly prepared, partly because of interference from higher headquarters which had resulted in last-minute changes of troop assignments. Also, there was a high parapet in front of the Union line, an abatis and other obstacles. A proper means of passing over and through these had not been made ready. The crater left by the explosion — 170 feet long, 80 feet wide and 30 feet deep — was itself an obstacle, and a column of troops went straight into the big hole, where it bogged down for the duration of the fight. Altogether the attack was so slow in getting started and so badly coordinated after it did get under way that the surprised Confederate forces had plenty of time to regroup, bring up additional troops and cannon and direct a withering fire upon the Union soldiers.

Portions of the Ninth Corps kept dribbling forward and were in nearly every case promptly pinned down, taking refuge in the crater, in the blasted earthworks and wherever else they could find shelter from the savage Confederate cross fire that was turning the area into a slaughter pen.

If the battleground was confused, the zone of approach was almost equally so, with units bumping into each other and getting tangled up in the crowded trenches. But Wentworth somehow got the 32nd Maine through the mess, over the parapets and into the fight. They entered a scene as infernally scary as anything the war had yet produced. The explosion had cast the ground up into strange forms and shapes, covered with a dense, stinking cloud of smoke and dust. The Union artillery was firing one of the heaviest concentrations of the war and enemy cannon were responding; the swishing of their projectiles, the shock and glare of exploding shells and the buzzing and whining of shell fragments combined with a mounting racket of rifle fire. Live and dead Confederate soldiers lay in various stages of burial in and around the crater — some with feet, others with heads or arms sticking out of the churned-up earth. There were also pieces of people scattered about; unthinkable slippery things underfoot; and the ground kept rising in spurts as though raked by the claws of a giant invisible cat. Stunned by the appalling noise, concussion and visible imminence of death, many soldiers simply fell and lay where they had fallen or tried to burrow into the earth; but through these disagreeable distractions the 32nd Maine followed Colonel Wentworth unsteadily forward into the smoke and dust — no semblance of a line, just a scramble of awkwardly moving figures, now seen and now unseen, disappearing into the murk.

The brigade of which the 32nd Maine was a part was attacking to the right of the crater and doing extremely well under the circumstances. An excited Union general appeared out of a dust cloud and shook Wentworth's hand, yelling something which was believed to have been of a laudatory nature. But congratulations were premature. The brigade surged on past the crater and managed to clean out a line of Confederate rifle pits; then it, too, was shattered by the violent counterattack.

Everything seemed to go to pieces at once. The colors went down, slashed to ribbons. A bullet struck Wentworth in the left side, took off a piece of his hip bone, went entirely through his body and destroyed the arm of 18-year-old Sergeant Ray P. Eaton, who was standing beside him.

Someone managed to get hold of Wentworth and drag him into the crater — the only visible refuge from the storm of fire. There he found himself lying next to one of his young officers, Lieutenant James J. Chase, aged 22. Young Chase was a sight that Wentworth was never able to forget; the lieutenant's face was a splotch of blood in which one eye seemed to be dangling. A bullet had struck him just behind the left eye, knocking it out of the socket and injuring the other eye as well.

As the few survivors in the crater contemplated their shattered colonel, it occurred to them that, while the crater was protection for them, it was no protection for Wentworth: he was going to bleed to death if he didn't get medical attention and get it in a hurry. However, if they tried to carry him back to the Union

144

trenches over the bullet-swept ground, they'd probably all be killed. The soldiers decided to give it a try anyway. A stretcher was found, Wentworth was put on it and a small carrying party made a dash. On the way a canister shot smashed into the ground beneath the stretcher, and there were other narrow misses. But the carrying party struggled on and in a final desperate effort rolled Wentworth down an embankment into a Union trench, where waiting hands caught him.

It was just one example of the uncommon bravery that had been all around the colonel on that bad morning at Petersburg, and it was the last he ever saw of the 32nd Maine. Safe behind the Union lines, he was patched up by doctors who told him he would pull through, but he'd better be careful. If he ever had a bad fall, the effects of the wound might kill him. Soon he was on his way north to a hospital in Washington. He reached home in Kittery in the middle of August, 1864.

As for the 32nd Maine, Calvin Hayes was the senior officer surviving the battle, so he was commanding what was left of the regiment. On July 31, the day after the fight at the crater, he wrote in his diary:

Everything looks lonesome, so many have gone; one hundred and twenty-eight killed, wounded and missing out of less than one hundred and fifty who went into the fight.

Out of sixteen officers who were engaged, three escaped unharmed. We now have in the regiment eighty-five men, including cooks, present sick and extra-duty men.

Captain Horace H. Burbank was one of those captured and taken in hand by the Confederates. He later recalled:

We soon got into rebel traverses, and thence through a covered way into a turnpike leading to Petersburg. On our way we passed Generals Lee, Beauregard, Mahone and others whom I did not recognize, and none of whom recognized us. Circumstances did not conduce to making personal acquaintance.

Burbank was lucky in living to tell about it. Many of the Maine men disappeared and were never heard of again.

On August 1, under the terms of a brief truce, the Confederates allowed the Union men to go out and bury their dead. One of the 32nd Maine men remembered that it was

. . . such a sight I hope never to see again. Men were swollen out of all human shape, and whites could not be told from blacks, except by their hair. So much were they swollen that their clothes were burst, and their waistbands would not reach half way around their bodies, and the stench was awful.

And that was just about the end of the war for the 32nd Maine — a war in which they had discovered that the pursuit of martial glory eventually requires a strong stomach. The regiment participated in three more engagements and lost heavily. By December it was nothing but a wraith, and so it was consolidated with the 31st Maine and ceased to exist as an independent unit.

On what might be called the honor roll of the Army of the Potomac, its General Orders naming the battles that regiments and batteries were entitled to have inscribed on their colors and guidons, the 32nd Maine was credited with seven. Its score was seven months, seven battles.

The epitaph of the regiment was pronounced years later by its historian, Henry Houston, who wrote:

> Many of our number sleep in unknown graves in far-off Virginia today whose brave young lives were quenched in blood before they had seen their eighteenth birthday. . . . And although they left many of their number on every battlefield, those who survive have no cause to blush either for themselves or for those who fell, because of any failure in the performance of the full measure of a soldier's duty. Ignorant of much that pertains to military life, because of the lack of opportunity for instruction, and sorely at a loss as regards the knowledge of intricate and complicated maneuvers, because they were permitted no

time in which to learn the details of drill, there was yet one order they never failed to understand and never hesitated to obey, and that was the command to advance against the enemy.

Recuperating at home, Colonel Wentworth could have had only similar thoughts of his regiment, remembering with emotion the once-fresh faces of his young soldiers who had gone up in a quick, bright flame. The crowning touch was a letter he received in October from Second Lieutenant James J. Chase, whose bloodied face he had last seen in the crater. Chase wrote that he was going back to the war — as soon as he could get fitted with a glass eye.

It was also Wentworth's intention to return to service, but a special order from the War Department in November put an end to that idea by announcing his discharge for wounds and disability. It was the Department's way of telling him that he couldn't run a regiment from a rocking chair.

It was while Wentworth was still sore from his wounds and his thoughts of the vanished regiment that the Medal of Honor again came to his attention, and it must be supposed that a decoration of this sort is seen in a unique light by a man who has a long bullet scar in him and who has just come through a bloody battle in which he has seen, and been the beneficiary of, heroism under fire. He also had gained a fairly complete understanding of the condition of valor in war. There was not really much glory to it . . . no bands or flag-waving to cheer the soul . . . the swollen dead men and horses would be more like it and the "excreta on the hillsides" at Cold Harbor and the noise and stink of the Crater and other things equally dismal and disheartening. And yet there were men who rose above all this, and men who were willing to go back to it with a glass eye.

A year previously, the Medal of Honor might have looked different to him — perhaps less significant, less important. But now the shadow of the 32nd Maine lay across it. This regiment had never received a Medal of Honor and never would, but somehow its story was entwined with the decoration, and Wentworth now had an insight into its potential value and meaning that no reading of laws and regulations would have ever been able to provide.

The Civil War and what men had done in it meant a great deal to Mark Wentworth. In later life he gave books of war stories to his grandsons at Christmas, first reading them himself, and his wife remembered that as he read, tears always ran down his cheeks.

It was against such a background of understanding and emotion that Wentworth considered a surprising letter written to him by Maine Governor Samuel Cony on January 30, 1865. The whereabouts of this letter — if it still exists — is not known, but from Wentworth's reply what it said is clear. The Governor had just received a thundering big shipment of medals for the 27th Maine — 864 of them — with a man's name inscribed on each one. What was all this about, and what was to be done?

The Governor of 1863, Abner Coburn, would have known all about the affair of the 27th Maine volunteers, for he was in office when it happened and had been reminded of it again by Hannibal Hamlin. But the new Governor, Cony, must have been in the dark and greatly bewildered.

How should Wentworth enlighten the Governor? Should he explain that the War Department had made an error? Or should he conclude that someone in Washington had decided to honor the regiment for the action of a representative part of it? The thoughts that passed through his mind are not of record.

What is definitely known, however, is Wentworth's decision — which was to get hold of the medals if he could and take the matter into his own hands. On February 2 he wrote to the Governor reviewing the circumstances under which the regiment had been appealed to in June of 1863 and stating that 315 officers and men had responded by volunteering to remain in the defenses of Washington. Secretary Stanton's promise of Medals of Honor was also mentioned.

Wentworth then pointed out in his letter that there ought to be some record of all this in the state capital at Augusta:

> Copies of the request & acknowledgment
> of the service offered, orders & morning re-
> ports of those that remained were forwarded
> the 1st of July 1863 to the adjutant general of
> the state by my adjutant and are probably in
> his office.

Did this mean that an official list of the volunteers (or nonvolunteers) had been sent to
Augusta? It seems doubtful. Conceivably, granting intense diligence on the part of the company
officers and clerks during the short period from
8 p.m. June 30 (when the nonvolunteers departed) to the morning of July 1 (when the
morning report was normally filed) the "morning reports of those that remained" might have
shown, under "remarks," the names of those
who were absent by reason of having gone home.
But it seems more likely that those morning reports of July 1 were simply reports of numbers,
not names, which was what a morning report
was primarily supposed to be.

Anyway, if there was any sort of a roster of
names, possibly the Governor's letter had said it
was lost, for it was now Wentworth's intention to
compile a list himself by writing to the company
commanders. His letter to the Governor continues:

> I have a list of a portion of the companies

151

and have today written to the Capts of those I have not to furnish me with a list of their men at once. I recorded most of the men myself.

If you will forward the medals to me I will see that they are properly distributed to the right persons & forward you the names of those that received them or their nearest relatives in the event of death of the persons entitled to it, or will assist in any other way you think best.

The Governor, probably only too happy to be rid of this avalanche of medals, complied with Wentworth's request. The decorations were sent to Kittery, from which place Wentworth made distribution.

But he gave them only to the officers and men who, he judged, had been the volunteers.

In his letter to the Governor in February, 1865, Wentworth had stated that these numbered 315. However, there is evidence that he modified this figure. Calvin Hayes years later produced a list which he said he had obtained from Wentworth and which he further stated was the list whereby the medals had been distributed. It numbered 299. The accompanying statement by Hayes indicated that a list of these volunteers was sent to the War Department, and it is also worth remembering that in his February, 1865, letter, just quoted, Wentworth promised to send a list to the Governor of Maine.

According to another responsible veteran of

the 27th Maine, following the distribution, Wentworth sent the unissued medals back to the state capital in Augusta, but some years later they were returned to him, and Wentworth then stored them in his stable in Kittery.

This stable has long since vanished. The best view we have of it now is through the recollections of Wentworth's only surviving granddaughter, Jessie Hobbs Dunshee, who as a little girl visited the Wentworth home nearly every weekend with her parents. Her most vivid memory is of coming upon a sand-colored dog named Mingie, who was lying just inside the stable door, half asleep, with its tongue out, panting. When she kindly attempted to cool Mingie with a palm-leaf fan, the animal awoke and bit her on the left hand. "What did you do to the dog?" Dr. Wentworth asked. "I only fanned it," Jessie replied, and the Doctor said, "I guess it didn't want to be fanned." He then applied ammonia to the wound, which hurt like blazes.

But Jessie was a fearless soul (as she still is today) and in spite of being nailed by the ungrateful beast, she went on and explored the stable. Combined with the stable under the one roof was a carriage house. This contained a single buggy and a double buggy, single and double sleighs and a seldom-used coach; the coach was sprinkled on the inside with red pepper, which kept out insects, vermin and, incidentally, children, whom it afflicted with violent fits of sneezing.

153

In the adjoining stable were stalls for the two sorrel horses Major and General, for the black mare Dolly and for a cow. There was also a Robe Room. In the Robe Room were shelves on which were stored the various robes appropriate to the seasons: Fringed linen robes for keeping off the dust of summer driving, heavier plush robes for fall or spring and thick buffalo robes for the dead of winter — all smelling of camphor. And beneath the shelves were large drawers containing, Jessie believed, parts of harnesses and other odds and ends.

Fortunately in the general case but unfortunately in this particular instance of historical retrospection, little girls are relatively civilized creatures who usually don't ransack a property, so we don't know exactly where the Medals of Honor were kept in the stable. If our observer had been a small boy, we would have known exactly where they were. The best we can do is to guess, and a good guess is that the decorations were stored in the drawers of the Robe Room, or in the attic over the carriage house, and let us hope they were guarded by liberal sprinklings of red pepper as well as, for a time, by the savage stable dog. (It is somewhat sad to relate that because of indiscriminate biting Mingie was soon afterward replaced by a fox terrier whose name has not descended to us, presumably because he never did anything spectacular.)

Once he had quietly disposed of the matter and stored the undistributed medals, Wentworth had nothing further to say to the Government, as far as the records in Washington reveal. Why hadn't he returned the unissued medals to Washington? Wentworth may have reasoned that once a Government bureau gets something tangled up it is very hazardous for a private citizen to try to untangle it. Presumably the original error was now embedded in the official records of the War Department in one of its more deeply lying strata, so it might repeat itself at some future time if disturbed. Suppose (he might have thought) the unissued medals were sent to Washington. Later a clerk might find them, check against a list which someone had neglected to change, and back to Maine they would come — perhaps to fall into the hands of some uninformed official who would promptly mail them to the unentitled veterans of the 27th Maine whose names would be found plainly engraved on the reverses.

And, as will be seen, that is just what might have happened.

Under the circumstances Wentworth decided that it was best to place the medals in escrow and to cast a cloak of silence over the whole affair.

It was a silence that would serve the Medal of Honor well. The 560 or so pieces that he kept out of circulation represented very nearly half of all the Army Medals of Honor that had been issued up to that time. Their public display might therefore have devalued the medal by almost 50 per cent.

Of course there were still the 300-odd medals that he had distributed on legal — but in the light of the developing reputation of the medal — unjustified grounds.

But these would eventually be taken care of by still another champion.

Its name was Confusion, and although stamped to earth it would repeatedly rise again in the finest traditions of the military service.

Let Not Thy Left Hand Know

When the volunteers of the 27th Maine took their two paces forward in July of 1863 they set in motion a series of events the unfolding of which no human eye could see, so complicated and long-continued was its course. Through this concatenation various actors struggled; some striking a blow for, some against, the integrity of the Medal of Honor; some calm, some impassioned; some moving in hidden, some in open ways; some contradicting or undoing what others had decided or done.

Yet through it all, as though supernaturally directed, a pattern of beneficent progress evolved for the medal over a period of more than half a century. During this time several manipulators appeared upon the scene, only to vanish, leaving the seemingly unguided threads of continuity to other hands.

The first to disappear was Edwin McMasters Stanton, the great Secretary of War. Stanton was a strong-willed man who was usually at cross-purposes with someone, and after Lincoln's death — even though he continued as a member of the Cabinet — he set his teeth against his own superior, President Andrew Johnson, taking the side of the Radical Republicans who were the

157

President's foes in Congress. There ensued a series of stormy scenes in which were involved Congressional support of Stanton, Stanton's dismissal by Johnson, Stanton's refusal to be dismissed, Johnson's unsuccessful impeachment and Stanton's final resignation followed by his death about a year and a half later.

As far as the Medal of Honor was concerned, the passing of Stanton removed an influence which, based upon the record up until then, must be regarded as pernicious. Under Stanton's direction the War Department had ordered from Wm. Wilson & Son a total of 10,000 of the medals. Stanton had been responsible for the wholesale issue to the 27th Maine and, as has been related, he offered to reward a couple of other regiments on the same basis. All this would seem to indicate that he considered the decoration as simply another tool for use in achieving military victory, which of course is largely what it is, but if Stanton's open-handed policy had continued the Medal of Honor would have become a very dull tool — a prize of little worth. The fact that he apparently had a legal right to bestow the decorations as he did must, however, be acknowledged.

Fortunately, the worst that Stanton was ever able to do was represented by the 864 medals issued for the 27th Maine, and this stroke of munificence was in large part foiled by the New England conscience of Mark F. Wentworth who, in his own quiet way, was almost as strong-willed as Stanton.

There had been, however, and there were to follow, a few other assaults on the integrity of the Medal of Honor which were of a relatively minor nature.

In the year 1865 Medals of Honor were awarded to 29 officers and noncommissioned officers who had escorted the remains of President Lincoln on its long and circuitous journey from Washington to Illinois. In view of the tragedy and majesty of this assignment, medals of some sort might well have been in order. But gallantry in action was not involved. The action was all over by then, for Lincoln and everybody else. The only justification for the award was the joint resolution which Lincoln himself had signed in 1862 providing for awards for bravery in action *"and other soldier-like qualities"* — and even this provision had to be rather liberally interpreted.

The laws as they stood did at least state clearly that any recipient of the Army Medal of Honor had to be an officer or an enlisted man. But one medal was awarded to a person who was not an officer, not an enlisted man and not a man. This was a woman's rights zealot named Dr. Mary E. Walker. She was the second woman ever to graduate from Syracuse University Medical School and, not satisfied with this accomplishment, she plunged into the Civil War as a contract surgeon. She was captured by the Confederates at Chattanooga and imprisoned for a time at Richmond. Dr. Walker was awarded the Medal of Honor in 1866.

After the war she made the most of this distinction. A reporter describing President Chester A. Arthur's first New Year's reception wrote:

Brilliant as were the diamonds of Madame de Struve, the wife of the Russian minister, and effective as was the bronze golden silk dress, trimmed with gold beads, of the wife of Attorney General Brewster, the "observed of all observers" was Dr. Mary Walker, who came tripping in with elastic step, shook hands with President Arthur, and was profusely poetical in wishing him the compliments of the season. She wore a black broadcloth frock coat and pantaloons, and carried a high black silk hat in her left hand, while in her right she flourished a slender cane. After leaving the President, she passed along the line of ladies who received with him, giving to each a sweeping bow, and then went into the East Room, where she was carefully scrutinized by the ladies.

And one of the things scrutinized was, of course, the Medal of Honor. Top *that*, ladies!

There were a few other unusual awards, but for some years after the close of the Civil War the recipients were largely officers and enlisted men of the Regular Army who received the Medal of Honor for gallantry in engagements with hostile Indians.

It was from the most famous battle of the Indian wars — the one in which Custer made his Last Stand — that an important contribution to Medal of Honor policy evolved. When approaching the Sioux encampment on the Little Big Horn, Custer rashly divided his force into three columns. He, with one column, suffered the massacre which bears his name. Meanwhile the rest of the 7th Cavalry was engaged in such a wild fracas that at the end of it the company commanders forwarded to higher headquarters a long list of soldiers who they felt ought to be awarded the Medal of Honor.

General Alfred H. Terry, the department commander, returned the list, saying it looked to him as though every man who had behaved ordinarily well had been recommended for the Medal of Honor, and that was not what the decoration was for. It was intended only for conspicuous acts of gallantry in action — acts which ought to be described at length opposite the name of each man recommended. He ordered the list to be revised.

The commander of the 7th Cavalry appointed a board of three officers to handle the revision. While saddled with this onerous task, the members of the board came up with what seemed to them an excellent standard for use in determining whether or not a man was entitled to the medal. As they put it:

. . . the conduct which deserves such recognition should not be the simple discharge of duty but such acts beyond this that if omitted or refused to be done should not justly subject the person to censure as for shortcomings or failure.

All 22 men approved by the board were awarded the medal, and the thought which the board had expressed passed on into law and Army Regulations, where it is found today as the "above and beyond the call of duty" requirement which is one of the governing considerations in Medal of Honor awards.

Among the men who earned the Medal of Honor fighting on the frontier, a few of the recipients were Indians themselves — braves who had signed up with the U.S. Army scouts. The peril of being an Indian fighting Indians and of becoming a mistaken target was illustrated by the citation for Co-rux-te-chod-ish, a sergeant of the Pawnee Scouts also known, or perhaps it should be said afterward known as Mad Bear, who "ran out from the command in pursuit of a dismounted Indian; was shot down and badly wounded by a bullet from his own command." Other medal holders who could only have been Indians were Elatsoosu, Nannasaddie, Nantje and Kosoha. One Indian recipient is listed merely as "Jim," another as "Rowdy," surely two of the most obscure heroes ever to appear on the Medal of Honor list.

In a few instances civilian scouts and guides were recognized — among them the famous Indian fighter, hunter and showman, Buffalo Bill (W. F. Cody), who received a Medal of Honor in 1872 for a daring gallop into a camp of the redmen, where he had shot two or three, put others to flight and had himself suffered a creased scalp. At the time he was serving as a civilian scout for the 3rd U.S. Cavalry near Fort McPherson, Nebraska.

A few other civilian scouts were similarly honored. Worthy as they may have been, the awards were not legal. The two laws governing the Army Medal of Honor had authorized awards to members of the Army and to no one else. However, these and other irregular issues of medals, apart from those which went to the 27th Maine, were small and constituted no great encroachment on the value of the medal. What was far more serious was something that came up in 1872. In that year a former captain in the 22nd New York State Militia, Asa B. Gardiner, reminded the War Department of General Orders No. 195, which it had published just before the battle of Gettysburg offering "Medals of Honor" to troops who "after the expiration of their term, have offered their service to the Government in the present emergency; and also for the volunteer troops from other states that have volunteered their temporary service in the States of Pennsylvania and Maryland." In requesting a medal on the basis of this order Gardiner wrote: "I understand there are a number of bronze medals for distribution to soldiers of the late war, and request may be allowed one as a souvenir of memorable times now past." He received the Medal of Honor.

This matter came up again in 1879, when Thomas C. Reed, formerly of the 27th New Jersey, also wrote in for a medal under the provisions of General Orders No. 195. Action on his application was deferred "indefinitely" on the basis that no money had ever been appropriated for obtaining the medals called for by G.O. 195. This was a highly significant decision; it implied that the G.O. 195 medal was a different medal from that commonly known as the Congressional Medal of Honor. The Army might well have stuck by this decision; but it did not, and the lid of a Pandora's Box began to open.

In 1884 Thomas Reed applied again, and in the meantime there had been either a change of personnel or a change of mind. Someone in the War Department made a notation on his application. "It is understood that there is a large stock of medals on hand from which this can be issued if deserved." A Medal of Honor was issued to Thomas Reed on May 17, 1884, whereupon there were applications on behalf of four other veterans of the 27th New Jersey, and medals were issued to all four.

The Secretary of War who approved these applications apparently did not realize that the recognition of General Orders No. 195 as a basis for awarding Medals of Honor left him way out on the end of a limb. Two classes of recipients had been provided for in this order: (1) those who had offered to extend their terms as did the 27th Maine, and (2) volunteer troops from other states who had offered their temporary services in the states of Pennsylvania and Maryland. According to an estimate made later on, around 50,000 men would have qualified under these terms. Many of them, in fact most of them, probably were alive in 1884, and had they all been alerted to rush through the breach that Gardiner and Reed had made, the remaining stock of about 8,300 medals would have been used up in no time, while the worth and prestige of the Medal of Honor would have suffered a corresponding decline.

Fortunately, this did not happen. But no sooner had this threat subsided when another one arose.

In 1886 the Adjutant General's Office published an official circular. It was entitled:

MEDALS OF HONOR
Awarded for
DISTINGUISHED SERVICE
During the
WAR OF THE REBELLION

And among the names listed were those of all 864 members of the 27th Maine — the unentitled as well as the entitled!

And there was nothing to indicate that some of these men had remained in the defenses of

Washington while others had gone home. In fact, this aspect of the story seems not to have been entered in the records of the War Department — seems to have escaped its attention entirely. Wentworth's list of the entitled men, if it had ever reached the Department, had been mislaid or lost, or had gotten into the wrong bureau so that the left hand had not been told what the right hand was doing, or even that there was a right hand.

Now somewhere around 560 unentitled veterans of the 27th Maine officially had just as much right to the medals as did the entitled!

It is easy to imagine what might have happened. If Wentworth had sent the undistributed medals back to Washington in 1865, a left hand would have stored them away somewhere. Later, after a passage of years and several changes of personnel in the War Department, a right hand would have issued the 1886 circular. Then all that one of the unentitled veterans had to do was to write to the Department, complain that he had never received the medal which the circular said was his, and apply for it. Someone then might have rummaged around, found the medals, checked them against the circular and mailed the medal for this veteran — or possibly all of them — back to Maine. (Medals of Honor were often awarded by mail in those days.)

But thanks to the prescience of Mark Wentworth, the medals were not in Washington. And there is no record in the file of the War Depart-

166

ment bearing on this case that any veterans of the 27th Maine ever did write in for a medal on the basis of the 1886 circular. Wentworth had handled the whole thing so quietly that it must have appeared, for many years, that the volunteers who had received medals were the only ones for whom these decorations had been issued. In all likelihood the veterans of the 27th Maine never heard of the circular, and probably many of them had never heard of the medal.

As for the War Department, it remained in blissful ignorance of this matter of the entitled *vs.* the unentitled veterans of the 27th Maine until 1891. Awakening came by chance. For the first time the Official Army Register included, in its issue of that year, a list of all holders of the Medal of Honor in the Regular Army. The Army was small — there were not more than 75 or so names of medal holders listed — and the chance of a 27th Maine veteran being in the Regular Army was slight. But it so happened that there was one among its legions. A former officer of the 27th, Henry B. Osgood, had been appointed to West Point on July 4, 1863, and had graduated from the Military Academy four years later. In 1891 he was a captain and he would eventually become a brigadier general.

By another chance — it was not intentional, for the oversight was later corrected — Osgood's name had been left off the Medal of Honor list.

Therefore in December of 1891 Captain

Osgood addressed a grievance to the War Department. He was a holder of the Medal of Honor, and why wasn't his name on the list?

The ensuing correspondence brought to the attention of the Department the surprising intelligence that some of the 27th Maine people, Osgood among them, had remained in the defenses of Washington while others had gone home. Who had stayed and who had gone? Did anybody know?

With this question the affair of the 27th Maine came fairly within the realm of a man whose opinions and actions with respect to the case would be decisive over the next 15 or 20 years: Colonel Fred C. Ainsworth. In 1892 Ainsworth was well on his way to becoming one of the two most powerful officers in the Army and one of the most influential figures in Washington. And he would attain this position of power largely because of his accomplishments as an archivist — which is a statement so at variance with what most people believe to be the scope and potential of archives-keeping that it needs considerable elaboration.

The explanation of Ainsworth's success, as is so often the case, is that of the right man arriving at the right place at the right time. Just as the Civil War had important aftereffects in industry, transportation and communications, so did it stimulate subsequent administrative work in the Government. The war had produced tons of paper having to do with the disbanded forces —

around 400,000 muster rolls plus added hundreds of thousands of medical, service and other records. It had also produced a large and influential group of veterans. More than 2,000,000 men had had a hand in saving the Union; more than 1,500,000 of the saviors were still around in 1886, and many of them had suffered, or said they had suffered, diseases, disabilities, injustices and other difficulties for which recompense of some sort was to be considered. Meanwhile the Congress, not a little influenced by the lobbying activities of the G.A.R. and veterans' claim agents, had enacted general and special legislation that was increasingly liberal in granting pensions and other benefits.

The main result was a torrential flow of applications to the Commissioner of Pensions and a corresponding burden of work in two other offices where military records had to be consulted and facts verified before claims could be settled: the Surgeon General's Office and the Office of the Adjutant General. Here armies of clerks pawed through mountains of records which had never been given any orderly arrangement to facilitate efficient searching. For example, in the Surgeon General's Office, hospital registers had to be scanned page by page to find the name and record of a man who said he had been sick or injured; the names had been entered chronologically in the order of the men's admissions to hospitals, and there was no other way to find the desired information. Both offices were

169

swamped. By November of 1886 the Surgeon General's Office was more than 9,500 cases in arrears and the Adjutant General was behind by about 50,000. The veterans whose cases were thus held in abeyance were not pleased, and rumblings of their displeasure were heard in Congress.

There then entered upon the scene Captain Fred Ainsworth, who had been serving since 1875 as a surgeon at Army posts in the West and Southwest and in whom glimmerings of administrative talent had been detected. In December of 1886 Ainsworth was called in to take charge of the Record and Pension Division of the Surgeon General's Office. In the situation that prevailed, his coming East was like that of Saul being summoned from the land of Benjamin.

A tall, powerfully built young man who never seemed to relax and whose piercing eyes glared intently above a sweeping cavalry mustache, Ainsworth proved to be as efficient as he looked — a natural-born administrative genius. He made an analysis of what was wrong and instantly applied corrective measures. The backlog of unanswered inquiries addressed to the Record and Pension Division was cleaned up in three months. Ainsworth then began a series of innovations which were to revolutionize record-keeping in the War Department; one example was a system of index-record cards which made it possible to obtain information in a fraction of the time it had taken before and which saved wear and tear on the precious original records.

When a Congressional committee conducted an investigation of inefficiency in Government departments, Ainsworth shone by comparison as a light in the wilderness. His career was meteoric from that point onward. Some men join departments, but in the case of Ainsworth departments joined *him* or were built around him. In 1889, in addition to his division of the Surgeon General's Office, he was given 13 divisions of the Adjutant General's Office; this consolidation resulted in a new bureau, the Record and Pension Division (later Office) of the War Department and eventually a promotion to colonel for Ainsworth, its head.

The Colonel's methods, which saved the taxpayers hundreds of thousands of dollars, were adopted in other divisions of the Government and even in private business. Ainsworth was careful to see that these accomplishments were heard of in the right places; his work was lauded by Congressmen and even praised in annual messages of the President to Congress.

But it was Ainsworth's control and mastery of the records and his legalistic approach to decisions based on them that was one of his greatest sources of power. From his vast storehouse of knowledge and precedent he could quickly assemble ammunition with which to shoot down projects of which he disapproved, or to advance those which he favored. He became a behind-the-scenes operator whose influence has rarely been surpassed in the history of Washington bureaucracy.

Controversial was a word that was frequently applied to Ainsworth, and aptly applied, for there were two sides to almost everything he did. He was dictatorial, hot-tempered and contemptuous of opposition; for these and other reasons he was hated and feared by many of his subordinates. Yet he worked long and effectively to improve pay, pensions and other benefits for soldiers and civil servants.

He was disliked by historians because he would not allow them access to original records; yet he brought to completion the publication of that great mine of historical information, *War of the Rebellion . . . Official Records of the Union and Confederate Armies*, and his work did much to help lay the foundations for the National Archives.

It was said that he curried favor with politicians. Yet when it seemed to him that the occasion demanded it, he did not hesitate to administer jarring reverses to prominent figures, and throughout his career he was usually in a fight with someone in high office.

However, two-sided as he may have been in several respects, there was one point on which Ainsworth did not waver. This had to do with the primacy, integrity and inviolability of the records; and the policies he championed in this regard have remained as an important legacy to the department he served. There were several aspects to this body of policy, but the one that was

172

finally to have the most to do with the 27th Maine and its Medals of Honor was the concept of what *constituted* an official record. It was, according to Ainsworth's views, a record that had been made by someone who had the authority to make it, who had personal knowledge of the facts and who had completed it at the time of the events chronicled or within a reasonable period thereafter. Moreover, it was a record that had been continually within the control of the Government, so that the likelihood of its being tampered with was reduced to a minimum. Further, a record of an organization no longer in existence should never be changed or altered, for if it were otherwise the failings of human memory or the equally human tendency to be self-persuaded and to state that acts were done which were not done — or that acts were not done which were done — would pollute the wellspring of information which Ainsworth wished to keep pure.

The point at which Ainsworth came upon the case of the 27th Maine was apparently early in 1892, soon after his Record and Pension Division had been raised to the status of an Office, with more than half of the employees of the War Department now under his supervision. One of the duties of the R&P Office was to assemble records and prepare briefs and opinions on cases having to do with the Medal of Honor, so that the Secretary of War would have all the information necessary to make a decision. Therefore

Ainsworth became concerned with obtaining a list of those who, in the 27th Maine, had remained in the defenses of Washington in 1863 and those who had gone home.

No such list could be found. Ainsworth even tried to find the transportation orders for the 27th Maine, believing that these might show which of the men had taken the train north on July 1, 1863, and which on July 4. But the transportation orders could not be found. True, Ainsworth had not completed his organization of the War Department records, nor were all of these records under his control at the time; but if he was not able to find an official list of the volunteers in Washington, its finding there by anyone else was and will be unlikely. If the list had been sent to the War Department back in 1865 — as Calvin Hayes later indicated it had — it must have been hopelessly buried in the pre-Ainsworth strata, which were jumbled to say the least.

The Adjutant General, whose office had been considerably diminished by its losses of divisions to Ainsworth's growing domain, attempted to secure a list of the 27th Maine volunteers from Maine, where the situation was equally discouraging. On January 16, 1892, he wrote to the Adjutant General of Maine:

Sir:
The records of this office show that eight hundred and sixty-four (864) medals were issued to the men of the 27th Maine Volunteers

174

in 1863 on representation that they had volunteered to remain in service during the Gettysburg crisis after the term of service of the regiment had expired. It now appears from the statements of a member of that regiment that the officers and men who actually volunteered for the service numbered but about 300. To complete the records of this office on this subject, I have the honor to request any information your records may afford showing the actual number of members of that regiment that volunteered as stated. A list of their names especially is desired, as none has ever been furnished this Department — also the whereabouts between date of expiration of their term of service of the regiment (June 30, 1863) and the date of its muster-out (July 17, 1863) of those who did not volunteer to remain and the present post office addresses of such surviving field officers of the regiment as may be known to you.

Very respectfully,
J. C. Kelton
Adjutant General

It will be remembered that Mark Wentworth, in his letter to Governor Cony in 1865, had promised to send him a list of the officers and men to whom he was about to distribute medals — the patriots who had responded to the call of extra duty in late June, 1863. But in 1892, in his reply to General Kelton, the Adjutant General of Maine said he knew nothing of the matter except what was shown by the published report of the Maine Adjutant General for 1863. The best he could do was to send Kelton clipped pages from this report; however, it simply gave the entire muster-out roster of the entire regiment and was of no help whatever.

Next the Adjutant General's Office in Washington established communication with Edward M. Rand, the former adjutant of the 27th Maine, and with seven of its former company officers, asking for lists of the men who had volunteered. Rand provided lists for Companies A and I, and the former company officers provided lists for B, C, E and G. However, there was no certainty that all were complete, and lists for D, F, H and K never did turn up. One former officer advised writing to Calvin Hayes in Kittery; another suggested that Mark Wentworth might have a list. But there is no record of correspondence with Hayes or Wentworth. Apparently the Adjutant General, recognizing the impossibility of compiling an accurate list in this way, threw up his hands and abandoned the investigation. There is no record, either, of Ainsworth's having had anything to do with this abortive search involving the former company officers in Maine; he may very well have considered the whole thing idiotic.

All that happened, apparently, was that the inquiries stirred the survivors of the 27th Maine to do something about a list. At a reunion in 1895 they voted to publish a history. This turned out to be essentially a reprint of a speech given by their former lieutenant colonel, James M. Stone, in 1889, with a list of the volunteers appended. It named 312 officers and men as being those who had remained in the defenses of Washington. A copy was sent to the War Department by Edward Rand, and there the matter rested for two more years.

In the meantime the policies of Colonel Ainsworth made themselves felt. Edward Rand and other veterans of the 27th were shocked when, in 1897, the War Department issued an official Medal of Honor circular which included the names of all 864 members of the regiment. Opposite the name of each 27th Maine man was an asterisk. The asterisk was explained by a note; and the note was pure Ainsworth; it gave exactly the information that was available from official records, no more and no less:

NOTE: The term of service of the 27th Maine Infantry being about to expire, the regiment was ordered to Arlington Heights, Virginia, where it arrived June 25, 1863, preparatory to being sent home for muster out. While the regiment was at that place the President requested it to remain in service a short time longer, on account of Lee's invasion of Pennsylvania. About 300 officers and enlisted men volunteered to remain, and did remain, at Arlington Heights, Virginia, in the defenses south of the Potomac, until the result of the battle of Gettysburg was known. They were sent home on July 4. The remainder of the regiment, consisting of about 560 officers and enlisted men was sent home on July 1. The entire regiment was mustered out of service at Portland, Maine, on July 17, 1863. On January 24, 1865, Medals of Honor, 864 in number, were issued to all members of the regiment who were mustered out with it. The official records show that it was intended to issue the medal to those who volunteered to remain in service beyond the expiration of their term, but, evidently through an inadvertence, the medal was also issued to about 560 members of the regiment who did not volunteer to remain in service. The records do not show either the names of those who volunteered to remain or of those who did not so volunteer.

(Of course there was one point on which the War Department was still in ignorance. The medal was not "also issued to about 560 members of the regiment who did not volunteer to remain in service," owing to the vigilance of Mark F. Wentworth.)

Edward M. Rand first became aware of the Medal of Honor circular when he saw an article in the *New York Times* of December 27, 1897. With reference to the 27th Maine, this article referred to a "hole in the new book" and it quoted the substance of the note saying that the records didn't show who had stayed and who hadn't.

Rand immediately got off a peppery letter to the War Department. He wouldn't discuss, he said, the question as to whether the medals were properly awarded to the 27th Maine soldiers. However, if the War Department was going to publish a list, the men who did remain in service were at least entitled to be distinguished from those who did not. The new list simply cast doubt and suspicion on everyone. Why hadn't the list made a proper distinction of the 312 men who had remained? Their names had been given in a history of the 27th Maine which he, Rand, the former adjutant, had sent to the War Department in 1895. He was now sending another copy, containing a correct and certified list. And if the Secretary of War wanted a character reference, he was referred to Thomas B. Reed, Speaker of the House.

Rand had undoubtedly made a careful and honest attempt to supply an accurate list. But he was up against problems in making it stick. In a couple of weeks he received the following letter:

Mr. Edward M. Rand
93 Exchange Street
Portland, Maine

Dear Mr. Rand:
  The official records of this Department do not show either the names of those members of the 27th Maine Infantry who volunteered to remain beyond the expiration of their term of

service, or of those who did not so volunteer, and the note to that effect in the recently published Medal of Honor list is absolutely correct.

The unofficial list compiled by you more than thirty years after the regiment was mustered out of service cannot be accepted by this Department as an official record, or as a basis upon which to make any official declaration relative to those members of the regiment who did or did not remain in service.

In addition to the fact that your compilation cannot be accepted as an official record, even if there were no reason to doubt its correctness, there is abundant evidence to show that the list furnished by you is very far from being correct. The consolidated morning report of the 27th Maine Infantry, the entries in which are verified by your own signature as adjutant, shows that only 301 officers and men remained at Arlington Heights after July 1, 1863, whereas your list contains the names of 312 officers and men, and it is stated on page 12 of the publication of which this list forms a part that those whose names are borne on the list "volunteered to remain and did remain, until the battle of Gettysburg had been fought and won."

Your list also contains the name of Major John D. Hill, but page 13 of the publication referred to above bears a statement to the effect that Major Hill went home in command of those members of the regiment who did not remain until after the battle of Gettysburg, and this statement is corroborated by the regimental morning report, which shows three field officers present prior to July 1, 1863, and only two field officers present on or after that date.

Your list also contains the name of Captain Frank A. Hutchins of Company K, but Captain Hutchins advised this Department, in a letter dated April 24, 1892, that Major Hill and himself went home with the men who left on July 1, and the morning report shows that the captain of Company K was absent on and after July 1, 1863, also that a field officer was absent on or after that date.

In view of the facts pointed out above, it is evident that your list cannot be relied upon as a source of accurate information as to the men who "volunteered to remain and did remain" in service after the majority of the regiment had gone home. The note with regard to this regiment that is contained in the Medal of Honor list recently published by this Department is an accurate statement of the showing of the official records. Without that statement the publication would be incomplete and misleading, and there is nothing to justify the Department in making any other statement with regard to the case.

G. D. Meiklejohn
Acting Secretary of War

While the signature is that of Meiklejohn, the attitude toward records and the keen analysis displayed in the letter are clearly those of Ainsworth. And while the letter was one that should quite properly have been signed by the Secretary of War or his assistant, it was also a typical result of something that Ainsworth quite frequently did — which was getting someone else to seem to be the author of his own unfavorable opinions; he apparently did not believe that the purveying of too much bad news was good for a department head or, in fact, that it was wise for a truly effective operator to be much in the limelight for any reason.

In his reply Rand admitted the error of the sentence which implied that 312 officers and men had actually remained in Washington. The list contained in the regimental history, he explained, was intended to give the names of those who had *volunteered* to remain; but not all of these were able to remain; Major Hill, Captain Hutchins and others were ordered to go home in command of troops who had not volunteered; these men could not very well be sent without officers; and this reduced the number actually staying to the 301 shown on the morning report. But 312 had volunteered to remain, and so they deserved to be listed. Rand closed on a somewhat sarcastic note saying that he had never worn the medal and never intended to, but he, at least, could prove he had been there in Washington on July 1, 1863; the War Department had *his* signature on the morning report.

Granting that the verbal laxity in the history had been simply an unfortunate slip of the pen, there was logic in Rand's explanation. On a handwritten list of volunteers which Captain Warren of Company C kept, there is still visible a note to the effect that one of the officers listed had in fact been ordered to go home with the nonvolunteers, and there may well have been others who did the same. However, a note of added vagueness was introduced. It was hard enough, years after the event, to say who had remained; to say who had *intended* to remain would have been even more difficult.

Soon after this exchange, Henry B. Osgood, the former officer of the 27th Maine who had precipitated the whole uproar by his inquiry in 1891 — now a major and commissary of subsistence — wrote to the War Department to reinforce Rand's statements. He had known Rand ever since 1862, he said, and the former adjutant's standing was beyond question; he was a lawyer, a most careful and painstaking keeper of records, and probably no volunteer regiment in the service had been the beneficiary of better paperwork.

But then Osgood, in all honesty and with the best of intentions, fell (or helped Rand fall deeper) into the pit that seems to await all makers of rolls and rosters. He stated that he himself had a list of the men in his former company (Company I) who had volunteered, and there were 56.

Rand's list of officers and men for Company I numbered 54.

Once an affair like this starts going bad, it gets worse every time someone touches it. A dusty pall had settled over the case of the 27th Maine, and nearly every person who ventured into it came out choking and sneezing.

Colonel Ainsworth himself answered Osgood's letter. In his reply he pointed out that what Rand had sent the War Department was not an original record made at the time of the event; it was nothing but a printed document. The printed list, Ainsworth continued, was inaccurate on its face, but even if its accuracy were not questioned, the Department could not properly accept it.

Rand and Osgood were not trying to hoodwink the War Department; they were apparently acting in perfectly good faith. The trouble was, their idea of what constitutes an official record was slightly different from Ainsworth's. Neither their endorsement nor that of anyone else could have induced him to recognize as official a list made so long after the war.

In his letter to Osgood, Ainsworth also brought to light something else:

Touching the present contention . . . it is proper to remark that there is on file in this office a letter of Edward M. Rand, dated January 27, 1892, addressed to the Adjutant General of the Army, in which Mr. Rand uses the following language: "Three hundred and fifteen officers and men volunteered to remain, but no list of their names has been preserved or was ever made to my knowledge. We thought little of it at the time as we considered that we were merely doing our duty." In view of this positive declaration on the part of Mr. Rand, and because of the manifest inaccuracies in the printed list, it is evident that that list is not one of which the Department can take official cognizance.

It may be remembered that 315 officers and men was also the number that Colonel Wentworth had in mind when he wrote to the Governor of Maine in February of 1865. However, after he consulted his company commanders and they consulted their own lists, Wentworth apparently modified this figure. There is evidence to support this belief in a letter which came to Colonel Ainsworth in 1898. This letter was from Frank M. Whitman, a past commander of the Medal of Honor Legion, an association of men who had earned the medal in action. Whitman said he had read the 1897 circular, including the note declaring that the records did not show which of the 27th Maine soldiers had volunteered and which had not, and he just happened to have in his possession a statement from a veteran of the 27th Maine with an appended list which purported to show who was who. He enclosed a copy of the statement and list. Whitman was a man who, like many of us, had a propensity for losing papers from time to time, and he had lost the last page of the statement, which would have shown the signature of the veteran. However, internal evidence proves that it was Calvin Hayes; the author identified himself as the former sergeant major of the regiment and referred to its colonel as his fellow townsman and lifelong friend. He also stated that as sergeant major of the 27th Maine he had assisted the adjutant and served as clerk to the colonel. The tense used in the statement referring to the colonel, fellow-townsman and so forth indicated that Wentworth was still alive when it was written. Further, Hayes stated that the appended list had been borrowed from Wentworth, and it was the list whereby the medals had been distributed to the men who had remained in the defenses of Washington.

The statement said that "about 300" had volunteered. The appended list which Whitman had copied and sent to Ainsworth numbered 299. This was close to the number given in the July 1, 1863, Morning Report, which had 301 officers and men present in the defenses of Washington on that date. Did this mean that the Hayes' list lacked only two of being officially accurate? Not necessarily — for this list also included the names of Major John D. Hill and Captain Frank A. Hutchins who, according to ample evidence, volunteered but were ordered to accompany the men who went home.

The War Department stuck to its position, and

again in 1904 it published another list of Medal of Honor holders which included the 864 men of the 27th Maine, along with the note saying that the official records did not show which had volunteered and which had not.

The conduct of the War Department in this matter, which was undoubtedly guided by Ainsworth, is deserving of a certain amount of admiration. The Secretary of War might have been persuaded to decide that none of the 27th Maine veterans was entitled to the medal and advised to sweep all 864 off the list. He might, for example, have ruled that the never-manufactured and nonexistent medals called for by General Orders No. 195 had actually been intended for this award and that therefore it had been made in error. He would have been enthusiastically supported in such a ruling by the Medal of Honor Legion.

Or, the War Department might have accepted the names of volunteers provided by Edward M. Rand and the survivors of the regiment; this acceptance would have at least cleaned up the official list to a considerable extent by wiping off more than 550 names.

Instead, the Department refused to take an easy way out. It would take no step that was not justified by what was revealed by authentic and official records. It apparently held that a number of the men of the regiment were legally entitled to Medals of Honor, these medals having been authorized by the joint resolution of 1862, which provided for awards in recognition of "other soldier-like qualities" as well as gallantry in action.

It was unfortunate, of course, that the War Department couldn't say who these good soldiers were, among the 864; and this was a state of affairs that was annoying and completely unsatisfactory to Edward M. Rand and the others who knew they had performed over and beyond the call of duty on that June day in 1863 when Lee was invading Pennsylvania.

But — it might be argued — measured against the high standards for the Medal of Honor awards that were emerging, even the 300 or so who had volunteered for four days of peaceful extra service had no real right to the decoration, even though legally they were entitled to it.

It was an argument, with merit on both sides, that would eventually have to be settled, but already circumstances were beginning to favor the side of those who would disqualify the volunteers. For if the War Department had officially and clearly recognized 312, or some other number, as being officially entitled to their medals, this would have given the men so recognized a position which the courts could hardly have failed to uphold if the case had ever come to adjudication.

Now, as matters stood, the legally entitled holders of the medal were so entangled with all the others, and so indistinguishable from them officially, that they were highly vulnerable; the whole body of 864 names made one large target, so conspicuously out of place that it could not escape attention.

Confusion was doing its work — beneficent work for the Medal of Honor, some might say.

Meanwhile, life had gone along quietly for Mark F. Wentworth, with shadow and sunshine passing over him as it did across the breeze-riffled reaches of Portsmouth Harbor. His first wife died in 1883. But he married again — a handsome lady — and his happy home life continued. Sometimes his old wound hurt him, but it did not materially slow him down. Behind his team of fine horses he drove about lower York County, attending to his medical and surgical patients, the Republican Party and certain affairs of the Navy Yard — seeing to it that the proper people worked there and that it continued to be prosperous and productive.

The controversy about the listing of the 27th Maine men in official War Department circulars did not arise in his lifetime. As far as the records reveal, none of the inquiries the War Department made in 1892 were addressed to him. He did not endorse the list sent to the War Department in 1895; nor was he, apparently, involved in this transaction, following which there was a long period of silence only broken when the Department issued its circular in October, 1897.

He sprang into action only when something seemed to affect the actual medals, as it did in the early 1890's. By that time the survivors of the

27th Maine had formed a regimental association, and they met in reunions at various places in York County where the veterans gathered to eat bean-hole beans, fish chowder and other Maine delicacies, to listen to speeches, sing the old war songs and reminisce. These seem to have been the only times when the medals were worn; most of the decorations were kept in their original cases laid away on closet shelves or in bureau drawers. Of the recipient of one it was remembered that he would never talk about it or display it because he felt he had no real right to it. Modesty on the part of the 27th Maine veterans themselves was certainly one of the factors in keeping public knowledge of the awards within narrow bounds.

The medals were, however, proudly worn at the 27th Maine reunions. These were great family, or social affairs, and there are several people alive today who attended them as children.

R. J. Libby of Fredonia, New York, was one of the children who was usually present, along with his father George Libby, who had served with Captain Joseph Warren in Company C. According to Mr. Libby, there was a considerable disturbance in the early 1890's, when some of the veterans who had *not* remained in the defenses of Washington appeared at a reunion wearing Medals of Honor.

Mr. Libby could remember Captain Warren and his father expressing their feelings about this

— one or the other of them saying, "If everybody has them, they don't mean a damned thing." Thereafter, during his father's lifetime he never saw him wear the medal or speak of it again.

Mark Wentworth's reaction was also one of anger. At a reunion in Biddeford, he mounted the speaker's platform and delivered an icy blast, the substance of which Mr. Libby remembers as being this: "It was my privilege to deliver the medals awarded by a grateful government to the men of the regiment who volunteered to remain in Washington beyond the term of their enlistment. It has come to my attention that additional medals, issued in error by the government, have been sent by persons unknown to me to other members of the regiment. I trust to the personal honor of the recipients that these will not be displayed."

How did these medals get into the hands of other-than-entitled veterans?

There is in War Department files in the National Archives a letter written to the Department in 1904 by Erastus Moulton, an officer in the 27th Maine regimental association and then or shortly afterward its president. Moulton wrote:

By some grave mistake the full Roster of the Reg't was given instead of the names of the comrades that vol. to remain. The Medals were sent to our Colonel, and he knowing the circumstances, issued the Medals only to

191

those entitled to them. The remaining Medals were stored at Augusta Me. in the City Hall.

It was the impression of R. J. Libby that while the medals were stored in the state capital someone in Augusta sent some of them to veterans of the 27th Maine. Few people knew the background of the medals, and it might have been very natural for an uninformed person, seeing a medal with a man's name engraved on it and knowing the man, to send the medal to him. After the passage of a number of years, this is the sort of thing that could very well have begun to happen.

The Erastus Moulton letter continues: "A few years after [ward?] the City Hall was remodeled and the person in charge sent the Medals to our Colonel Mark F. Wentworth. He stored them in his stable."

But even in the stable the medals were not entirely safe. Moulton's letter goes on to relate that one day the 27th Maine was having a reunion in Kittery, and "some of our comrades" got into the stable and made off with medals, offering some of them later to the men whose names were engraved on the backs, whereupon "Many would not receive them. Others did and wore them much to our surprise and indignation for we considered it a disgrace to ourselves as well as the 27th Regiment."

However, even though there were these leakages of undeserved medals, a variety of controls were in effect. There was the social pressure of disapproval by the entitled survivors and their families who attended the reunions. A miserably disposed small boy with a shrill voice could make the wearing of one of these unwarranted medals a very uncomfortable experience, not to speak of the acid womanly gossip set in motion, or the black scowls of the survivors themselves. Then there was the displeasure of Dr. Mark F. Wentworth, which was not easily borne or prudently incurred in York County. Add the refusal on the part of many of the unentitled veterans to wear the medals even if someone had brought or mailed them to their homes, and there is adequate explanation of why the general public was not made aware that any unusual number of Medals of Honor had been awarded to the 27th Maine.

And this was remarkable, because it was the most decorated regiment in the history of the United States and perhaps of the world.

Other information on what happened to the medals descends to us from Calvin Hayes, who was living in Kittery until his death in 1914. Calvin Hayes had a grandson, Calvin Hayes Cobb, who as a child was very close to him and who grew up to become a vice-admiral in the U.S. Navy. Some time in the late 1950's Admiral Cobb, who had his grandfather's Medal of Honor but who had never given it much thought, suddenly became interested in the whole affair and set off along the trail of investigation that the author of this narrative was to follow a few years later. Death cut short his researches, but he left notes and correspondence behind — some of it based on remembered conversations with his grandfather. These were kindly made available by his family.

It was Admiral Cobb's understanding that the undistributed medals were still in Wentworth's possession at the time of his death.

Whatever internal dissension there was among the survivors of the 27th Maine appears to have been of a minor nature, quietly suppressed. The real controversy was that with the War Department, precipitated when the Department published its 1897 circular which unjustly, the survivors thought, lumped the entitled men with the unentitled. But Mark Wentworth was spared all this.

About four months before the controversial circular appeared, something which Civil War doctors had feared would happen to Mark Wentworth did happen; he fell, and in his fall a Confederate bullet fired at Petersburg 33 years before may have finally struck home. The *Portsmouth Daily Chronicle* of Saturday, July 10, 1897, told about it. "Dr. Mark Wentworth fell at his home in Kittery on Thursday and remained unconscious through the night and at least part of Friday forenoon . . ." He died at 3:50 on the following Monday, July 12. In the course of a long story about him, the newspaper saluted Wentworth as a staunch Republican from the earliest days of the Party, as a valued physician, great civic leader and distinguished soldier. The paper might have added that he had also been a great friend and protector of the Medal of Honor.

But now that he was gone, was this protection to vanish? After all, death had visited Dr. Wentworth suddenly. He had been unconscious after his fall, all or most of the time. What would happen to his unissued stock of Medals of Honor, a large part of which, as later events were to indicate, still remained in his possession?

According to the information gathered by Vice-Admiral Calvin Hayes Cobb, shortly after Wentworth's funeral the undistributed medals vanished from his property.

And the Vice-Admiral couldn't say for sure, but he had a strong suspicion that Grandfather Calvin Hayes might have had something to do with the disappearance.

Wherein the Mouths of Lions Are Stopped

The next two champions of the Medal of Honor to enter the fray which centered about the 27th Maine were Frank M. Whitman and Theodore Roosevelt. In vigor and belligerency, and to some extent in appearance, they bore a decided resemblance to each other.

Frank M. Whitman was the sort of man who would grapple with the Devil himself. A photograph taken along toward the turn of the century portrays him as a somewhat aged gentleman with head thrust forward on bulky shoulders, white bristling mustache, black bow tie, watch chain across ample vest, white hair and fierce light eyes glinting behind steel-rimmed spectacles.

While serving in the Civil War, Whitman had not only received one Medal of Honor but had been recommended for another. He had been one of the first men to storm across Burnside's Bridge at Antietam, later spending the night between opposing lines carrying wounded comrades to safety. At Spotsylvania Court House, Whitman was one of the first men to charge over the Confederate works, and there he had lost a leg.

In 1891 Whitman was a lawyer and the commander of the Medal of Honor Legion, an organization of medal recipients which included a number of influential people. One of its more prominent members was Dan Sickles, who some people thought deserved a medal for self-assurance if not for courage.

Another member and early commander was General Oliver Otis Howard of Maine, who had served with distinction all through the war after losing an arm at Fair Oaks. (It was here on the morning following the amputation that he made his famous wisecrack to General Phil Kearny, who had lost the opposite arm in the Mexican War: "I suggested that he and I thereafter buy our gloves together.")

After the formation of the Medal of Honor Legion in 1890, there was a marked increase in applications for the decoration on behalf of former members of the volunteer forces in the Civil War. And the number of awards increased accordingly. To illustrate: Up through 1866 about 1,300 Army Medals of Honor were issued, including those for the 27th Maine. Only another 400, approximately, were awarded between then and 1890, and these mostly to members of the Regular Army for service in the Indian campaigns.

But in the 1890's more than 800 Army Medals of Honor were issued, most of them to former volunteers for acts of bravery performed in the Great Rebellion.

Not counting the members of the 27th Maine, about 1,500 men of all services finally received Medals of Honor for service in the Civil War. The degree of heroism which was involved in each case is difficult to determine from the citations, which are laconic as compared with those of modern times. Careful records were not kept. Proofs of performance were not as rigid as they are today. A man might even send in his own application or have his Congressman or some other third party do it, with whatever supporting evidence he could get together. Many of the deeds for which Medals of Honor were awarded probably would not merit one today.

However, let no one suppose that the Civil War awards were not of respectable quality in general, or that a distinguished tradition was not firmly established to cast its reflections of honor and renown on subsequent recipients of all ages. When these awards were finally reviewed by a Medal of Honor Board in 1917, the board stated, "In a large majority of cases the medals have been awarded for distinguished conduct in action, measuring that term by the highest standard, and there can be no question as to propriety of the award." Even concerning the more liberal awards that were made under the then-prevailing law, the board commented that "with few exceptions these cases set forth the acts of brave men under trying circumstances."

Like most things pertaining to the Civil War, its Medal of Honor awards have a flavor all their own. For example, one reads of J. C. Julius Langbein, a drummer boy, who "voluntarily and under a heavy fire went to the aid of a wounded officer, procured medical assistance for him, and aided in carrying him to a place of safety" — this deed performed when Langbein was 15 years of age.

Distinctive also is the fact that more than 400 of the 1,200 or so Civil War Army awards (these not including the 27th Maine medals) were what might be called "flag awards" because they were made for actions having something to do with the flags that troops carried — usually with capturing a flag from the enemy. One soldier who obtained the Medal of Honor in this way said:

It's easy enough. All one has to do is be there and go in with the crowd, and be careful not to let too many get ahead of him, else the first choice of flags is lost. There are some risks, however. If the fellow who carries the flag is obstinate, and don't want to give it up, you can hand him your card, or use any other inducement which may occur to you at the time.

The soldier may have been indulging in a bit of sardonic humor at the expense of people who said that capturing flags must not be difficult — there were so many men receiving medals on this account. And indeed this impression might have been easy to come by. Secretary Stanton loved to receive captured Confederate flags, and the Army often gave leaves and furloughs or published special orders so that the captors of the flags could carry them to Washington and have a ceremony with the Secretary. Shortly after the end-of-the-war Confederate debacle at Sailor's Creek, Mrs. George Custer, then in Washington, saw "a street-car filled with soldiers, and with flags streaming from every window as the horses were urged rapidly to the War Department."

Nevertheless, a man could get hurt trying to lay hands on one of these trophies. The Civil War was the last of our big wars in which massed soldiers followed banners into battle. As weapons improved, this practice became too dangerous; in fact it was too dangerous in the Civil War. As the colors swept forward at the head of advancing battalions, they were the principal targets of enemy fire, lurching downward as their bearers fell, tossing upward again as other men grabbed the staffs from the hands of wounded comrades. If the attack fell back, disorganized, the flags became rallying points. If the assault reached the enemy lines, the colors of the contending forces became the centers of vicious hand-to-hand fighting. Flags were not only tactical instruments but symbols emblematic of honor and pride that was more than regimental, it was personal. Men wept when they were lost. At Appomattox, many soldiers of Lee's regiments tore up their flags and secreted the battle-worn bits of cloth about their persons, placing only the bare staffs on the stacks of surrendered arms and equipment. It was not strange that so many Civil War Medals of Honor were awarded for bearing colors while desperately wounded, for seizing fallen colors and carrying them onward to revive faltering attacks, for capturing enemy flags and for otherwise performing heroically at these focal points of danger.

Other Civil War awards had to do with rescuing comrades under fire, picking up and carrying or throwing away live shells that had fallen into a group, leading storming parties and otherwise displaying conspicuous determination to close with the enemy. Of this latter class, Private Samuel E. Eddy of the 37th Massachusetts provided a good example; he

. . . saved the life of the adjutant of his regiment by voluntarily going beyond the line and there killing one of the enemy who was in the act of firing upon the wounded officer. Was assailed by several of the enemy, run through the body with a bayonet, and pinned to the ground, but while so situated he shot and killed his assailant.

The sort of raw, red courage and aggressive fighting spirit that is the foundation of the Medal of Honor tradition was abundant in the Civil War, and if recommendations had been made and citations had been written as explicitly as they were in later years, the record would have been even more impressive.

The Medal of Honor Legion — one of whose commanders, incidentally, was to be former Drummer Boy Langbein — had much to do with establishing high standards for the awards. One of its first efforts was aimed at having the names of the 27th Maine veterans removed from the official list. In 1890 the 27th Maine accounted for about half of the entire Army list.

In November of 1891 Frank Whitman wrote to the Adjutant General saying that the 27th Maine men were not eligible for membership in the Medal of Honor Legion, and yet they had been issued the same medal. What reasonable explanation could there be for such a state of affairs as this?

The reply of the Adjutant General is worth quoting in full, because it gave Whitman some ammunition which he turned against the War Department later on:

Mr. Frank Whitman
Commander in Chief,
Medal of Honor Legion
296 State Street, Boston, Mass.

Dear Sir:

In reply to your inquiry of the 18th ultimo, regarding the issue of Medals of Honor to members of the 27th Maine Vols., I have the honor to inform you that Acts of Congress approved July 12, 1862 and March 3, 1863, authorize the President to cause Medals of Honor to be prepared and "to direct that the same be presented, in the name of Congress, to such non-commissioned officers and privates as shall most distinguish themselves for their gallantry in action and other soldier-like qualities during the present insurrection."

General Order 195, June 29, 1863, from this office directs the Adjutant General to provide an "appropriate Medal of Honor for the troops who, after the expiration of their term, have offered their services to the Government in the present emergency and also for volunteer troops from other States that have volunteered their temporary services in the States of Pennsylvania and Maryland." No funds being available for preparing these medals, no further steps were taken to carry out the provisions of the order, except in the case of the 27th Maine Vols., which organization the Secretary of War directed should be furnished with the medals provided for by the Act of March 3, 1863, and the medals were prepared and sent to and receipted for by the State authorities. In issuing these medals the Department had to be guided by the lists of names as furnished by the officers of the regiment.

Very respectfully,
J. C. Kelton
Adjutant General

Whitman had never heard of General Orders No. 195, but he would never forget it from then on. What the Adjutant General had imprudently done was to suggest to him that the 27th Maine medals had been improperly or illegally awarded under this General Order instead of the acts of Congress of 1862 and 1863. Whitman lost or mislaid the Adjutant General's letter, but he remembered its substance very accurately, and he would open an attack on this point later on.

In the story of the Medal of Honor, General Orders No. 195 keeps popping up again and again. In 1895 a joint resolution was introduced in Congress proposing that money be appropriated to carry out its provisions. The resolution did not pass, whereupon it might have been supposed that G.O. 195 would not raise its head again. Not so. It was a hard snake to kill and it would continue on its sinuous way through a couple of decades of the next century.

In 1896 a new ribbon for the Medal of Honor was authorized, along with a rosette or knot to be worn in lieu of the medal. The ribbon was designed with a vertical white stripe down the center, with a blue and red stripe on either side. The rosette combined the same colors. Tiffany and Co. received the contract, and the ribbon was made in Paris. Holders of the medal could get the new ribbon and bow knot by application to the War Department, the applicant to be identified by the sworn testimony of two reputable people who had known him for at least five years;

or they could purchase them from Tiffany's by showing an official statement from the War Department, a certificate of membership in the Medal of Honor Legion or the medal itself. Several veterans of the 27th Maine procured the new ribbon for their medals, and no question was raised at that time as to their right to wear it.

June 26, 1897, marked another and much more important milestone in the history of the Medal of Honor. On that date, by direction of the President, Army Regulations were amended to knock out forever, in effect, the provision of the 1862 law which allowed medals to be awarded for "other soldier-like qualities." The amended regulation read, in part:

> In order that the Congressional Medal of Honor may be deserved, service must have been performed in action of such conspicuous character as to clearly distinguish the man for gallantry and intrepidity above his comrades — service that involved extreme jeopardy of life or the performance of extraordinarily hazardous duty. Recommendations for the decoration will be judged by this standard of extraordinary merit, and incontestable proof of performance of the service will be exacted.

This was a great step forward, and it must have been extremely pleasing to Frank Whitman and the Medal of Honor Legion. That fall, however, there appeared the controversial War Department circular which listed all 864 members of the 27th Maine as holders of the medal, with the explanatory note saying the Department didn't know which ones were entitled to it and which were not. This enraged Whitman, and he returned to the attack with his silvery mustache bristling. He wrote Colonel Ainsworth an angry letter in which he said that he didn't suppose the War Department cared a snap for his opinion but he was going to give it just the same. He understood that when President Lincoln's request to the 27th Maine to remain in service was made, a promise of a medal was also made. He wasn't going to say the President and the Secretary of War didn't have the right to promise a medal, but he would say they didn't have any right to promise the Congressional Medal, and he ventured to assert that they actually hadn't promised any such thing, because there was no authority for it under the law.

In Whitman's opinion, the medal promised was the medal authorized by General Orders No. 195, and that was some *other* medal; it wasn't the Medal of Honor. And therefore it followed that when the War Department issued the Medal of Honor to the 27th Maine, it was doing something absolutely illegal and wrong. In fact, it was grand larceny. The excuse that there was no money appropriated to manufacture or issue the medals authorized by G.O. No. 195 was no excuse for issuing Congressional Medals. And here

Frank Whitman referred back to the letter the Adjutant General had written to him in 1891, which he had lost, but which he could remember clearly. Whitman had struck the Department a loud, clanging blow.

Within a few years he was to have an important ally.

Early in the 20th century a new opportunity presented itself to those who wished the names of the 27th Maine veterans expunged from the lists. This came about by reason of the fact that a number of organizations had begun to imitate the Congressional Medal of Honor in their own emblematic devices. The worst offender was the Grand Army of the Republic, which had a star-shaped badge, very similar in outline at least to the Medal of Honor, with a ribbon that was quite similar in color and design.

The War Department decided that it was time for a new Medal of Honor. Several drawings were prepared and submitted to officers of the Medal of Honor Legion, who were deeply involved in the project. Secretary of War Elihu Root approved the chosen design on January 28, 1904, and ordered it used for the preparation of a new die whenever the next appropriation became available. This was soon. An act of Congress approved April 23, 1904, authorized 3,000 medals of the new design, together with appropriate rosettes and other insignia to be worn in lieu of the medal and appropriated $12,000 for the manufacture. The new law called for the medals to be presented by direction of the President, in the name of Congress, to such officers, noncommissioned officers and privates "as have most distinguished, or may hereafter most distinguish, themselves by their gallantry in action." Thus, the requirements of the award were the same as those of the act of 1863, which had specified that the medal must be earned in action. However, the new law authorized *replacement* of medals issued not only under the 1863 act but also under the broader 1862 legislation which permitted awards for "gallantry in action and other soldier-like qualities."

In other words, the 1904 act continued to sanction both of the old acts insofar as they applied to men who had been awarded their medals under the provision of these laws in previous years.

Almost immediately following the announcement of the new medal the War Department began to receive a barrage of letters from officers of the Medal of Honor Legion demanding that none of the new medals be issued to veterans of the 27th Maine. Now, they pointed out, would be a good time to correct what everyone recognized as a terrible mistake. Dan Sickles was especially vehement; he wrote saying that the 27th Maine medals had been improvidently issued, in violation of an act of Congress. (He was right about the improvidence but wrong about the violation.) The War Department was also warned that on September 21 and 22 the Medal of Honor

208

Legion was going to meet at Atlantic City, where it would probably "take action." Just what this move was going to be was not stated, but it went without saying that any action by so many men of valor was bound to be fearsome.

It was a strong effort by a band of heroes to safeguard the Medal of Honor for the glory of all future heroes. But they failed to reckon with a man who sat in the middle of a great arsenal of rules, records, laws and regulations, who thought these matters were important and who was a very tough customer. Most of their letters of protest came under the hand of F. C. Ainsworth, who as chief of the Record and Pension Office had been in the middle of this whole mess for years. But he had now risen to a much greater height. In 1899, while still Chief of the Record and Pension Office, he had been promoted to brigadier general. This office, as has been related, had absorbed parts of the Adjutant General's office. In 1904 it gobbled it up entirely; the Record and Pension and Adjutant General's Offices were merged to form a new bureau: the Military Secretary's Office, with Ainsworth being promoted to major general and named the Military Secretary. Three years later Congress would rename the Military Secretary's Department the Adjutant General's Department, and Ainsworth would emerge as the Adjutant General — the *anschluss* completed.

It was shortly after General Ainsworth had become the Military Secretary, which was close to being the most powerful office in the War Department, that he had to deal with the Medal of Honor Legion and its protests regarding the 27th Maine medals. Aware of the fulminations of the Legion and suspecting or being informed by his intelligence sources that these would soon reach the Commander-in-Chief himself, he set about preparing a massive road block, for he had no intention to giving in to this particular pressure group.

Ainsworth didn't mind doing the politic thing now and then, nor is it to be supposed that he personally cared one way or the other about the issue of the new 1904 Medals of Honor to the 27th Maine men. But this move of the Medal of Honor Legion was threatening to hit him where he lived; these people, who didn't know what they were talking about, were invading an area where they didn't belong: the sacred official records and the legalistic process of decision-making that ought to be based on those records. This was his, Ainsworth's, domain, and he would not be moved by hosts of angels, bands of devils or President Theodore Roosevelt himself.

Ainsworth prepared a long memorandum in which he precisely stated the facts of the 27th Maine situation as revealed by the records. On September 12 he sent this to the Judge Advocate General with the request that he get started on writing an opinion as to whether the Secretary of War, under the law, had any right to withhold the new medals from the survivors of the 27th

Maine. Ainsworth then sat back to await the completion of one of his finest ploys.

The Judge Advocate General who assisted him was Brigadier General George Breckenridge Davis, whose career, if not spectacular, had been almost as remarkable as that of Ainsworth. Davis had enlisted in a Civil War cavalry outfit at the age of 16 and had served all through the Rebellion. He had then gone to West Point, and after graduation he had alternated between fighting Indians on the western frontier and serving as a member of the West Point faculty. Somewhere along the way he had developed an unusual capacity for scholarship and writing. He had attended law school, served as professor of law at West Point and had written a number of books on constitutional, military and international law, some of which had become standard textbooks. He was also a respected contributor to historical and military journals. Now the Judge Advocate General at the age of 57, Davis was an individual who was immensely well qualified to comply with the little note that Ainsworth sent along with his formal memorandum request on September 12. The note said: "It is requested that this case be *made special*."

Thus alerted, Davis immediately set to work among the law books and records, and eight days later he delivered his opinion to Ainsworth. It was powerful ammunition. Ainsworth, with his guns loaded, then awaited further developments.

He didn't have long to wait, for presently the following letter arrived in the War Department:

WHITE HOUSE,
WASHINGTON

October 8, 1904

To the Secretary of War:

I call your attention to the enclosed memorandum from the Medal of Honor Legion. It is of course a rank absurdity that the highly prized Congressional Medal of Honor should have been issued to the Twenty-seventh Maine Regiment under the circumstances enumerated in this protest.

If it be true that a new medal of honor is about to be exchanged for the medals now held by those to whom Congressional Medals of Honor have been awarded in the past, I direct that the memorial of the Medal of Honor Legion be complied with as concerns the issuing of these medals. Consult me about this before any new medals are issued, and before taking any actions in relation thereto.

Theodore Roosevelt

This was just the sort of direct, fearless and forthright action that might have been expected from the hero of San Juan Hill. An injustice existed. Wipe it out with a stroke of the pen!

But as Roosevelt picked up the pen to sign the letter, he experienced a chill — an unwonted seizure of caution. He inked out the word "direct" and inserted the words "believe" and "should" so that the affected part of the sentence read, "I believe that the memorial of the Medal of Honor Legion should be complied with."

These were fortunate scribbles on the part of the President, for there is a time when boldness may not be rewarded, as was the case with the man who cried, "Nothing is impossible!" only to be asked if he had ever tried to swallow an umbrella without closing it.

After reading the letter, Ainsworth waited for a decent interval — the minimum in which a reply might have been prepared if it had not been prepared already — and then provided the Secretary of War with the Davis opinion, which was then forwarded to the President.

In this opinion Judge Advocate General Davis had thrown up a wall of logic and precedent against which even a Rough Rider might have dashed to his own embarrassment. Davis did not quite go back to Moses and Hammurabi, but he went back far enough to get a long running start in pointing out that President Roosevelt and Secretary of War Taft had better respect the awards that President Lincoln and Secretary of War Stanton had made to the 27th Maine.

In his opinion he first cited a case that had come before President John Quincy Adams, involving two pursers who had been dismissed from the Navy during the prior administration of President Monroe and who wanted Adams to restore them retroactively. Adams' Attorney General opined that one Executive had no business upsetting the act of another who has been his predecessor, for it if were otherwise,

> . . . the Executive which is to follow us must have the like authority to review and unsettle our decisions, and to set up again those of our predecessors; and upon this principle, no question can be considered as finally settled. . . . I have understood it to be a rule of action prescribed to itself by each administration, to consider the acts of its predecessors conclusive, as far as the Executive is concerned. It is but a decent degree of respect for each administration to entertain of its predecessor, to suppose it as well qualified as itself to execute the laws according to the intention of their makers; and not to set an example of review and reversal, which, in its turn, may be brought to bear upon itself, and thus to keep the acts of the Executive perpetually unsettled and afloat.

One can almost picture Roosevelt stroking his mustache thoughtfully and considering this argument. He himself was a reformer — a maker of what he hoped would be far-reaching decisions tending toward the betterment of society. Would *he* wish to set a precedent whereby something that *he* had decided or done could be unsettled and set afloat by a subsequent President? Davis also quoted from another decision of a previous Attorney General arising from a land dispute:

... an act done by one President of the United States, vesting a right in a citizen, is not subject to review and reversal by his successor; for if it were, there would be no stability or security for any rights of property acquired under the action of the Government.

And Davis cited several other opinions of Attorneys General to the same effect.

A medal, of course, could be called a piece of property.

Davis then moved on to a Supreme Court decision and other court decisions, following which he summarized all his findings in the following salvo:

— If an act, or decision, of the President, or of a subordinate officer of the Executive who has authority to decide questions arising in the execution of statutes, has operated to pass or convey title to, or ownership of, property, real or personal, to an individual, a property right has been vested in the grantee which can only be divested by the action of a court, and the result of legal proceedings.

— If the President, or his subordinate officer, acts by way of execution, and applies the law to a particular set of facts, his act in giving effect to the statute constitutes complete execution, as to the particular case to which the statute has been applied, and no additional or different execution can be given, by himself or a successor, to a statute which has once been completely executed.

— If the act of an officer of the Executive has been in opposition to or is not warranted by the statute, the courts alone can apply the remedy. This on account of the requirements of the Fifth Amendment to the Constitution that "No person shall . . . be deprived of life, liberty or property, without due process of law," and the judicial department of the Government is the branch whose function it is to determine questions affecting the ownership of property and the validity of titles thereto.

Davis also held that the awards to the 27th Maine had been made on the basis of the 1862 law granting the Medal of Honor to those who distinguished themselves "by gallantry in action and other soldier-like qualities."

His concluding opinion was that the Secretary of War had no authority to review the action of President Lincoln and Secretary Stanton in awarding medals to the 27th Maine, and that the survivors of the regiment should receive the medals of the new design authorized by the law of 1904 for replacement of their old medals.

It was a good example of what sometimes happens when bold deeds are contemplated but — before anyone can say "Let 'er rip!" — the advice of lawyers is sought. With one concerted roar the heroes of the Medal of Honor Legion, reinforced by the voice of Roosevelt, might have swept the names of the 27th Maine men from the Medal of Honor list. But now the mouths of lions were stopped. Nothing more was heard from Roosevelt. The Secretary of War concurred in the Judge Advocate General's opinion and decided that all the old medals, including those of the 27th Maine, should be replaced with new ones of the 1904 design upon application and proper identification of the veteran in case.

In his opinion Davis also stated:

What has been said as to the finality of executive acts applied with equal force to the decision of the Secretary of War upon the list prepared by the survivors of the 27th Maine Infantry and submitted to the Department on December 30, 1897, and to his subsequent decision that: "the testimony of survivors, or unofficial lists of names made after the disbandment of the regiment, cannot be accepted by the Department as a basis for any decision with regard to this matter."

This doctrine of what-has-been-done-cannot-be-undone tied the Gordian knot of the 27th Maine list even tighter. Now there seemed no possibility that the names of the 300-odd men, whoever they were, who were legally entitled to the medal could be extricated from the tangled mass of 864 names.

In its Medal of Honor list issued in 1904 the War Department continued to list all 864 of the 27th Maine men, along with the footnote saying in effect, "A mistake was made, but there is no way of telling from the records which men it applied to."

The appearance of this list caused Frank M. Whitman to return to the assault as vigorously as he had stormed the Bloody Angle at Spotsylvania 40 years before. Writing to the Military Secretary, he declared that it caused him grief and anguish that the Judge Advocate General — he of all people — he who was supposed to uphold the law, had taken the law unto himself and ruled that the 27th Maine medals had been awarded under the legislation of 1862, when Whitman himself had received a letter from the Adjutant General (he had looked for it the other night but couldn't find it, but it must have been received some time between August, 1891, and September, 1892, and if the Military Secretary would look in the files he would probably find a copy) — a letter which said that these medals to the Maine men had been issued under General Orders No. 195, which was no authorization at all for the Medal of Honor, and the whole thing was a crime and a disaster.

Military Secretary Ainsworth did look in the

files, and he did find the letter. He then wrote Whitman in part:

An exhaustive search of the records on file in this Department has been made but nothing has been found to show that the medal of honor authorized by the joint resolution of Congress approved July 12, 1862, and section 6 of the act of Congress approved March 3, 1863 was awarded to the members of the 27th Maine Infantry Volunteers because of lack of funds to prepare medals for them under the provisions of General Orders No. 195, from the Adjutant General's Office, dated June 29, 1863, as you were erroneously informed in a letter addressed to you by the Adjutant General of the Army on December 3, 1891.

Nothing whatever has been found to show or indicate that the medals issued to members of this regiment were not awarded under the provisions of the joint resolution and act of Congress mentioned.

Whitman next wrote to his Congressman, who sent his protest on to the President. But Roosevelt had had enough of the whole affair; he referred the protest to Secretary of War William Howard Taft, and Taft gave the Congressman the same story that Ainsworth had given Whitman directly: the 27th Maine medals had been legally awarded under the legislation of 1862;

the former Adjutant General had erred in stating otherwise; and the War Department was willing to replace with new medals all of the old medals that had been issued to the regiment.

Did this mean that some 560 unentitled veterans of the 27th, or those of them who were alive, could now write to the War Department and get Medals of Honor?

No, the dead hand of Mark F. Wentworth was still effective. The regulations arising from the 1904 law said that a current holder of the old Medal of Honor would have to turn it in before a new one would be issued. Wentworth's impoundment of the medals, and their subsequent disappearance following his death, had left the unentitled, or most of them, with no old Medal of Honor to turn in.

This protection for the medal continued until 1907, when the Medal of Honor Legion unwittingly helped to destroy it. There had been a clamor about the rule which said that the old medals had to be turned in in order to get new ones. Many of the old veterans had become attached to the medal with the Civil War design; it had much to recommend it, sentimentally and artistically, when compared with the 1904 medal.

The 1904 design, which has continued in its essential details to the present day although the ribbon has undergone further changes, still embodies a bronze star with Minerva in the center. But only Minerva's head shows, with a reversion to the ancient style of deep-bowled helmet and classic crest, and the medallic star is gold-finished and surrounded by a wreath in green enamel.

By contrast, the old Civil War star, as befits a medal for heroism, is stark and simple, deriving its strength not from finishes or embellishments but from the material of which it is made; its shadows are deep and rich; the dusky bronze, darkening with age, has the tone of gun metal, battle smoke, tragedy and terrors.

The 1904 design leans upon inscriptions: THE UNITED STATES OF AMERICA around Minerva's head, VALOR on a suspension bar. The 1862 design is wordless; it speaks in symbols with greater subtlety and substance. The new and the old eagles, by which both medals are attached to their ribbons, also invite comment. The new eagle is certainly more graceful. But his neck is stretched and his head is pointed upward in such a way that a casual glance conveys the impression that the eagle is ingloriously hanging onto the suspension by its beak; whereas the head of the old eagle, who is suspended by his wing tips, is left free and fiercely glaring about as if watching for the enemy.

All these observations are, of course, matters of opinion which may or may not have been shared by the Civil War veterans following the appearance of the 1904 design. What is recorded is the fact that the veterans didn't mind Congress issuing a new medal, but they certainly objected to giving up the old one which they cherished with such affection. They wanted to keep the solid and satisfying medallic picture of Minerva Repulsing Discord, which told the whole story of what they had done in the great war. The Medal of Honor Legion brought their wishes to the attention of Congress, and in 1907 Congress passed a joint resolution which provided that former recipients need not turn in their old medals to get the new ones, and if they had already turned in their old medals, these were to be returned to them, but that both medals could not be worn at the same time.

After 1907 it would have been possible for anyone on the Medal of Honor list, including any of the 864 members of the 27th Maine who were alive, entitled or not, to apply to the War Department and receive one of the new Medals of Honor. Thus the Legion unknowingly broke down the last defense.

However, the passage of years which had already swept Mark Wentworth away was beginning to serve his purpose in safeguarding the unissued medals. At a reunion of the 27th Maine about this time it was estimated that no more than 375 of its members still survived.

Calvin Hayes was one of those who kept his old medal and got a new one, issued to him in 1909 along with a rosette. Many years later his grandson, Vice-Admiral Calvin H. Cobb, wrote to the War Department asking how many veterans of the 27th Maine applied for and received the new medals; the answer was that complete statistics were not maintained, but it appeared that about 50 of the new medals were issued to veterans of the 27th Maine between 1905 and 1911.

That surely did not represent any serious encroachment upon the integrity of the medal, as actually worn or displayed by either the entitled or the unentitled segments of the regiment. From about 1910 on, thanks largely to Mark F. Wentworth and his loyal coadjutors who followed him, it might be said that the 27th Maine no longer constituted a serious threat to the Medal of Honor except on the record where, it is true, its 864 names still made a large, black blot.

The War Department continued to be harassed by several applications from veterans who had volunteered for extra service in the Civil War, including members of a couple of Ohio regiments who had offered this extra service at the time of the first battle of Bull Run. The War Department flatly refused all such application, continuing with the stand it had established in 1904–05. It asserted that the 27th Maine had been issued the medals under no General Order but by direction of the President and Secretary of War in accord with the original legislation of 1862 . . . that General Orders No. 195 was not a valid authorization for issue . . . that a lot of units besides the 27th Maine had volunteered extra service at one time or another, but if these people wanted Medals of Honor they would have to have a special act of Congress to get them — medals would not be issued by the War Department.

Thus it turned out that through a curious convolution of events all 864 of the 27th Maine awards were supported by the executive department of the Government; all 864 were recorded on the official Medal of Honor list, where one was as good as another, and the medal in its new design was readily available to any of these men who happened to be alive and who wanted it.

It was a low point in the fortunes of the Medal of Honor. But often things are darkest just before dawn, and there would soon be an upturn. At this time it is somewhat surprising to realize that the Medal of Honor was the only decoration the Army had for rewarding individual distinguished service on the part of both officers and enlisted men; there was a Certificate of Merit with an accompanying medal, but this was available only to enlisted men. Soon, however, other decorations would be authorized for lesser degrees of distinction, and measures would be taken to isolate the Medal of Honor in heightened splendor at the top of the medallic structure — to be known as the "Pyramid of Honor."

The Medal of Honor had been moving toward this pinnacle ever since 1862, its story like nothing so much as that of Christian's journey in *Pilgrim's Progress* — through a Wicket Gate and along narrow ways with many false branchings leading to Danger and Destruction, its progress menaced by Mr. Worldly-Wise Stanton, helped by Faithful Wentworth, somewhat impeded by Mr. Legality Davis, cheered onward by Evangelist Whitman, and so on through the 27th Maine quagmire and past other perils until it arrived at Mount Zion.

Now it had just one more stony ridge to surmount, and somehow that one would be the most trying and puzzling of all, for it brought, once again, Principle and Progress into a poignant conflict.

A Fast Shuffle on Capitol Hill

Before Minerva and the medal she adorned could ascend to the exalted heights they occupy today, there inevitably had to be a human sacrifice.

And the humans to be sacrificed were mainly the legally entitled but officially unknown holders of the award among the veterans of the 27th Maine. Events started moving toward this sad but necessary consummation about 1914.

One might reason that if 300 or so of the Maine soldiers had been legally put on the list, they would have to be illegally put off. It was this thought that had bothered a few Old Army people in the great controversy of 1904, bothered them to the extent that they had battled the Medal of Honor Legion, their own Commander-in-Chief and everybody else to a surprising standstill when efforts were made to deny the new medal to the Maine veterans.

But now the great, solid phalanx that had protected the 27th Maine, consisting of William Howard Taft flanked on one hand by the redoubtable Ainsworth and on the other by the learned George B. Davis, was gone. Taft had advanced, Davis had retired, and Ainsworth had exploded at the apex of his career. As one of the two top officers in the Army, Ainsworth had become involved in a struggle with the other, Chief of Staff General Leonard Wood, who was also, as it happened, a doctor-turned-soldier. Wood had invaded the area of Army paperwork which Ainsworth, as the Adjutant General, considered to be his own inviolable domain, and had fostered a proposal for Army record-keeping to which Ainsworth had responded with a caustic, angry letter. The letter was so intemperate the Secretary of War, Henry L. Stimson, relieved Ainsworth from duty, and with the prospect of charges being brought against him, Ainsworth had resigned February 16, 1912, to avert a court-martial which would have shaken the entire War Department. Now he was in retirement, and instead of being found in the maze of Army records which had been his lair for more than a quarter of a century, he was often seen enjoying long walks along the pathways of Rock Creek Park, chewing tobacco and wearing a bright red necktie.

Meanwhile the Medal of Honor Legion had pressed onward persistently and with a long view, as might have been expected from so heroically constituted an organization. The Legion wished to obtain, in the words of one of its declarations, "such legislation from Congress as will tend to give the Medal of Honor the same position among the military orders of the world which similar medals occupy." Ever since its formation in 1890, the Legion had been working to

227

have bills aimed at this sort of legislation put through Congress. None of them had made the grade.

A successful bill was finally introduced by Representative Isaac R. Sherwood of Ohio. Sherwood was not a Medal of Honor holder — such a person could not properly have presented the bill — but he did have a military record of some distinction. He had fought in 43 battles of the Civil War, had been mentioned in special orders for gallantry and had been brevetted brigadier general.

The bill Sherwood introduced called for the establishment of an "Army and Navy Medal of Honor Roll." On this roll were to be recorded the names of all surviving honorably discharged holders of the Medal of Honor who had reached the age of 65 *and who had been awarded the medal for action involving actual conflict with the enemy, distinguished by conspicuous gallantry or intrepidity, at the risk of life, above and beyond the call of duty.*

The people so enrolled would receive a special pension of $10 a month for life.

Sherwood made an able presentation of his bill. He appealed to the pride of the Congressmen, pointing to the monetary rewards that England, France, Germany and other countries bestowed upon their holders of equivalent medals. He played upon their patriotic emotions with an appropriate flight of eloquence capped by a quotation of poetry. He laid statistics before them, including a table showing "The conditions of the presentation of medals of honor in every civilized country on the globe."

And one of the points he made, possibly as an appeal to the economy-minded, was that the conditions of the law would exclude any of the 864 veterans of the 27th Maine who might still be alive and who might take it into their heads to apply.

Congress passed and President Wilson approved an act establishing an "Army and Navy Medal of Honor Roll" in the spring of 1916. Certain of the survivors of the 27th Maine heard of it and did not realize that the gate had been shut as far as they were concerned. The $10 a month was attractive, so some of them applied, only to discover, to their disappointment, that they were not eligible. The wording of the act provided for a man's listing on the roll only after the Secretary of the Army or Navy had caused the citation or, if necessary, the supporting documents to be examined to make sure that he had received the medal for gallantry in action.

What was to be done with the medal recipients whose service did not meet this standard?

The answer to that question made its appearance under somewhat mysterious circumstances soon afterward. During that spring a national defense act was being considered by the Congress. It was a long act, consisting of more than 100 sections. With a European war in progress — with "the world on fire and sparks falling all around," as one Representative put it — the discussions were heated. The proposed inclusion of a multimillion-dollar "water power nitrate scheme" added to the controversy. In the midst of all this someone slipped in the following section, which was passed and approved along with the rest of the act:

SEC. 122: *Investigation concerning medals of honor.* A board to consist of five general officers on the retired list of the Army shall be convened by the Secretary of War, within sixty days after the approval of this Act, for the purpose of investigating and reporting upon past awards or issues of the so-called congressional medal of honor by or through the War Department; this with a view to ascertain what medals of honor, if any, have been awarded or issued for any cause other than distinguished conduct by an officer or enlisted man in action involving actual conflict with an enemy by such officer or enlisted man or by troops with which he was serving at the time of such action. And in any case in which said board shall find and report that said medal was issued for any cause other than that hereinbefore specified the name of the recipient of the medal so issued shall be stricken permanently from the official medal of honor list. It shall be a misdemeanor for him to wear or publicly display said medal, and, if he shall still be in the Army, he shall be required to return said medal to the War Department for cancellation. Said board shall have full and free access to and use of all records pertaining to the award or issue of medals of honor by or through the War Department . . .

Certain provisions of the defense act of which this section was but a tiny part had been drafted by the General Staff. A story appearing in the *Army and Navy Journal* about that time noted that Sections 120–124 went "beyond the recommendations of the General Staff." However, the War Department had an opportunity to review the legislation again before it was passed, and the General Staff major who wrote the analysis, either failing to recognize the anti-personnel mine that someone had planted in the form of Section 122 or not wishing to raise an issue, gave it approval with the sort of virtuous but superficial statement with which no one can quarrel. He wrote, "If any person obtained the medal in a manner not authorized by law, he certainly has no right to it, and any person who obtained it in the manner authorized by the law can have no objection to an investigation into the merits of the award in his case." He was either deliberately or in ignorance missing the point that the section would take medals away from many people who *did* have a legal right to them — a right of many years' standing. The law was approved with Section 122 included.

The board of retired officers appointed to

carry out the provisions of the new law consisted of Lieutenant Generals Nelson A. Miles and Samuel B. M. Young, Major General Joseph P. Sanger and Brigadier Generals Butler D. Price and Oswald H. Ernst; its quality was indicated by the fact that Young was a former chief of staff, while Miles had been at one time commanding general of the Army.

General Miles was president of the board. A man of imposing appearance, with a fine sweeping mustache, a distinguished face and resolute but rather kindly eyes, Miles in full-dress uniform was a model of everything fine that anyone might ever have thought about the Army. And his record just about lived up to his looks. He'd been one of the youngest generals in the Civil War, commanding a corps at the age of 25. He had been in many of the great battles — Antietam, Fredericksburg, Chancellorsville, the Wilderness, Spotsylvania Court House, Cold Harbor, Petersburg. After the war he had fought Indians with conspicuous success. General Miles was himself a holder of the Medal of Honor and a past commander of the Medal of Honor Legion. The Legion was on record as being bitterly opposed to the 27th Maine awards and the names of the Maine men still flooded the Medal of Honor list. On this official list the name of General Nelson A. Miles appeared between those of Private George S. Miles and Corporal Thomas P. Miles of the 27th Maine, which must have moved the General many times to the

232

thought that while these two Maine men may have been nice fellows they were hardly distinguished company for such as himself and others who had risked life and limb in the presence of the enemy. Surely, if anyone wanted to see the prestige of the medal safeguarded and even enhanced, it was General Miles.

Yet when Miles read and fully understood the section of the act of Congress under which his board was supposed to proceed and when he applied his understanding to a cursory reading of the Medal of Honor list with briefly summarized citations, his conscience began to trouble him. So apparently did the consciences of the other members of the board, yet none could have felt the predicament they were getting into as keenly as did Nelson Miles because of something that had involved him more than 40 years before.

He was an old man now but he could still remember vividly a certain September in 1874 when, in command of an infantry-cavalry force, he was pursuing Kiowas and Comanches on the western plains. Near the Washita River, Indian Territory, 125 of the warring Indians had suddenly descended on six of his men who were traveling between commands carrying dispatches. Four of these six men were soldiers of the 6th Cavalry. Two — Amos Chapman and William Dixon — were civilian scouts. In the exchange of fire that followed all four of the soldiers were wounded, Private George W. Smith fatally. All but Smith managed to reach partial shelter in a buffalo wallow, which they improved by digging with knives and hands.

Smith, lying outside these improvised earthworks, was thought to be dead, but seeing him move, Amos Chapman ran out under fire and carried the wounded soldier to shelter in the buffalo wallow. "Amos," said Dixon, "you are badly hurt." Chapman replied, "No, I'm not." Dixon pointed to his friend's leg; it was shot through just above the ankle joint, and Chapman had been running on the bare bone, dragging his foot behind him and not feeling any pain. Now five of the six were wounded. Private Smith, although dying, sat upright to make the little group seem as uncrippled as possible. Around them the Indians, in their barbaric war paint and bright feathered bonnets, yelling and doing gymnastics on the backs of their ponies, rode in a tightening circle of doom.

What happened is best told in words that General Miles himself wrote in an official report made shortly after the event:

From early morning till dark, outnumbered, twenty-five to one, under almost constant fire, and at such short range that they sometimes used their pistols, retaining the last charge to prevent capture and torture, this little party of five defended their lives and the person of their dying comrade; without food, and their only drink the rain-water that collected in a pool mingled with their own blood. There is no doubt but that they killed more than double their number, besides those that were wounded. . . .

The simple recital of their deeds and the mention of the odds against which they fought; how the wounded defended the dying, and the dying aided the wounded by exposure to fresh wounds after the power of action was gone, these alone present a scene of cool courage, heroism and self-sacrifice, which duty as well as inclination prompt us to recognize, but which we cannot fitly honor.

The night passed and next morning Dixon went for help. Taking with him just four cartridges from the meager ammunition supply, he stole out of the rifle pit in a drizzling rain, traveled on foot until he met a body of cavalry and then guided the horsemen back to the relief of the besieged party.

Miles had written the recommendation whereby all six men who made the epic stand had been awarded the Medal of Honor — one posthumously. Now, if he did what the law told him he must do, Miles would have to strike the names of Amos Chapman and William Dixon from the list, for they were not — as the law stated they had to be — officers or enlisted men in the Army. Both had been serving in a civilian capacity.

That was one side of the coin to be seen in the board's instructions from Congress — in this case the Law and what seemed to be morally right in utter conflict.

And on the other side — this concerning those fellows from the 27th Maine who had volunteered in 1863 — there was the Law in conflict with itself. Maybe it wasn't desirable that the Maine men should have the medals, but the legislation as it stood in 1863 certainly entitled them to it. So here was a matter of overriding a principle that, in quite another way, didn't seem right either.

The more General Miles thought about it, the more peculiar the whole thing seemed. He finally decided that he ought to have a look behind the scenery and went to see the chairmen of the two military affairs committees in Congress. What he learned from these gentlemen prompted him, after a conference with the other members of the board, to address a letter to the Secretary of War which read in part:

> While some medals of honor have been given to officers and soldiers not in accordance with the law, and to civilians for heroic acts, without authority of law, it is assumed it is not the intention of Congress to deprive anyone of this distinguished honor where it has been worthily bestowed for most extraordinary, hazardous and dangerous service. Section 122 of the Act of Congress approved June 3, 1916, makes no mention of the acts of 1862 and 1863, and would seem to repeal, or

at least, annul, those acts that have been on the statute books for more than 50 years. The board is informed that said paragraph, or Section 122, was not in either of the Senate or House bills, but was inserted for some purpose in conference. If the provisions of Section 122 are strictly complied with, the board is of the opinion that grave injustice would be done to a class of public servants who have rendered most conspicuous acts of heroism that would be recognized by any army of the world. It leaves the board and the Honorable Secretary of War no discretion, and would be a cruel act towards a class that the government has manifestly desired to honor. The board, therefore, respectfully requests that the Honorable Secretary of War will ask that the Army Appropriations Bill, now pending in Congress, be amended by adding the following paragraph, to wit:

Section 122 of the Act of Congress approved June 3, 1916, shall not apply to persons who have lawfully received their medals of honor, nor to anyone who has rendered most extraordinary, hazardous and dangerous service to the Government.

If this paragraph is added, as the board hopes it may be, the duties of the board will be better defined and more practicable of execution. A memorandum of facts and the effect of the law of June 3, 1916, is herewith enclosed for reference and consideration.

Very respectfully,
Nelson A. Miles
Lieutenant General, United States Army
President of the Board

Whose hand it was that had aimed the sacrificial blow embodied in Section 122 is not of record, since minutes of conference committees are not kept, and Miles, of course, made no personal references in the report of the Medal of Honor Board. This report merely stated the belief that "the practical working of the law had not been understood by Congress, which had unwittingly committed an act of injustice, which, if called to their attention, would result in a modification of the language of the Act." Secretary of War Newton D. Baker agreed with the board's proposed amendment and laid the matter before the military committees. Late on the hot afternoon of July 26, 1916, no less a personage than Senator Henry Cabot Lodge of Massachusetts arose and presented the amendment. Senator James K. Vardaman of Mississippi wanted to know the purpose of the amendment, whereupon the following dialogue ensued:

MR. LODGE: Mr. President, in the Army act approved in June there was inserted a section numbered 122, concerning investigations with regard to medals of honor. That section was entirely new matter, put in in conference. It never was before the House. It never was before the Senate. It is not connected, so far as I can make out, with anything in the bill. In providing for that investigation it is said: [*Lodge then quoted most of Section 122*] Under the act of 1862 it is provided that medals should be given for distinguished gallantry in action or other soldierly acts. A second provision in 1863 provided simply gallantry in action. Many medals were granted for soldierly acts properly under that law and were given in accordance with the act of 1862. Now it is proposed to apply rigidly to all those medals a new definition, making it absolutely retroactive. If medals were improperly issued under the terms of the act of 1862 or 1863, it is all very well perhaps to take them away; but if they were properly issued under the acts of 1862 and 1863 they ought not to be taken away by a new definition adopted last June. It is to cure that that I offer this amendment.

MR. VARDAMAN: Mr. President, I think the amendment is subject to a point of order, and I shall have to make that point.

MR. LODGE: Undoubtedly it is subject to a point of order; I do not dispute that, but I think we are likely to have some very serious cases of injustices to men who received, and justly received, medals of honor in the Civil War and in the Spanish War in accordance with the law at that time. I do not believe myself it can be done or would be done by any board of officers, but I do think that it is a very bad precedent to have a clause that was put into a bill in conference, never before either House of Congress, under which such a wrong might be done.

MR. VARDAMAN: I have no fear whatever that wrong will be done by a board of officers composed of retired Army officers of character.

MR. LODGE: I will say, Mr. President, this amendment is suggested by the board.

MR. VARDAMAN: I make the point of order that it is legislation upon an appropriations bill.

THE VICE PRESIDENT: The point of order is sustained.

And so the amendment which was intended to save the legally justified awards was rejected. In having no fear whatever that wrong would be done by a board composed of retired Army officers of character, Mr. Vardaman obviously disregarded the fact that with Section 122 unamended, officers of character would have no choice as to what they could or could not do.

General Miles and his board made no further attempt to secure a modification of the law, believing that the session of Congress was too far advanced to make the effort practicable at that time. However, such an attempt was still in their minds, for after their review had been completed they stated in their report: "The board begs leave to express the hope that the War Department will defer action, in certain cases to be specified hereafter, until the matter can receive the careful consideration of Congress."

As the report of the board proceeded, it became clear that the affair of the 27th Maine men — since so few others were affected — had been the prime target of the whole investigation. The pertinent sections of this report follow:

The records of all persons on the Medal of Honor list, numbering 2,625 have been carefully examined by the board.

In a large majority of cases the medals have been awarded for distinguished conduct in action, measuring that term by the highest standard, and there can be no question as to the propriety of the award.

In some cases the papers are missing and those on file do not furnish evidence, which of itself would be satisfactory to this board, except for the corroborative evidence contained in the action of the proper authorities at the time. The evidence was satisfactory to them and should not be questioned now, after a lapse of so many years, the death of important witnesses, and of the recipients of the medals, and the loss of valuable papers. In

some cases also the term "distinguished conduct in action," is defined by the authorities
making the award, as well as by applicants for
the medal, with much greater liberality than
is now exercised under the regulations of the
War Department in awarding medals of
honor. With but few exceptions these cases
set forth the acts of brave men under trying
circumstances. The rewards which these men
received were greater than would now be
given for the same acts, but the acts were
highly meritorious nevertheless and, in the
absence of adverse evidence and because
there has been no high judicial interpretation
of the medal of honor laws, the board has felt
bound to measure the act by the standards established by the authorities at the time of the
award, rather than by that now observed,
thus avoiding as far as practicable, retroactive
judgment on the course of the War Department in a matter lawfully within its discretion, and so closely affecting the honor of so
many patriotic citizens living and dead.

The report of the board then began to set forth
the instances wherein the medal had not been
awarded for distinguished service, including
those of the 27th Maine.
It is apparent that General Miles and his distinguished companions, in approaching the records of the Maine regiment, did not realize that
they were venturing into a sort of administrative

Everglades. Before they knew it, they were in the quicksands.

In cataloging the cases of those who were not entitled to the medal, they began boldly: "The first is that of 555 members of the 27th Regiment of Maine Volunteer Infantry . . ." There then followed a brief recapitulation of what happened in Washington in late June of 1863, with Lee invading the North, the Maine men about to go home, President Lincoln and Secretary of War Stanton appealing to them, a promise of medals and so forth.

But then the board assumed that these medals had been awarded under General Orders No. 195, and quoted the order in full!

This, of course, was completely at odds with previous rulings made by the War Department, to the effect that the 27th Maine medals had nothing to do with G.O. No. 195 — that they were the real McCoy, awarded under the original legislation of 1862 and 1863.

After the board had stated that 555 officers and men of the 27th Maine had gone home its report continued:

Nevertheless, by some "inadvertence" medals of honor were awarded them as well as to those who remained. The medals issued to those who went home were undeserved. Those awarded to the 309 who remained in service, while not given for "distinguished conduct in action" were given by the Secretary of War in accordance with law and in ful-

243

fillment of the promise of the President.

How did the board arrive at the finding, which had eluded everybody else in the War Department, of an exact number of those who went home and those who remained in service?

Here again they had disregarded a previous decision of the War Department: its refusal to recognize a list of the volunteers as presented in a history prepared by certain survivors of the regiment in 1895. Unaware or unmindful of this previous ruling, the board explained itself as follows:

The figures of the Twenty-seventh Maine regiment are taken from History of the Twenty-seventh Maine Volunteer Infantry by Col. James M. Stone, Aug. 27, 1895, the Thurston Print, Portland, Maine. Colonel Stone was major of this regiment when it was organized, Sept. 10, 1862. He gives a list of those who volunteered to remain, numbering in all 312. In his list appear the names: L. Nason, private Company B, George Hobbs and Justin Spinney, volunteer recruits, which are not included in the official medal of honor list and received no medals. Deducting these three from the 312 named by him, there remain 309 on the official list who actually remained in the defenses of Washington after their term of service had expired. . . .

Alas!

The board was not only unaware of the vast-
ness of the labyrinthine tangle it had entered, but
it had also added a bit of confusion of its own
making, as everyone seemed to who had anything to do with the records of the 27th Maine.

The board was right about George Hobbs and
Justin Spinney, but there was no L. Nason on
Stone's list. There was a Luther Nason, but Luther did not answer the description implied by
the board's phrase, "which are not included in
the official Medal of Honor list and received no
medals." He was on the official list and did receive a medal, so far as is known. The only man
in Company B who answered the board's description of being on Stone's list but not on the
official list was Elwell Nason. (From "Elwell
Nason" to "L. Nason" sounds like a slip in a
verbal transmission.)

Over the years there had apparently been a
great many slips having to do with the lists of the
27th Maine, and what had happened provides an
excellent case history attesting the value of original records as compared with later generations
of the same records in transcribed or printed
form. In a 27th Maine company the primary
document, when it came to getting a man's name
right, was the enlistment roll, on which the new
recruit signed his full name in his own hand-
writing, or if he could not write made an "X his
mark" upon his name after someone else had
written it for him. The roll was signed in duplicate, and one copy was kept with the company to

245

which the recruit was assigned. By consulting this roll, on which the names were as correct as they were ever going to be, it should have been possible for the clerks to keep on writing the names correctly, but in actual practice a slow erosion of accuracy set in as the various additional rolls were made. A "Jr." would be dropped here and there, an initial "R" replaced with a "P," a name "Bussell" would be changed to "Buzzell" and later perhaps to "Buzzard," and so on. The poor souls who were responsible for these wandering transcriptions during the Civil War would have been more careful had they realized the scrutiny to which these military records would later be subjected as the Government granted more and more pensions and other benefits. The clerks and company officers of the 27th Maine might have been particularly careful had they known that, because of their involvement with the Medal of Honor, the names they wrote and rewrote would appear in many printed records, including several War Department circulars and a U.S. Senate document. In this further process printers and proofreaders contributed errors of their own. As examples of the final results, a man who had signed his last name as "Jeffery" on the enlistment roll appeared in Medal of Honor circulars as "Jeffords," and a man who had signed "Lougee" (a fairly common name in Maine) appeared as "Longee." Between the spellings as given in the final record of the 27th Maine printed in the

1863 Maine Adjutant General's Report and the War Department circulars there were more than 100 disagreements in spelling. Sometimes the Maine Adjutant General had a name right and the War Department had it wrong; sometimes it was the other way around; and occasionally they both had it wrong.

The record-keeping also developed a few minor mysteries such as that having to do with the Harmons of Company C; a Corporal Leonard C. Harmon appears on the enlistment roll and other original records of the company as well as on Stone's list of volunteers, but he does not appear in the Medal of Honor circulars. On the other hand a Samuel C. Harmon of Company C appears in the Medal of Honor circulars and a medal was issued for him, but as far as the records of the regiment are concerned, no such person ever existed. Perhaps Mark Wentworth had the nonexistent Samuel's medal reengraved for Leonard.

Another bit of confusion which the board added (it really didn't matter in the long run, but it is typical of the way in which guardian spirits — or something — kept frustrating everybody who tried to penetrate the affair of the 27th Maine) had to do with numbers. Prior to beginning deliberations, one of the members of the board had suggested that in order to filter out all strains of possible kinship, friendship or other personal interest, the recorder should assign to each case a number and withhold the actual name from the board until after the man's case had been considered and a decision had been reached. Consequently there were 864 numbers to be assigned to the 27th Maine men.

The recorder did quite well; he only made one mistake, assigning the same number to two men; but when the report of the board and all its proceedings were published in a Senate document, the printers added six more errors of numbering. Inasmuch as the same printed report listed the volunteers, or those whom the board had judged to be volunteers, only by numbers, someone might conceivably have been chaffered out of his rightful place by this laxity.

But in the end it was all an exercise — a dry run as the Army says — and the only reason for going into detail is that it was a good example of the fact that it's no easy thing to prepare a correct list of soldiers for pay, for muster, for medals or for anything else. The company clerk's manual had warned about this way back in Civil War days, but no one would ever take the warning seriously. And the five generals had not been invulnerable.

Having indicated the 555 men of the 27th Maine who it felt ought to be stricken from the list, the board continued with a toll of other undeserving recipients, and these were few: four officers and 25 first sergeants who had served as Abraham Lincoln's funeral guard and seven miscellaneous people including Dr. Mary E. Walker.

Concerning the 309 men of the 27th Maine

designated by the board as the volunteers, plus five veterans of the 27th New Jersey and one veteran of the 22nd New York State Militia who had been awarded their medals under General Orders No. 195, the report stated: "In view of the circumstances attending the award of these medals, the board recommends that action by the War Department be deferred pending a possible reconsideration of the law by Congress."

(There was a curious coincidence among the five cases of the 27th New Jersey. It so happened that George W. Mindil had been awarded *two* Medals of Honor, a rare occurrence, and one of them had been given for gallantry in action in 1862. In fact, Mindil had served with distinction in the Civil War, and his name was to remain on the official Medal of Honor list by virtue of his one "gallantry in action" award.)

In the case of the five civilian scouts which included Buffalo Bill, the report had this to say: "They rendered distinguished service in action, and, in the opinion of the board, they fully earned their medals. It is hoped that a modification of the law will permit them to retain them."

Outside of the traps it had fallen into in dealing with the inscrutable 27th Maine, the board made recommendations which were reasonable, fair and far-reaching. The conclusion of its report, which was tinged with indignation at the legislative instructions under which the board had been forced to operate, did much to put the whole matter into perspective:

. . . the board invites attention to the large number of officers and enlisted men who have served in the army of the United States from 1861 to date, estimated at 3,200,000, and to the small number of medals of honor issued. It is well known, however, that there have been many cases of heroic conduct deserving of medals which have not been so rewarded. On the other hand, the board has noted some cases which would have been sufficiently and more appropriately rewarded by brevets, certificates of merit, or mention in orders.

In this connection the board ventures to suggest that other insignia, in addition to the medal of honor, be established by Congress to be awarded for distinguished or highly meritorious services not only in action but also in other spheres of duty. Such rewards are recognized in all armies and are a great incentive to extraordinary effort and the display of soldierly qualities.

As the military profession offers no reward to its members except for distinguished and meritorious services, the board suggests that medals of honor should not be issued to civilians who, if occasion requires, should be rewarded in some other way. Medals of honor should be reserved as the highest military decoration to be awarded to officers and enlisted men only and as now prescribed in the Army Regulations, which, in the opinion of the board should be enacted into law to prevent future meddling and misunderstandings and to enhance the value of the award. And once a medal of honor or other insignia has been duly awarded to an officer or enlisted man according to law, he should not be deprived of it except by the judgment of a military court or for causes disgraceful to the military service.

Thus the board concluded its report, which could be summarized as follows:

THE AWARD TO	REPORTED
555 members of the 27th Maine	Made in error. Not justified.
29 members of Lincoln's funeral guard	Not earned in action.
7 miscellaneous recipients	Not earned in action.
309 members of the 27th Maine	Not earned in action but awarded legally. Rescission should be deferred pending possible reconsideration of the 1916 law by Congress.

| 6 recipients under G.O. 195 | Not earned in action but awarded legally. Rescission should be deferred pending possible reconsideration of the 1916 law by Congress. |
| 5 civilian scouts and guides | Earned in action but not awarded according to law. Law should be modified to allow their retention. |

911 *Total*

The Adjutant General then asked the Judge Advocate General what he could do about the recommendation that action be deferred on the 309 of the 27th Maine and the few others involved. The Judge Advocate General returned the opinion that the recent law as written left the War Department with no choice.

Therefore, all 911 awards were stricken from the Medal of Honor list. One result which was somewhat ironic was that, while the five famous civilian Indian fighters lost the right to their decorations, several members of the Indian Scouts remained on the list — Elatsoosu, Kosoha, Mad

252

Bear, Nannasaddie and the others who were recognized as having had military rather than civilian status.

A minor mercy was seen in the fact that the popular hero Buffalo Bill never learned of his loss. He had died a week before the report of the board was signed; his body had just been viewed by immense throngs at the capitol in Denver, and he would be exalted to safe immortality in a tomb blasted out of solid rock on the top of Lookout Mountain.

The only woman recipient, Dr. Mary Walker, was still alive and, it must be presumed, capable of considerable rage at the phraseology with which her award had been dismissed. The report of the board had said, "This was a contract surgeon whose service does not appear to have been distinguished in action or otherwise."

Perhaps it was just as well for the members of the board personally that the Judge Advocate General ruled as he did and that their recommendations for reconsideration were not accepted. Further study might have subjected them to the embarrassment of defending findings which were at variance with two previous War Department decisions: those ruling that the 27th Maine medals had *not* been awarded under General Orders No. 195 and that the list of volunteers as given in Stone's history could not be accepted as official.

Further, even if these conditions had not existed it probably would have been almost impossible at that late date to get the whole mess untangled with respect to the entitled and the unentitled veterans of the 27th Maine.

Nevertheless, the board had illuminated a principle.

The United States is supposed to be a country of law. And if a medal is awarded, or anything else is legally done by the executive department of the Government, shall a Congress have the right, 50 years later, to reverse that action? If so, Congress could, if it wished, begin to write history. It could decide, for example, that Ulysses S. Grant should never have been appointed a lieutenant general, and that henceforth official records should refer to him as Major General Grant.

But at that time the clouds of World War I were hanging heavy over the nation, and people in Washington had a great many things to think about besides the grumbling of five old generals and honors awarded to men who were mostly all dead anyway.

The War Department handled the matter as decently as it was able to. Although nothing in the law indicated that he had to do so, the Adjutant General set about assembling a list of names and addresses of survivors of the 27th Maine, so that he could write to them and tell them what happened. He applied to the Commissioner of Pensions for help. Addresses were found for 183 survivors, which did not necessarily mean that all of these were alive. Those known to be dead numbered 521. And 160 had never had any business with the Pension Office so there was no way of telling where they were or how many were alive; it is a safe guess that far fewer than 200 were still around; survivors had numbered an estimated 300 in 1912 and they had been fading fast during the five years since then.

On March 3, 1917, the Adjutant General sent letters to the 183 addresses that had been found, and the War Department files do not show much reaction. Perhaps to some old soldiers, who had treasured the medal all their lives, the letter was a cause for disappointment and grief. Perhaps for others, whose names were about to be stricken from the lists of life, it didn't much matter. There were some to whom the letter must have been a source of much bewilderment; these were men who had never received the medal or heard anything about it. In writing the letters, the Adjutant General did not realize that what the Medal of Honor Board wanted to accomplish with respect to unearned medals had been taken care of by Mark F. Wentworth more than half a century before. Like the rain which falleth upon the just and the unjust, the Adjutant General's messages went to both the entitled and the unentitled alike.

What must have been the bewilderment, and the strange emotions, of one of these unmedaled and uninformed old men upon receiving, on a March morning in 1917, one of these letters, the content of which if received today would be roughly comparable to the following: "The Congressional Medal of Honor which you received in the Spanish-American War has been taken away from you by an act of Congress, and if you wear it any more in public, you will be guilty of a misdemeanor."

One old gentleman who had never received the medal was nevertheless thrown into a towering rage when thus informed of being deprived of his nonexistent decoration. Once he had recovered from his astonishment, he loosed an Olympian blast at the Federal Government. In his reply to the Adjutant General he said that he didn't have a Congressional Medal of Honor, but if he did have one he would not give it back to the War Department or to anyone else. He would keep and wear it indoors or out, or wherever he pleased. He would go right out and walk up and down the street with it on if it suited him to do so. Further, if his name and others had been found on any Medal of Honor list, why it must have been placed there by authority of Congress 50 years before, and the people who placed the names on the list must have had adequate legal reasons for doing it. And if those fellows down in Washington were now taking satisfaction in striking from such lists the names of old veterans who had risked their lives to save the Union, they could get a lot *more* pleasure if they would go around and destroy all the old muster rolls, which were the genuine rolls of honor!

It was a strange commentary on the way things

were going down there in Washington, the old veteran continued, when Medals of Honor given by Congress could be repudiated by the same government 50 years afterward.

Only 183 letters of notification were sent by the Adjutant General; and some of the intended recipients had never received medals, so some of the letters were meaningless. This meant that a few entitled veterans and many families of deceased medal holders to whom the decorations had descended were still left in the dark; it would have been nearly impossible for the Army to determine, in 1917, the whereabouts of so many Medals of Honor issued 52 years before. One of the people who never got the word was Vice-Admiral Calvin H. Cobb, the grandson of Calvin Hayes previously mentioned. (Calvin Hayes died in 1914.) Admiral Cobb had in his possession the medals issued to his grandfather, both the original and the 1904 design. However, it occurred to him that there ought to be some sort of citation to go with the medals and so he wrote to the Department of Defense in 1959 to ask for a copy. He then received the bad news, which he had never heard before, that all of the 27th Medals of Honor had been rescinded.

It was this shock that started Admiral Cobb on his investigation of the affair, and when he learned the whole story he was even further distressed. One of his comments was to the effect that if the 1916 law was constitutional and just, then a precedent had been established whereby in the future U.S. medals awarded in World War I could be cancelled or readjusted according to the standards of World War II, which he believed to be higher in certain instances having to do with the Distinguished Service Cross and Medal.

In 1960, shortly before his death, Admiral Cobb — according to one of his notes on the subject — suggested to Senator Margaret Chase Smith of Maine that legislation be initiated to restore to the Medal of Honor list the 312 names given in Stone's history; however, he had little hope that a U.S. Senator, so busy with matters so much more important, would be able to act on the suggestion very speedily. Had Admiral Cobb lived to pursue his study further, he might also have recognized that Senator Smith, or anyone else attempting to set the matter straight, would undoubtedly run into the same difficulty that bedeviled the War Department in the 1890's, and the difficulty that was overlooked by the Medal of Honor review board in 1916–17 — the improbability of determining with absolute certainty from available official records which of the men of the regiment had remained in Washington and which had gone home.

The key to the perplexity of the unpleasant task with which the Medal of Honor board was saddled in 1916–17 was simply this: they had been given the assignment of doing what many people would consider a wrong in order to correct what many other people believed to be a greater wrong. The "other soldier-like qualities" phrase in the joint resolution of 1862 was an unwise provision — but it was still the law. That this part of the law would be made largely inoperative and its unwisdom thwarted — in spite of everything the people in Washington did or failed to do — was because of two things:

1. A baffling cloud of confusion which confounded administrators and effectively obscured the exact number of 27th Maine men who were legally entitled to the medal.

2. A singular prescience and directness of action on the part of Mark F. Wentworth, who foresaw how by the compounding of a clerical error some 560 medals might be redistributed if returned to the Government, and who simply kept them out of harm's way.

Wentworth, long silent in his granite tomb when the new Medal of Honor was issued, probably would not have liked it. There was no red in the ribbon. Also, the figure of Minerva had been chopped off. Now just her head showed in the design. But if Minerva could look down, she would at least see that her garments were considerably more luminous.

And Wentworth probably would have approved of that.

"This Sole Remaining Seal of Honor"

The foregoing has had much to do with laws and regulations during the period 1862–1917. But in the meantime, how had the Medal of Honor made out where it mattered most: in its public reputation?

Many things can never be much more than what people think they are. In that sense the Law of Aerodynamics — illustrations of which represent currents of air flowing over a cross-section of an airplane wing, a vacuum created above the wing, the plane thus drawn upward, and so on — might be one of the greatest hoaxes ever perpetrated. What causes airplanes to go up is a form of levitation: mass confidence on the part of millions of people who climb aboard *expecting* the planes to go up; without this trust Wilbur and Orville Wright might just as well have remained in the bicycle business.

And something of this sort of widespread public regard was likewise essential to the ascent of the Medal of Honor to its present status. No matter what laws had been enacted, if a large number of these decorations had been worn by people of no particular military distinction, the medal would have come to be held in correspondingly low esteem, especially in the State of

Maine, where the veterans of the 27th Maine were at large.

Did any such thing happen?

The best comment available is that of General Joshua Chamberlain, who had not only a deep interest in the Medal of Honor but the opportunity to observe what was going on in veterans' affairs during the period 1865–1914.

Chamberlain himself was a recipient of the Medal of Honor, and there is no question of his deserving it, even under present-day standards. Late on the second day of Gettysburg, Chamberlain and the 20th Maine defended the extreme left of the Union line on Little Round Top against an attack by an overwhelming number of Confederate troops; the Southerners made repeated charges, which were beaten off in hand-to-hand fighting; after more than an hour of this, with the 20th Maine out of ammunition, Chamberlain routed his attackers and captured more than 400 prisoners by launching a surprise bayonet charge down the slopes of the hill — a charge that succeeded partly because it seemed to be impossible. When the fight was over, nearly 300 men of Maine, Texas and Alabama were sprawled, dead or wounded, around Little Round Top, and blood lay in puddles on the rocks.

For that afternoon's work Chamberlain received the Medal of Honor in 1893. He was Governor of Maine for four terms immediately following the Civil War, and he spoke or was present at many veterans' reunions up through the first decade of the 20th century. If the decoration had been in any way devalued by public display or wide public knowledge of the 27th Maine medals, Chamberlain certainly would have known about it.

Something that Chamberlain wrote shortly before his death in 1914 is therefore significant. He was discussing some of the more dubious honors of the Civil War and deploring the indiscriminate bestowal of brevet commissions which, in the words of a wit of the day, had done everything but brevet mules to horses. He then went on to state:

Only the Congressional Medal of Honor had been held sacred — not to be bought or sold, or recklessly conferred. It was held to be the highest honor — recognition of some act of conspicuous personal gallantry beyond what military duty required. Knowing what has happened with the cross of the Legion of Honor in France, and how sacred the Victoria Cross is held in England, we trust that no self-seeking plea nor political pressure shall avail to belittle the estimation of this sole-remaining seal of honor whose very meaning and worth is that it notes conduct in which manhood rises above self. May this award ever be for him who has won it, at the peril of life, in storm of battle, but let us not behold the sublime spectacle of vicarious suffering travestied by the imposition of vicarious honors.

This speaks well for the way in which Wentworth had managed the whole affair, and for a commendable restraint on the part of the more than 300 veterans of the 27th Maine who figuratively and often literally had kept the medals "up attic." If the 27th had ever adopted a regimental flower it might well have been the night-blooming cereus.

The strict legal and other safeguards for the Medal of Honor which Chamberlain advocated and which the Medal of Honor Board had advised went into effect in 1918. That year the President approved an act of Congress which included the following requirement:

> That the provisions of existing law relating to the award of Medals of Honor to officers, noncommissioned officers, and privates of the Army be, and they hereby are, amended so that the President is authorized to present, in the name of the Congress, a medal of honor only to each person who, while an officer or enlisted man of the Army, shall hereafter, in action involving actual conflict with an enemy, distinguish himself conspicuously by gallantry and intrepidity at the risk of his life above and beyond the call of duty.

The 1918 legislation also set a time limit for

awards, something that was badly needed. At that time applications for Medals of Honor for Civil War service were still being received, and eyewitness reports and other documents of this sort were becoming, to say the least, unreliable. These applications had been particularly burdensome around the turn of the century, when Secretary of War Elihu Root had grumbled that much of the time and attention of the War Department was being taken up with investigations of purported deeds of heroism performed more than 40 years before. The 1918 law said that henceforth, with certain exceptions, the award would have to be made within three years of the deed, and that the supporting statements or recommendations would have to be made within two years.

The law also did something else which was to serve as a protection and buffer for the Medal of Honor. Part of its vulnerability at the time was the fact that it was, in Chamberlain's words, the sole seal of honor available to both officers and enlisted men in the Army. The new legislation provided for the award of the Distinguished Service Cross for remarkable but lesser degrees of heroism in action, and for the award of a Distinguished Service Medal for meritorious service in duties of great responsibility. Similar awards were established for the Navy at about the same time. These Army and Navy medals were the precursors of a whole series of decorations for combat and noncombat achievements, so that almost any act of distinction could be recognized. Also, a series of campaign or service medals which had begun in 1905 was steadily expanded. The result was that by the time of World War II the United States was a well-medaled army. It was a saying among soldiers that certain medals "came in your K-ration" and it was a rare veteran of World War II who did not come home entitled to two or more service medals including the World War II Victory Medal, which he could hardly avoid being entitled to.

While this "Pyramid of Honor" was a-building, the so-called Congressional Medal of Honor was, of course, rising higher and higher, by displacement, to an almost sacred status.

After 1918 there were very few instances of the Medal of Honor being awarded for anything other than gallantry in combat. Several were awarded by special acts of Congress, but these were unusual. Commander Richard E. Byrd, Jr., and Machinist Floyd Bennett were given Medals of Honor for flying over the North Pole, Captain Charles A. Lindbergh for flying the Atlantic, but as restrictions have continued to grow more severe, comparable awards would be unlikely today.

At least two awards made by special acts of Congress seem to have been in the nature of elaborate apologies, similar in a way to the medal that was awarded to Sergeant Co-rux-te-chod-ish (Mad Bear) in 1869 when he ran out ahead of the troops and was mistakenly shot by members of his own command. One of these went in 1935 to a retired officer, Major General Adolphus W. Greely, for activities covering a remarkably long span of life; Greely, a veteran of the Civil War, had suffered hardship — and, some people thought, neglect and injustice — as a result of an expedition he led to the Arctic in the 1880's; but he had nevertheless gone on to render distinguished services to the Army and the Government.

Another award, this one posthumous, was authorized by Congress in 1946 for William C. Mitchell, "formerly a colonel, United States Army, in recognition of his outstanding pioneer service and foresight in the field of American military aviation." (The story of Billy Mitchell's running out ahead of the troops is too well known to need repetition here.) The title of the act was *An Act authorizing the President of the United States to award posthumously in the name of Congress a Medal of Honor to William Mitchell*, so it certainly could be called a Congressional Medal of Honor. However, it was not *the* Medal of Honor but a special decoration; the words of the act called for "a gold medal to be struck with suitable emblems, devices and inscriptions."

This illustrates a confusion in terminology that has grown up around the medal. On many occasions — beginning with the gold medal authorized for George Washington — Congress has awarded a special medal which could be referred to as a Congressional medal, but not as *the* medal which represents the nation's highest military honor. In order to avoid this confusion, the armed forces refer to their supreme decoration simply as the Medal of Honor. However, because the medal is, by law, awarded "in the name of Congress," the word Congressional has clung to it firmly, and the public seems to know it best as the Congressional Medal of Honor.

By special acts of Congress, Medals of Honor have been awarded posthumously to the Unknown Soldiers of World Wars I and II and the Korean War — also to the Unknown Soldiers of Great Britain and France (buried in Westminster Abbey and the Arc de Triomphe) and to the Unknown Soldiers of Belgium, Rumania and Italy. All of the awards going to foreign countries were made immediately following World War I, when the same countries awarded their highest decorations to the American Unknown Soldier at Arlington.

Since 1918 a few Medals of Honor have also been awarded by the Navy for noncombat services, these usually being connected with rescue and salvage operations, such as those which followed the sinking of the *Squalus* in 1939, or with fires, accidents or other emergencies. These were justified by legislation which was slightly different from that governing Army awards; it provided Medals of Honor for acts involving actual conflict with the enemy or "in the line of profession." Nevertheless, the "line of profession" awards seem to have declined steadily, and nearly all Navy Medals of Honor in World War II were earned under combat conditions. Finally, in an amendment of the law in 1963, the words "line of profession" were eliminated.

The Army, simply because of the greater numbers it normally has engaged in time of war, has been and continues to be the most important custodian of the Medal of Honor. This is shown by the best count now available of the numbers of medals awarded by the services (not including those of the 27th Maine and others rescinded) through 1965:

Army	2,200
Navy	729
Marine Corps	236
Air Force	4 [*]
Coast Guard	1

---

[*]The Air Corps was part of the Army from 1907 to 1947, during which time it received 43 Medals of Honor. These are included in the Army total.

No one can charge the military services with any laxity in their guardianship of the Medal of Honor in the major wars of this century. Those who are alive to wear the medal may be recognized as having performed acts characterized by almost incredible courage — acts which sometimes can be hardly comprehended, perhaps even by the recipients themselves.

The theme of many of these awards is simple self-sacrifice for the sake of others. A common Army and Marine Corps citation (yet how can it be called common!) reads:

When an enemy grenade fell within his group he shouted a warning to his comrades and then unhesitatingly dived upon the missile, absorbing the shattering impact of the exploding charge within his own body and so saving those around him from death or serious injury.

More than 60 Medal of Honor recipients threw themselves upon grenades in exactly this manner; almost always the award was posthumous, although at least nine survived the blast. A Navy counterpart to one of these acts took place in World War I, when Ensign Daniel A. J. Sullivan threw himself upon some depth charges which had been thrown about the deck by an accident of battle and which had been set for firing; Sullivan was able to secure the charges and thus he saved the ship from disaster.

Other men have made gifts of their lives in many other ways. In World War I, Marine Gunnery Sergeant Fred W. Stockham, in the midst of a gas attack, gave his gas mask to a wounded man who had none, and so perished in the fumes. On the deck of the submarine *Growler* in World War II, Commander Howard W. Gilmore, riddled by machine-gun bullets, saved the vessel and crew but consigned himself to an ocean burial by giving the order, "Take her down." Near Valmontone, Italy, caught under the glaring light of flares, Army Private Herbert F. Christian singly attacked 60 enemy riflemen, three machine guns, and three tanks so that his patrol could escape from an ambush. With his right leg severed above the knee, he steadily advanced on his left knee and the bloody stump of his right thigh, firing his submachine gun, killing a number of the enemy and being killed himself while his 12-man patrol made good its escape.

On a bombing flight over Japan, a faulty phosphorus bomb exploded in the launching chute, flying back into the plane and into the face of Staff Sergeant Henry E. Erwin. White phosphorus is one of the most fearsome substances used in modern warfare. It makes an enormous amount of dense smoke suddenly and burns with a flame that is terribly intense and destructive. The phosphorus bomb which shot back into Erwin's face obliterated his nose, blinded him and fell at his feet, where it threatened to burn its way right through the deck and into a load of bombs below. The plane, filled with smoke which choked the pilots and obscured their vision, went into a dive. Seemingly, for all that anyone could humanly do, the aircraft was a goner — and everyone in it. But Sergeant Erwin somehow picked the flaming bomb up. While it ate at his flesh, he crawled around the gun turret and headed for the copilot's window. The navigator's table stopped him; but he grasped the white-hot, hissing bomb between his forearm and body, felt around and released a spring lock, raised the table, groped his way onward through a narrow passage, located the window and threw the bomb out. Erwin then fell back on the deck completely aflame, but the plane and its crew were saved and the Sergeant lived to remember it, if he ever cared to.

These stories are typical of the nearly super-human degree of courage to which the Medal of Honor has become affixed. But they are not completely representative of all the acts which have earned the decoration. A greater number of awards in modern times have emphasized not succor of the wounded or self-sacrifice for the sake of comrades — although these accomplishments are often involved as part of the act recognized — but a heroic determination to close with the enemy which has resulted in remarkable, and remarkably effective personal onslaughts.

These one-man attacks have been delivered with rifles, machine guns, grenades, carbines, pistols, cannon, bombs, bazookas, empty guns used as clubs, fists, rocks, entrenching tools and nearly every weapon imaginable. This is rough stuff — no fare for a weak stomach. Yet as long as war continues to be an instrument of national policy, the citations may be reviewed with at least the profit of understanding what sort of work is important in winning a battle once people are in one. From such a review at least

271

two impressions emerge. One has to do with the inordinate amount of panic, slaughter and destruction that can be inflicted by one resolute human being; the other with the inspirational effect upon troops with whom the hero is serving. The two effects combined can make the Medal of Honor holder a very formidable factor in the equation of a battle.

Typical was the exploit of Army Lieutenant Samuel Woodfill in World War I. Woodfill found the advance of his company halted by enemy machine gunners — who are both the villains and the victims of so many Medal of Honor stories. Woodfill rushed three machine-gun nests one after another and destroyed them personally, killing at least a dozen of the gunners. Two of these he dispatched with a pick-ax. His men were so inspired by this example that they pressed on to their objective under severe fire.

However, the leaders of these one-man-inspired attacks haven't always been officers or noncommissioned officers. Private soldiers have led many of them. For example, on a slope of Hen Hill, Okinawa, Army Private First Class Clarence B. Craft suddenly stood up and faced an entrenched Japanese force that had been repelling attacks made in battalion strength. His companions thought Craft was trying to commit suicide. Instead, he simply walked up the hill, shooting Japanese wherever one stuck his head up and driving others to deeper cover. Reaching the crest of the hill, where he stood silhouetted against the sky, he was supported by a chain of grenade passers and throwers, and Craft threw two cases of grenades himself while directing the throws of others. Then, with grenades from both sides flying over him and bursting on either slope, he pressed on with his rapid-fire attack, cleaning out the main Japanese trench and destroying a heavy machine gun nest. The citation says, "By this time the Japanese were in complete rout and American forces were swarming over the hill."

With Okinawa and World II won and the Atomic Age upon us, it might be thought that such primitive combat would no longer be necessary. But typical of several award-earning actions in Korea was that of Army Captain Lewis L. Millett, who led a hand-to-hand assault up another fire-swept hill, personally grenading, bayonetting, clubbing and otherwise doing to death a number of the foe, his men storming after him and sending the enemy fleeing in disorder.

Often these Medal of Honor attacks have been characterized by exemplary thought as well as action on the part of the men who have led or delivered them. A medal holder of Civil War days saw it thus: "In times like these every man in the ranks must, for the time, be a general himself; that is, he must be brave, use good judgment, make up his mind in a moment and take advantage of every opportunity to overcome the enemy." Many award-winning deeds have been performed, in the midst of harrowing danger, with a cool exercise of great skill or technical knowledge.

As an instance, Navy Lieutenant Edward H. O'Hare in February of 1942 interposed his single plane between his carrier and an attacking formation of nine enemy bombers, shot down five of these aircraft and damaged a sixth. This was a great feat of flying and marksmanship as well as an outstanding display of courage, and it undoubtedly saved the carrier from destruction or serious damage.

In quite another way Army Corporal Charles E. Kelly, although his citation does not fully explain it, performed a technical feat while throwing 60-mm. mortar shells by hand from the window of a beleaguered storehouse. The citation, which appeared early in 1944, said that Kelly "picked up 60-mm. mortar shells, pulled the safety pins and used the shells as grenades, killing at least five of the enemy." This puzzled many people who were familiar with the operation of mortars. Even though the safety pin is drawn, a mortar shell will not ordinarily explode unless it is fully armed; and it is normally armed by the jar of propulsion in being fired, which actuates another safety device. The jar causes a "setback" pin to drop, which in turn allows an interrupter pin to fly to one side and other things to happen productive of an explosion when the shell lands. The July *Infantry Journal* of that year explained how Kelly did it. He duplicated the jarring effect by banging the base of the mortar shell on a solid surface before he fired it. The article pointed out that this is a trick anyone can do, provided that he isn't overly concerned about banging a half-pound of TNT around.

More explicit was the citation for Technical Sergeant Beaufort T. Anderson of the Army, who on Okinawa personally halted a screaming wave of Japanese: "Securing a box of mortar shells, he extracted the safety pins, banged the bases upon a rock to arm them and then proceeded alternately to hurl shells and fire his piece among the fanatical foe, finally forcing them to withdraw."

Anderson did away with 25 of the enemy in this manner. And in Korea, Army Lieutenant Lloyd L. Burke, in the course of an attack in which he killed more than 100, caught several grenades in the air and threw them back at the enemy. But the casualties he inflicted fell far short of being a record. One Medal of Honor recipient is credited with 250 enemy deaths in a single action, another with 150, another with 105 and so on — modern automatic and semi-automatic weapons multiplying the effectiveness of individual valor.

A willingness to sacrifice himself — an unquenchable desire to destroy and defeat the enemy — an implacable determination to complete a mission, self-assigned or otherwise: these appear to be the chief characteristics of Medal of Honor holders. A conspicuous example of all three was provided by Army Lieutenant

Bernard J. Ray, whose company was halted under heavy fire by a wire barrier in the Hürtgen Forest in November, 1944. Lieutenant Ray placed explosive caps in his pockets, picked up several bangalore torpedoes and wrapped a length of highly explosive primer cord about his body. Then he dashed forward and started to place his demolition charges under the wire. Enemy mortar bursts began walking toward him. One severely wounded him just as he had placed his torpedoes. Realizing that he would fail unless he completed the job promptly, he arranged a hasty wiring system. Then, with the caps still in his pockets and the explosive cord still wound around his body, he pushed down on the handle of his charger and blew himself and the barricade to glory. On through the gap went the attack, which, in the words of Ray's citation, "was of positive significance in gaining the approaches to the Cologne Plain."

Equally spectacular was the act of Lieutenant Lloyd H. Hughes who, in the low-level raid on Ploesti on August 1, 1943, flew his shot-up, gasoline-spewing bomber through a wall of flame which had arisen from burning oil tanks — thereby turning his aircraft into a blowtorch — in order to drop his bombs and avoid jeopardizing the formation.

As was the case with Lieutenant Hughes, many Medal of Honor recipients have made the decision to sacrifice not only themselves but men under their command if necessary. This was the hard choice that fell, by way of example, to Captain William E. Barber, holding an important pass in Korea with a company of Marines. Savagely attacked and surrounded by a force of estimated regimental strength, and having received orders by radio to fight his way back to safety, Barber nevertheless requested permission to hold on and be supplied by air drops. His citation tells the rest of the story:

Aware that leaving the position would sever contact with the 8,000 Marines trapped at Yudam-ni and jeopardize their chances of joining the 3,000 more awaiting their arrival in Hagaru-ri for the continued drive to the sea, he chose to risk loss of his command rather than sacrifice more men if the enemy seized control and forced a renewed battle to regain the position, or abandon his many wounded who were unable to walk. Although severely wounded in the leg . . . Captain Barber continued to maintain personal control, often moving up and down the lines on a stretcher to direct the defense and consistently encouraging and inspiring his men to supreme efforts despite the staggering opposition. Waging desperate battle throughout 5 days and 6 nights of repeated onslaughts launched by the fanatical aggressors, he and his heroic command accounted for approximately 1,000 enemy dead in this epic stand in bitter subzero weather, and when the company was relieved, only 82 of his original 220 men were able to walk away from the position so valiantly defended against insuperable odds. His profound faith and courage, great personal valor, and unwavering fortitude were decisive factors in the successful withdrawal of the division from the deathtrap in the Chosin Reservoir sector and reflect the highest credit upon Captain Barber, his intrepid officers and men, and the United States naval service.

The intrepid officers and men, it should be added, were those of Company F, 2nd Battalion, 7th Marines, 1st Marine Division.

And so it is that hundreds of American fighting men — carrying out desperate assignments even though wounded, burning, freezing, bleeding, staggering from concussion or otherwise beset — have given the word VALOR on this medal a great and terrible meaning.

So lofty a height of bravery does the decoration mark today that in the Korean War, of 131 Medals of Honor awarded, only 37 went to living men.

In fact, it may be wondered if the armed services are not making this a medal for illustrious ghosts, whose comrades in Valhalla presumably need no boost to morale, rather than an award to living soldiers, sailors and airmen, whose companions often do.

Shortly after VE Day in 1945, someone had

the thought that Medals of Honor should be awarded to General Dwight D. Eisenhower and also, posthumously to General John J. Pershing, who led the American Expeditionary Force in World War I.

Eisenhower disapproved of the idea. So did the War Department. Strike a special gold medal for such awards, the Department suggested, but let the Medal of Honor continue to be reserved for those whose deeds in actual combat merit it. Even General George S. Patton, Jr., whose daring leadership was a major factor in the success of our arms in Europe, never received the Medal of Honor.

On May 5, 1961, when millions of television viewers watched Alan B. Shepard, Jr., roar aloft on the nose of a flaming rocket — the first American to soar into space — the thought must have occurred to many people that this was one of the bravest things that mortal man had ever done and that Shepard ought to have the Medal of Honor. However, Shepard didn't get the medal, nor is it likely that he or any of the other astronauts ever will except by a special dispensation of Congress or unless they become engaged in combat.

All this by way of illustrating that the Medal of Honor is now, according to law, an award not for heroic action alone, no matter how outstanding, but for heroic action at the risk of life, above and beyond the call of duty, in some form of conflict. The action does not necessarily have to be in a declared war. In fact, the eligibility requirements have recently been somewhat enlarged to provide for the responsibilities the United States has assumed in various parts of the world. An act of Congress of July 25, 1963, made these requirements uniform for all the armed forces and made the Medal of Honor available for acts performed by our military people while engaged in an action against an enemy of the United States, while engaged in military operations involving conflict with an opposing foreign force or while serving with friendly foreign forces engaged in an armed conflict against an opposing armed force in which the United States is not a belligerent party.

And that is what the Medal of Honor stands for today. The serenity of the Army design — the static head of Minerva with the quiet blue of the ribbon and the cool green and gold of the wreathed star — belies the fact that it is actually a badge of bloody battle. The dusky, smoky bronze of the old 1862 design with its scene of conflict in the center of the star and its ribbon striped with red is somehow more suggestive of the conditions under which most of these medals have been earned. There are, in fact, good arguments for a return on the part of the Army to the old medallic star. Regarding the present Army medal, there should properly be great hesitation in advancing criticisms of any symbol so hallowed by superhuman deeds of valor during the past 50 years.

However, there are criticisms on record which deserve to be looked at again. Immediately after

World War I, possibly stimulated by firsthand observation of the medals of foreign countries, there was an expression of dissatisfaction with the Medal of Honor designs, including one which the Navy had developed in the form of a cross for combat heroism. (This was issued for a relatively short period of time beginning around 1919, while the old Medal of Honor continued to be awarded for deeds of heroism not performed in combat action.) The criticism was spearheaded by the National Commission of Fine Arts, which took a whack at both the Army medal and the Navy decoration just mentioned. The commission criticized the Army medal on several counts: For being finished on only one side, for having a "cheap and insignificant appearance," for suspension by two points of the star instead of one and for a confusing conflict between the enameled green oak leaves on the star and the laurel leaves of the surrounding wreath. Its report stated, "This highest award to American valor now resembles a bit of jewelry and lacks the elegance and simplicity characteristic of high military medals of other countries." And of the general subject it said:

Medals are not playthings. They represent valor, achievement, service. They are worn on occasions of the highest ceremony. Consequently they should be perfect works of art. They may be simple and inexpensive, but they ought to be good.

Since then the Navy has dropped its cross-type design and resumed the issue of the old 1862 bronze star for all its Medal of Honor awards. Today, with a different ribbon and a minor variation or two, the star of the Navy hangs from its anchor and Minerva Repulses Discord just as she did 100 years ago.

For a time the Air Force was content with the Army design, but in 1965, in a characteristic show of independence, it announced its own Medal of Honor. This appears to be basically the old 1862 star in gold-finished bronze four-fifths surrounded by a wreath of laurel in green enamel. However, the center of the star for some reason bears the head of the Statue of Liberty, and Minerva has been ousted altogether. (It is to be hoped that the Secretary of the Air Force was prudent enough to order the necessary propitiatory rites to placate the evicted goddess before she was pitched out.) The greatly modified star is suspended from a trophy consisting of a bar bearing the word VALOR above an adaptation of thunderbolts from the U.S. Air Force coat of arms.

Quite apart from the reservations that may be expressed concerning their designs, it is to be regretted that the Army and Air Force do not follow the Navy in going back to the old bronze star, suspending it with devices emblematic of their own services with the exception of a ribbon which could be uniform for Army, Navy and Air Force.

Better still, all services might recognize that this is the only medal awarded in the name of Congress; the only U.S. medal with more than a century of tradition, and the decoration that people have known for years as *the* Congressional Medal of Honor. This would imply doing away with separate symbols and — for all three services — simply suspending the star from the ribbon by one point (turning Minerva and her foe a bit to stand them upright). Thus, public awareness of the medal could be multiplied and enhanced through having one design instead of three. And thus would be utilized the importance of the old star — valuable historically and, if you happen to think so, in the beauty and interest of its symbolism.

This old Star of the Union was bestowed for about two-thirds of the approximately 3,170 awards now on the official list. It therefore has been an important part of the Medal of Honor tradition, and if the medal had been meticulously preserved by all our services it would now have an unbroken history comparable to that of England's Victoria Cross, for it is very nearly as ancient.

The Victoria Cross, the highest British decoration, was instituted in 1856, retroactive through 1854 to include the Crimean War. It has always been manufactured by the same firm, Hancock & Company of London. It has always been made from the gun metal of cannon captured at Sevastopol. It is awarded in exactly the same form to all military services and even to civilians serving under the direction of the armed forces who perform acts of gallantry in the presence of the enemy. The only alteration that has ever been made in the medal took place in 1918, and that was in the interest of uniformity. Before 1918, the ribbon was blue for the Royal Navy; since then it has been claret (red) for everybody. Through 1965, awards of the Victoria Cross numbered 1,346. It is not the sort of honor represented by an "order," and therefore it is not suspended from the neck but pinned on the uniform, and there are those who say the Medal of Honor should be worn the same way, for the same reason.

But no matter in what form it is issued, the Congressional Medal of Honor today stands for a great tradition. The fact that this tradition came into the present century so remarkably unstained is due to the efforts and attitudes of hundreds of people, including many in Congress, in the Medal of Honor societies and in the armed service departments. To be counted as not the least of these must be the modest forbearance, on the part of some 300 Maine veterans, to make any notable public display of their legally awarded medals, and the decision on the part of Mark F. Wentworth to keep the other 560 or so in Maine rather than to send them back to Washington, from which place they might well have been redistributed.

In summary it may be said that no other U.S.

medal was born of such imprecise legislation or has suffered so much administrative abuse. Yet it has triumphed over all obstacles to become an object of awe and veneration unmatched in our secular history.

This veneration will soon be given an unusual expression. Having observed that there is nowhere any major public display or institution memorializing the Medal of Honor and the men who have earned it, Freedoms Foundation at Valley Forge is establishing a Medal of Honor Grove. The Foundation has acquired more than 50 acres of natural woodland and quiet streams at Valley Forge, adjoining the site of the encampment hallowed by the patriots of the Revolution. A section of the tract will be designated for each of the 50 states, Puerto Rico and the District of Columbia, and on each section will stand a monument bearing the names of the Medal of Honor winners from that state or region. In addition, a living tree will be marked with the name of each man now on the official Medal of Honor list.

Several miles of winding pathways will connect the state areas, with formal gardens at intervals. A central building will house archives of the Medal of Honor awards — something that will satisfy a long-existing need, for there is no central depository for these records and much information pertaining to them is inaccessible except through laborious research. Thus, for the first time, a major monument to the Medal of Honor

285

is taking shape. The effect of such a monument and of the tradition it makes visually real is of course incalculable. Are the youngsters of today interested in such concepts as valor, duty and plain old-fashioned love of country? Those who visualize them as beatniks, black-jacketed motorcyclists or incomprehensible pseudo-sophisticates might take some comfort from a visit to Valley Forge or to any of our historic sites during the summer months when school is out. The common scene is that of thousands of boys and girls and their parents trudging happily through such places in what can only be regarded as a demonstration of keen and continuing interest in our American heritage. The parking lots are Unions in themselves — with license plates proclaiming Kansas, Indiana, Oregon, Oklahoma, Georgia, Florida, Vermont and every other state. The cars are more elegant, the cameras more expensive, the camping outfits more opulent than ever before, but the kids look entirely normal. In fact, there is something extremely healthy and wholesome in this massive tide of wide-eyed pilgrims which yearly flows through Williamsburg, Lexington, Independence Hall, Gettysburg and all our patriotic shrines. Observing it, one cannot fail to believe that under the surface froth, which gets most of the attention, America is still made of pretty good stuff. But good stuff alone does not make good citizens. There are certain things that need to be held up so that they can be personally

286

seen and understood. As the youngsters walk the hills of Valley Forge, where the faith of Washington's soldiers still speaks to them, and then through the winding ways of the Medal of Honor Grove with its visible testimony of continued devotion, who knows but what a seed will be planted in some single individual that may one day save us all.

As for the arboreal and somewhat druidical nature of the remarkable monument planned by Freedoms Foundation, this also has much to recommend it. When it comes to things of the spirit, sacred groves are among man's oldest institutions, probably antedating cathedrals and monuments of stone. Yet the majesty of the Medal of Honor Grove will have a somber tone; winds will be hushed within it; blue and khaki ghosts will haunt the leafy corridors, perhaps looking for something to lighten the grimness associated with war, as they often did in life.

It may therefore be appropriate to suggest that in order to provide a note of relief in the Medal of Honor Grove a coppice of small northern pines be planted somewhere among the lofty and long-lived maples, oaks and elms. The quantity should be in the neighborhood of 300 but actually undetermined; and the trees should be planted in a dense thicket so that nobody will ever be able to grasp their number.

The little tangle of pines would aptly represent Mark F. Wentworth and the other volunteers of the 27th Maine who — even though they may not deserve to stand tall in this splendid company — at least performed "over and above the call of duty" as far as was necessary when their call came.

Alarums & Excavations

What happened to the medals that are reported to have vanished following the death of Mark Wentworth in 1897?

A New England minister, the Reverend Ephraim Peabody, perhaps from the memory of his college days in Maine, once wrote a poem entitled "Night in the Woods," which began:

> The deep unfathomable cope of heaven!
> The deep and silent sky!
> Through the narrow forest opening
> Looks down its peaceful eye.

Maine is certainly a place of such silences . . . of ocean deeps and vast forest reaches disturbed only by the soundless shadows of passing clouds . . . of kitchens where the clocks tick loud . . . and of a people who, perhaps because of their surroundings, have as one of their maxims, "Say nothin' and saw wood."

Aside from this natural-born reticence, over a period of a century there is also the difficulty of preserving communications left by the people of changing generations; always some are rising like fireflies over a warm meadow, with little personal knowledge of what has gone before, while others are sinking down and taking much information with them.

Perhaps when Maine gets its official attic in order through the Maine State Archives authorized by its legislature in 1965, or if undiscovered informants are discovered, or if people who "ain't talkin' " talk, more about this matter will be revealed. Or perhaps never.

For the present, it is against a background of silence and of hearsay, speculation and theory that a few scattered clues may be examined.

The first has to do with something that took place on Walker Street in Kittery in the early 1950's. Even today an observer will note that when a shift of the Navy Yard is getting out, there is a tremendous surge of workers' automobiles through the village toward the main highways, a movement not unlike the upstream rush of Chinook salmon. At the time spoken of, this congestion must have been even more severe, for the Kittery authorities decided to widen and extend Walker Street to provide additional egress.

When this work commenced, one thing that had to be done was to move a house, standing near the corner of Walker and Dame Streets, back some distance in order to make way for the widening process.

At the same time, it is said, it so happened that the people living in a house next to the one being moved were cleaning out a detached shed standing upon their property and hauling much material away to the dump. During the cleaning-out they invited one of the carpenters who was engaged in the house-moving job to visit the shed, look over the junk it contained and take anything that he thought might be useful to him — these being the circumstances as remembered by the carpenter. Much more vividly he recalls what happened inside the shed. In the course of his rummaging about, he climbed up into the attic, and while pawing around in the dim light he saw, low under the slanting roof, what he could make out as a wooden box partially covered by an accumulation of other attic objects.

When he opened the box he discovered that it contained a large number of small black cases. They resembled jewelry cases and were obviously very old. He opened several, and they were empty. He saw many other empty cases scattered about the floor of the attic.

Reflecting that he had very little use for old beaten-up jewelry cases, the carpenter was about to move away when something caused him to take hold of the large wooden box and heft it. The box was somewhat heavier than it should have been if it had contained only empty cases. Digging down to the bottom of the box, he found that about 50 of the cases contained medals. Some of the medals were in good shape; the ribbons on others were badly stained or had partially disintegrated. There was a name engraved on the back of each medal; there were also names printed on slips of paper pasted to the cases; but the name on the case seldom corresponded to the name on the medal.

Although the carpenter at the time did not recognize these as Medals of Honor, what he had found was part of the lot of 27th Maine medals which Wentworth had kept from the unentitled.

How had the medals come to be in the attic of the old shed?

Richard Rogers had remembered that Mark Wentworth carried many of his military habits into civilian life — that he "always liked to have a crew of men around him." His second-in-command in many undertakings had been his old adjutant, Calvin Hayes. A man who was also close to Wentworth and who might be described in military terms as an aide was Charles Farwell.

At the time when Wentworth was at the height of his power in Kittery, Charles Farwell was a young man working at the Navy Yard in the capacity of a clerk. He was an excellent penman, and handy at all sorts of things. With a small, well-trimmed mustache and an erect, slender build, he was also rather distinguished in appearance. Sometimes the guard at the gate of the Navy Yard would salute Farwell as he entered or departed, taking him to be one of the naval officers in civilian clothes.

In addition to his duties at the Navy Yard, Farwell also did work of various kinds for Mark Wentworth. The young man had sound, patriotic sentiments; he was well liked and respected in the community, and Wentworth took an interest in him. When young Farwell married,

Wentworth helped him get settled, and the homestead which the Farwells came to occupy was on the corner of Dame and Walker Streets.

It was the property where the carpenter, decades later, found the Medals of Honor.

Whether Farwell was directed to take custody of the medals by Mark Wentworth in the event of his death . . . whether he acted in consort with Calvin Hayes — or whether he took this custody upon himself is all a matter for speculation. No one has been discovered who knows exactly how it happened. However, his daughter and his grandchildren can vouch for the fact that Farwell did have possession of the unissued medals.

Both Calvin Hayes and Charles Farwell were chief clerks at the Navy Yard — Hayes in the construction department, Farwell in ordnance. Calvin Hayes, if he did have anything to do with the disposition of the medals after Wentworth's death — an involvement which his grandson Vice-Admiral Calvin H. Cobb suspected — died in 1914, leaving Farwell as the sole custodian.

Chronologically, the next glimpse of the medals comes to us through the memories of two of Farwell's grandsons, who, as boys, were members of the household at the corner of Dame and Walker Streets. Both remember having seen a box full of medals in the attic of the shed, although neither knows what finally happened to them after they grew up and left the home. One places a date of seeing the box as between the years 1915 and 1920; he says it was a heavy

293

wooden box such as the Government might have used, and his best estimate was that it contained around 150 medals. This number leaves many medals unaccounted for, considering that Mark Wentworth kept some 560 from distribution and even allowing that some of these may have fallen by devious means into the hands of the unentitled. What had happened to the others?

At this point, a whole series of incidents deserves to be recorded.

One of the observations which the reader may remember from the opening chapter of this narrative had to do with the loss of control and its attendant shocks and surprises inherent in the Bumblebee Method of research, which, briefly described, consists of starting somewhere, anywhere, and simply letting one thing lead to another. It may also be remembered that the investigation had begun with the firing of a sizable volley of letters into southern Maine, heedless of who might be energized to do what, and risking the consequences of unexpected chain reactions.

In the spring of 1963, I received an anxious telephone call from Frank Neal. He had picked up a story to the effect that the unissued medals were buried in the ground, and his informant had given him the approximate location. I immediately shared his concern. Our feeling was that the letters of inquiry, which had been rattling around in York County for some time, must have aroused a dormant interest in the medals. Further, if one person knew the story of the buried medals, then others must know it as well, and it was possible that someone might take an interest in hunting for them and digging them up. Our joint decision was that the medals should be made the object of a search and that if found they should be placed in the custody of a reputable museum, removing them from the possibility of uses that might be inappropriate to the Medal of Honor. With that I hastened to Maine.

Once in Kittery, there wasn't much to go on. The story which Frank had picked up in vague outline was that the medals were buried on the old Wentworth place under the base of a flagpole. Inasmuch as there was now no flagpole on the property, it was necessary to determine where one had been. The house of Mark Wentworth and part of his former land are now owned by Dr. Paul E. Taylor, who uses the house as an office building. We decided to acquaint Dr. Taylor with the story and ask his permission to explore.

At Dr. Taylor's place, a large white house with a barn and other outbuildings on the outskirts of Kittery, we found the doctor — a square-built, dark-browed, balding, no-nonsense sort of man — in his kitchen, where he was performing some sort of minor household repair. He was armed with a screwdriver and clad in old clothes; a tear below the knees of his work pants was patched with surgical tape. When presented with our request, Dr. Taylor regarded us warily and with a certain clinical interest — an entirely proper attitude for a physician who has just been confronted by people who say they wish to dig up his lawn because there are Medals of Honor in it.

In answer Dr. Taylor informed us that one other owner of the old Wentworth house had intervened between him and the widow of Dr. Wentworth. Possibly there had also been tenants. He had never seen any medals; in fact he had found very little relating to the Civil War around the place. As for any medals being buried on the property, he was skeptical. However, we could dig if we wanted to, just so long as we didn't tear up any of his sanitation pipes. The ground, he pointed out, was an odd conglomeration of ledge and swampy spots, and he had had a devil of a time getting these pipes laid.

The aid of E. C. Tobey was enlisted. We drove to the old Wentworth place and walked around it. On the south side there was very little space between the house and the adjoining property, and it was an unlikely area for a flagpole to begin with. The ground west of the house, in its rear, was low and wet. But in the north lawn we noticed a small rounded swell. Tobey walked over to it, shuffled away a covering of grass with his foot and said, "This could be it." Just level with the sod at the top of the little knoll was an arrangement of flat stones centered about a hole such as might have accommodated the base of a flagpole. If there had been a flagpole on the lawn, this seemed to have been the place for it. And if medals had been buried under a flagpole they were very likely here.

One difficulty which was at once apparent was the central location in the village. Any digging here was sure to attract a lot of attention. We decided to meet here at sunrise the next day, Sunday, when nearly everyone would still be asleep. At this point it would have been understandable if Frank Neal, a respected member of the professional community, had excused himself from the possibility of being seen with two out-of-towners digging up the lawn of a leading physician. But by now he had been thoroughly seized with the peculiar infection which this affair seemed to generate in most people who came in contact with it, and he insisted on being present with pick and shovel.

A fine spring morning was just rising from the Atlantic when we next assembled, with the low rays of brilliant early sunlight casting long shadows across the lawn of the old Wentworth place. Kittery was quiet except for a state policeman who drove past and looked at us curiously. Frank Neal informed us that we had no need to worry about being arrested; he had thought it wise to inform the police of our permission.

Tobey loosened and overturned the flat stones. He went to work vigorously with pick and shovel. At a depth of about seven inches his pick struck something that gave forth a dull unmistakable thud.

We had struck solid ledge.

The well-graded, artificial surface of the lawn had deceived us. What we had taken to be a man-made elevation was really a thinly covered out-cropping of coastal bed rock.

We reexamined the surface of the lawn intently on all sides of the house, but there was no place more likely to have been the site of a flagpole than the one where we had dug. Further, we had to remind ourselves that the entire lot, as it now existed, had been only a part of the former Wentworth estate, which originally had included much more extensive grounds.

"If they are here anywhere, it will take a mine detector to find them," Frank Neal said. "And I think I know where I can buy one."

I tried to dissuade him, pointing out that a mine or metal detector would undoubtedly cost a large sum of money. But it was quite obvious that Neal had a streak of bulldog in him. Once he started something, he would hang to it.

By now the village of Kittery was beginning to awake from its slumber. We parted with the agreement that I would return later in the summer while on my vacation.

Later in the day I visited Dr. Taylor at his residence. The doctor was still in old clothes and was engaged with a couple of helpers in a spring clean-up of the yard. I reported our lack of success. "Exactly where did you dig?" the doctor asked. I told him. "My God! There isn't more than eight inches of soil there!" he exclaimed. I assured him that this was correct.

However, before we had talked very long it became apparent that Dr. Taylor was becoming affected — somewhat against his will — by what Tobey had called "medal fever." He very kindly offered to go with me to look through the old Wentworth house itself. We drove back to the house and began the search in the cellar. There was nothing there and seemingly no possibility of anything being buried there, for the floor of the cellar was the same ledge that had brought our sunrise excavation to such a sudden end. The first floor was occupied by a waiting room, examining and surgical rooms and other facilities of Dr. Taylor's medical practice. These rooms had been remodeled and extensively worked over; no medals had ever been found. The rooms of the second story were largely vacant and easy to inspect. They yielded nothing. We went up to the third story immediately under the roof. It was hot there, the sun beating down strongly on the shingles above us. There were a few boxes of odds and ends on the floor. We rummaged through them unsuccessfully. Then we turned our attention to something else. The room was much narrower than the ones below; its walls had been erected under the slanting roof at a point where head room was no longer sufficient. There was, therefore, an occult space behind each wall. There was a boat hook lying on the floor. Dr. Taylor, a sturdy man, picked up the boat hook and swung it at one of the walls, striking several crashing blows and loosening boards which he pried off with a loud skreaking of nails and clouds of dust, to make an entrance. Dr. Taylor then crouched down and disappeared into the dark cavern thus exposed. His voice came echoing out, "Oh, my poor bald head among these cobwebs!" I followed him in and we examined this hidden space thoroughly, as well as the space behind the opposite wall. No results. And a search of a shed attached to the house produced nothing. One fact was well established: there are no Medals of Honor in the old Wentworth house.

We drove back to Dr. Taylor's residence to discover smoke and flames rolling up behind his barn. In his absence a grass fire had started and we spent the next hour subduing it. He must have been relieved to see me depart.

Tobey wrote me a couple of weeks later:

Mr. Neal has got the loan of a metal detector and we tried it out. He did some experiments with it yesterday. We went to some old cellars and found a few pieces of tableware, buckles, etc. This instrument doesn't go more than six inches deep, so not much use. He has another one coming.

The other one came and Tobey wrote that it would go to tremendous depths. If there were Medals of Honor anywhere in the earth's crust, it would find them. It was late June or early July when I passed through Kittery again, on my way to northern Maine for a vacation. I stopped to see Neal's detector mechanism. It mainly consisted of two black boxes, one of which bore dials on its face. The two black boxes were connected by a rod and fitted with cords and earphones. Held by a handle, the apparatus could be played over the surface of the ground, and when subterranean metal was detected, there was a scream in the earphones and a pointer on one of the dials flung itself violently to the right. We detected and unearthed several underground objects, which proved to be nails, around the site of an old garrison house out in the country. It was obvious that Frank was delighted with the detector. It provided a relief from his law practice and was a change from golf. He speculated on whether the Medals of Honor, if found, would be legally classified as treasure trove or buried chattels.

We had planned to do some exploring on the following day, but next day was rainy and Frank became involved in a law case; there were other difficulties and I was anxious to go fishing. The exploration was postponed with the intention of resuming it when I returned from up north. As I drove on up through Maine the next day, the sky was blue, the sun was bright and there was a profusion of wild flowers everywhere . . . the barbaric reds and yellows of hawkweed in old fields and beside some of the country roads carpets of little yellow buds that smell like pineapple when they are crushed, the name of which I do not know, and also the fragrance of wild strawberries ripening in the grass. And furthermore, the fish were biting. Soon I was completely out of touch with the world at a lakeside camp, deliberately not listening to radio or reading newspapers. However, there was an intrusion on the evening of July 18. I had just returned to the camp after having been out in a boat all day. Now the stars were coming out, the shadows of the surrounding forest were moving out upon the water and the loons were beginning their night cries. Into this tranquillity, shattering it completely, came four newspaper clippings, sent in by relatives.

The news stories were about the 27th Maine medals. There had been a commotion in southern Maine, and what sounded like chaos in Kittery. There had been an excavation.

It took a while to piece the whole story together, but what had happened was simply one of the chain reactions arising from the Bumblebee Method. One of the letter inquiries which I had mailed months before had lain all this time in the possession of a lady in Kennebunk. Finally she had had the happy and helpful thought of sending my inquiry to "The Clearing House," in the *Portland Press Herald*. This is a column to which people send the "Does any reader know the answer to *this?*" sort of question. My inquiry appeared in the column of July 9, and someone *did* know the answer.

The reply appeared in the column of July 12 under the heading, COULD IT BE THAT 27TH

302

Maine Regiment Medals Are Buried? The respondent was Mrs. Jean E. Weare of Portland, a granddaughter of Charles Farwell and cousin of the grandsons previously mentioned. Her story is here somewhat enlarged from the version that appeared in the column, the author having had the benefit of later conversation with Mrs. Weare, who was kind enough to add several details. But it is essentially the same and goes as follows:

Jean Weare, visiting the Farwell place as a child, had seen a nail keg full of mysterious metal objects (which she believed to have been the medals) in the shed. These were things that Grandfather Farwell didn't want children to touch; in fact, she recalled that he had finally put the keg up in the attic of the shed in an attempt to keep them out of the way of the youngsters. In addition, Jean had another reason for not touching the strange metal objects: a few years before, while she was poking into something else, a rake had fallen on her head and inflicted a painful wound. It was another wound, of an altogether different sort, that had fixed in her mind an incident that took place, she thought, one day in the summer of either 1927 or 1928. On this particular day her grandfather had shouted at her angrily, and this was so unlike his usual kindly disposition toward her that she could never forget the circumstances that caused the display of temper.

It seems that her grandfather was putting up a

flagpole in his yard. He was a patriotic man, and this was a very natural thing for him to be doing. What was unusual was the base for the pole which was being set into the ground. It was the nail keg she had seen the metal objects in; the keg contained newly made cement, and further, the cement was of an angular texture and lumpiness which indicated to her that the metal objects had been mixed into it.

When Jean sought to examine this supposed concrete casserole more closely, her grandfather angrily shouted at her to go away and stay away.

The flagpole, Mrs. Weare said, had been in the back yard, near the edge of Dame Street. The pole was no longer there, but she believed the objects she had seen as a child were Medals of Honor and that they were still there in the ground where the pole had once stood.

This, then, was the origin of the flagpole story. Mrs. Weare had mentioned it to other people over the years and in passing from one person to another the story had undergone the usual deletions and transformations. All that had reached Frank Neal was that the medals were buried under a flagpole, and Frank had thought they were on the old Wentworth place, not the former Farwell property.

All this was cause for interesting speculation. Charles Farwell died in 1930. By that time he had outlasted nearly all of the veterans of the 27th Maine. But in the later years of his life had he sought to dispose of his perplexing responsibility by burying quantities of medals here and there, as by interment under the Stars and Stripes in his yard?

The rest of the story was unfolded by two clippings from the *Portsmouth Herald* indicating that the focus of excitement had centered upon Kittery following the publication of Mrs. Weare's story. The clipping dated July 13 bore a long black headline: 500 MEDALS OF HONOR BURIED IN KITTERY? And the one dated July 15 indicated that the owner of the former Farwell property had taken heroic action: he had dug up the lawn. Subsequent inquires revealed that an earth-moving machine had gone to work on the area beneath which, it was hoped, the medals would be found encased in concrete like slices of banana in a blob of Jell-O. The excavation, which took place while I was away on the fishing trip, proceeded to a considerable depth, and every shovelful of earth was carefully examined, but no hunk of concrete was found. Thus, the theory was never proved or disproved. If there had been a concrete flagpole base, someone had dug it out and hauled it away, perhaps to repose in some ditch or embankment.

And so all of us were confounded and our diggings brought to naught — possibly by a continuation of the same inscrutable series of balks and bewilderments that had thwarted almost everyone who had tried to pry into the affair of the 27th Maine medals for nearly a century.

If a quantity of the medals is ever discovered,

whoever finds them will also find himself in a puzzling predicament as to what to do with them. Whom would they belong to? The finder? The person on whose property they are found? The State of Maine? The Federal Government? Or the families of the men whose names are inscribed on the back and whose legal right to them has never been officially disproved? (The 1916 law said that only recipients still in the Army would be obliged to turn them in.) Also, could they be sold? There are laws forbidding the sale of U.S. medals, but could these medals, now obsolete for more than 60 years, be seriously considered to be U.S. decorations?

The finder would probably be well advised to turn around and bury them again.

As for the medals that were in the big box in the attic — aside from the 50 which still remained there in the early 1950's — what became of them is also a matter for speculation. One of the grandsons of Charles Farwell remembered that when the old gentleman died in 1930 the medals were still there; but after that several people, including children, may have had access to the attic. Another recalls that small boys of the neighborhood used the medals while playing cops and robbers — the bronze star serving as an excellent sheriff's badge. He also recalls that the box of medals was still there when he left the property.

The imagined spectacle of an urchin stealing down from the attic with a Medal of Honor and speeding off on his velocipede is a dreadful one, but it accords well with the tradition of the small boy as a despoiler of historical artifacts. As has been previously noted, civilization would be greatly advanced if small boys were given regular canings, with or without observable cause; *they* will always know what it's for.

Other of these attic medals may have found their way to a stretch of street and highway extending for many miles north and south of Kittery — that portion of U.S. Route No. 1 which might be called Antique Alley. Driving along this route, the husband of the antique-minded woman runs a nervous and often expensive gantlet of old churns, sleigh bells, iron pots, milking stools and other objects of this kind as well as innumerable items of bric-a-brac. Some of the colorful old medals may have floated away by this route.

More fortunate are the medals that have found their way into the hands of studious collectors who preserve and cherish them and often make them available for public display.

Working together or singly, many of these devotees of the Medal of Honor have gathered collections of information about it which would be difficult to duplicate. For example, Jane Kenworthy of Bucks County, Pennsylvania, took on the staggering assignment of preparing a correct list of Medal of Honor recipients in all services since 1863. It might be supposed that the U.S. Government would have such a list, but it does not. During the early years of the award in particular, careful records were not kept. And the official bestowal of the decoration was not what it is today, with the President normally making the award at the White House and citations receiving the most careful scrutiny from unit commanders on up. During much of the 19th-century period the medals were often simply sent by mail with an accompanying letter. What happened in at least one instance — that concerning Sergeant Daniel Miller of the 8th Ohio Volunteer Infantry who won the medal at Gettysburg — was related by Brigadier General Theophilus F. Rodenbough:

Through some inexcusable blunder the gallant Sergeant Miller . . . never received the medal for which he was recommended by his regimental commander, but it was sent by the War Department to another man of similar surname in the same company. The poor fellow died some years since, and never ceased to feel that "Republics are ungrateful."

It seemed to Jane Kenworthy that someone in the Republic should be sufficiently grateful to its heroes to make a careful examination of all available records and revise the Medal of Honor list for correctness of names, places, ranks, organizations and other information which is now faulty in many instances.

This represents a monumental task. On a list of the more than 3,000 recognized recipients giving even the minimum essentials of information, there are at least 50,000 opportunities to get something wrong. Roster-making has the appearance of being simple on first thought, but it is an exceedingly tricky business, as the Civil War clerk's manual warned to no avail. When, in 1964, the Senate Subcommittee on Veterans' Affairs of the Committee on Labor and Public Welfare published its excellent book, *Medal of Honor Recipients — 1863–1963*, the chairman, Senator Ralph W. Yarborough, was smart enough to write in the foreword, "Undoubtedly there have been mistakes made in this record," going on to solicit corrective information from any reader who might have it. With greater fairness the Senator might have said, "Probably a few mistakes have been made in compiling this record, and undoubtedly dozens have been passed along which somebody else made forty or fifty years ago, or more." Yet the correct information exists somewhere, and it may be possible to dig it out. Jane Kenworthy's prodigious effort to do so has already brought the Medal of Honor list many steps nearer to perfection.

Another person who is probably unsurpassed in his knowledge of the Medal of Honor in many of its aspects is Charles P. Hey of Philadelphia, who has photographed the medals of several periods with a fidelity and care which technical skill alone could not produce.

With the help of Jane Kenworthy, Charles Hey, Frank Neal, E. C. Tobey and many other people in the United States and England, a considerable effort covering about four years was made to determine the whereabouts of the 27th Maine medals today. For many years collectors have been aware of the 27th Maine medals which have been in circulation, but their interest has been mostly in the medals — not in tracing their history to any great depth. In the words of Mr. Hey, "Many of them have been seen and little noted. We, however, who have long been interested and who have a kind of affection for the old Bronze Star have filed in our memories these frustrated wanderers as they have crossed our paths."

Some trace or location of nearly 100 of these medals was found. Numerically at least, this is what pollsters would certainly call an adequate "sample." Whether it is "protectable" or not is another question. All that can be said is that the research revealed nothing unexpected. Nearly all the "entitled" medals located are still in possession of families descended from their volunteer recipients — or those who were volunteers as far as unofficial records reveal. Most of the "unentitled" medals, classified on the same basis, are in widely scattered public and private collections, but there appear to be *not as many of these as one would look for if 400 or 500 had been set loose*. Of the largest lot of unissued medals, estimated as 82 for Company F, not a single one was found, which may or may not be significant.

And so some elements of the mystery still remain. And this is exactly as it should be, for as many people have discovered, the 27th Maine medals have always had about them what the Reverend Ephraim Peabody called an unfathomable cope.

The final notes to be entered in this record are those of the last trip to Maine having to do with the medals, on August 20, 1965, one of those days when brilliant sunlight and Maine's remarkable clarity of air combine to make the landscape resemble one of those old paintings in which every twig and blade of grass is separately seen — when the sun is reflected from poplars seemingly hung with thousands of tiny twinkling mirrors and the trunks of white birches shine across great distances. It was the sort of day on which a revelation might have been expected.

In Augusta, at the Adjutant General's Office, the author was conducted to a basement room to have a look at the official records of the 27th Maine. True, the War Department in 1892 — when it was trying to find a list of the 27th Maine men who had remained in the defenses of Washington — had been told by the Maine Adjutant General of that year that he knew nothing about the medals except what was shown in the printed report of the Maine Adjutant General for 1863. But there was always the chance that something might have turned up in a favorable shuffle of the papers since then.

Part of the basement room was in considerable disorder, with bales of unsorted and uncatalogued documents jammed into drawers and filing cabinets. Yet it was quickly apparent that some topnotch archival work had been done. Certain essential records of the Civil War are in an admirable state of organization. In one set of filing cabinets the name of every Maine man who served in the Rebellion is recorded on a card along with his basic service information; and the cards also bear numbers referring to the pages of large, atlas-like books in which muster rolls and other original records are bound. This system makes it possible for the Maine Adjutant General to answer quickly and accurately any inquiry about a Civil War soldier — and he still receives many such inquiries.

When drawers of giant steel cases containing these bound original records were opened, it was also evident that someone had performed a prodigious task with infinite patience and care. Original rolls obviously once dilapidated from much handling and disorderly storage had been repaired with strong transparent paper and properly backed, and much other work of restoration had been done. All documents had been put in meticulous order and bound interleaved with tough, durable paper. The bindings were solid and looked relatively new. When had all this been done?

A later examination of the reports of the Maine Adjutant General and Paymaster General for the years 1890 onward told the story. In 1893 one of Maine's great former Civil War officers, General Selden Connor, was appointed Adjutant General for the state. In his report at the end of that year he observed that the supply of printed reports for the Civil War years (which contain listings of Maine soldiers) was running out, and further:

Those reports are very full and accurate considering the imperfect data from which they were prepared and the pressure of work upon the office at the time they were made. The researches made through all the years that have passed since they were issued have disclosed many clerical mistakes and errors in fact, in many cases doing great injustice to worthy soldiers. Maine owes it to her soldiers to cause a trustworthy and easily accessible record of their services to be published.

In early 1895 the Maine legislature authorized the work which Connor recommended. But he changed his mind about having the records published again; something less susceptible to error was suggested. An item in the Paymaster General's report for that year bearing upon the project shows that Connor spent $53 for a trip to Washington "to procure information at the Record and Pension Office." This undoubtedly means that he consulted Colonel F. C. Ainsworth, who was head of the Record and Pension

Office at that time and who was engaged in the preparation of a system for the War Department which made use of index-record cards referring to rolls preserved in their original form. It was this reliable system which Selden Connor adopted for Maine. The work began in 1895 or 1896. It took nearly 20 years and many thousands of dollars to complete. It is still being used today to answer inquiries about Maine soldiers in the Civil War, and it is just as fast and efficient as it ever was.

However, this organization of the records came far too late to be of service in answering the inquiry about the 27th Maine volunteers which the War Department addressed to the Maine Adjutant General in 1892. What, if anything, had turned up later on as the work proceeded?

The answers came to light on the visit to the basement room in August, 1965, previously described. The drawer containing the original records for the 27th Maine was tugged open. The large books were removed.

The process of going through the pages began. Pages 5810–5820, enlistment rolls . . . pages 5821–5835, descriptive rolls . . . pages 5836–5857, muster-in rolls . . . pages 5858–5869, muster-out rolls.

And in the last book, pages 5870–5876, monthly returns. But what is this on the last two pages of the last book? A list entitled, "Roll of Officers & Men in the 27th Maine Regiment who volunteered in June 1863 to remain after their term of service had expired and assist in the defense of Washington."

The list is not signed or dated, but it is very old, and in all likelihood it is the list which Mark Wentworth, in 1865, promised he would send to the Governor of Maine after he had completed distribution of the medals. It is certainly not the list which appeared in Stone's history in 1895 (which had 312 names) for it has only 299 names, including those of the "volunteer recruits," George Hobbs and Justin Spinney. Further, it corresponds with minor exceptions to the list which Calvin Hayes sent to Frank Whitman and Frank Whitman sent to the War Department in 1898 — the list which Hayes said he had obtained from Wentworth and which he also said was the one whereby the medals had been distributed. The exceptions: On the Hayes list appear the names of two Kittery men which do not appear on the presumed Wentworth list, while on the Hayes list Hobbs and Spinney do not appear; thus both lists number 299. Otherwise, both lists correspond in the sequence of names and the names themselves.

It is interesting to speculate what might have been the effect of this list now in the office of the Maine Adjutant General if it had been found and sent to the War Department in 1892, when the Department was trying to determine who had stayed in Washington and who had not. In all probability Ainsworth would not have recognized a list made after the disbandment of the

315

regiment, even if it had been made in 1865. But in 1892 Ainsworth still had far to go in reaching the peak of his influence. Granting this, what if the then Maine Adjutant General — among the official records of whose office the list now certainly is — had certified it as official?

And what if the Secretary of War *had* accepted it — thereby being able to reduce the Medal of Honor list by 565 names?

Would the Medal of Honor review board of 1916–17 then have been considered necessary?

Or if it had, following the Great Rescission of 1917, what would have happened if one of the 27th Maine veterans, with his name solidly and officially recorded, had taken his case to the courts?

All that can be said is that it didn't happen. And one can only conclude that here, too, Minerva must have been present to cast her protective spell, for better or worse, over the Medal of Honor. In her capacity as patroness of useful arts she would have been generally welcome in Maine, although the same cannot be said for some of the gods and goddesses she used to hang out with.

And her auspices, speaking of her in this case as Athena, may very well have extended to attics as well as Attica.

Acknowledgments

So many people have contributed to this work that another book would be needed to record all their names, occupations and the varied details of their generosity. The first words of thanks go to the author's wife, Jean A. Pullen, for sustenance and support of many kinds in the long and arduous process of putting a book together — and for contributing the title.

Many individuals who have been of invaluable assistance are mentioned in the main text or the Notes; without repeating their names here, the author simply reaffirms his gratitude. The nature of their help seems clear in all cases except those of Jane Kenworthy and Charles P. Hey, who contributed information on U.S. medals and read the manuscript. Mr. Hey also provided photographs and illustrative ideas.

Howard K. Bauernfeind, chairman of the board, and George Stevens, vice-president of J. B. Lippincott Company, gave needed encouragement at a time when the project was in its most doubtful and difficult stage. The book has also been fortunate in being under the editorial surveillance of Mr. Stevens — to the great benefit of its readers — also in having Betty Jane Corson as its copy editor and Dan Walden as its designer.

A fellow writer and a son by adoption of Maine, Lt. Col. John Paul Heffernan, suggested many sources of information and illustrative material. His interest has been a cheerful and helpful influence.

Dr. Mabel E. Deutrich, author of *The Struggle for Supremacy: The Career of General Fred C. Ainsworth*, was good enough to read the manuscript. This review was particularly appreciated because of Dr. Deutrich's knowledge of military record-keeping gained in her research on the Ainsworth book and in her work at the National Archives. However, it should be understood that the author is completely responsible for the correctness of all facts and figures as well as their interpretation. Further acknowledgment to Dr. Deutrich is found in the Notes pertaining to Chapter 6.

The author also appreciates a reading of the manuscript by Dr. Ernest C. Marriner, chairman of the Maine Archives Committee, educator, historian, and devoted chronicler of the folk and folkways of Maine.

Many institutions and government agencies, through helpful officers and staff members, provided answers to questions, access to resources, books, pictures, photostats, microfilm and other help. The author's sincere thanks go to all of these organizations and to the indicated individuals associated with them: The Athenaeum of Philadelphia, Edwin T. P. Boone, Jr., Jacquelyn Gwyn and Theresa Walters; Bangor Public Library, Robert C. Woodward; Bowdoin College Alumni Office, Robert M. Cross; The Civil War Centennial Commission, Edmund C. Gass; *Coin World*, Margo Russell; Congressional Medal of Honor Society, United States of America, Thomas J. Kelly; Freedoms Foundation at Valley Forge, Hamilton G. Reeve; The Free Library of Philadelphia, staff members of the Public Documents and Art Departments; Haverford College Library, Ruth H. Reese, and L. A. Post, Professor of Greek, Haverford College; The Historical Society of Pennsylvania, library staff; Legion of Valor of the United States of America, Inc., Lt. Col. Robert M. Gaynor; The Library of Congress, Reference Department; Maine Historical Society, Elizabeth Ring; Moore College of Art, Sylvia Heyl; National Archives and Records Service — Specialist in Iconography Josephine Cobb, Supervisory Archivist Elmer O. Parker and members of his staff of the Army and Navy Branch, and Chief of the Diplomatic, Legal and Fiscal Branch W. Neil Franklin and members of his staff; The Pennsylvania Academy of the Fine Arts, Louise Wallman; the Portsmouth (N.H.) Public Library, Dorothy M. Vaughan; Spink & Son, Ltd., of London, D. G. Liddell; State of Maine, The Adjutant General Maj. Gen. E. W. Heywood, Deputy Adjutant General Brig. Gen. L. B. Webster and Lucille DeRocher of their office staff; State of Maine, Department of State, Linwood F. Ross; Treasury Department, U.S. Mint Service,

Philadelphia, Superintendent Michael H. Sura; U.S. Army War College, Alan J. Blanchard; U.S. Department of the Air Force, Flint O. DuPre; U.S. Department of the Army, The Adjutant General Maj. Gen. J. C. Lambert; U.S. Department of Defense, Col. C. V. Glines; The Institute of Heraldry, U.S. Army, Major Joseph M. Massaro; U.S. Military Academy Library, Egon Weiss — Archives & History Section, Joseph M. O'Donnell; Veterans Administration, Office of General Counsel, Assistant General Counsel T. F. Daley; and the War Library and Museum of the Military Order of the Loyal Legion of the United States, Stephanie Benko.

So many individuals replied to inquiries about 27th Maine men and their medals that it would be impractical to list all of their names here. To any of these kind respondents who may read this, the author repeats the thanks previously expressed in letters. In several cases the inquiries developed into extended correspondence, interviews, the providing of books, letters, diaries and pictures and permission to directly quote or to use certain materials. Some of these have been acknowledged in the text, but acknowledgments are also due the following people: Marion Bucholtz, Marjorie J. Burbank, Gladys Hasty Carroll, Calvin H. Cobb, Jr., Charles L. Cobb, Edwin O. Cogan, Eleanor N. Clapp and her mother the late Geneva W. Neal, Marion Emery Cole, R. T. Cole, Joseph P. Copley, Winnifred M. Dyer, Mr. and Mrs. Paul Fellows, Dr. Hilda Fife,

Norm Flayderman, Joseph W. P. Frost, Mary L. Goodwin, Mary Clement Hall, Bevery Hewins, Joseph W. Hobbs, Mrs. Leo J. Irish, Adelbert H. Merrill, Ruth Pullen, Haskell Richardson, Charles W. Seaward, Russell Seaward, Addie B. Small, George H. Smith, Milton A. Smith, Reginald Tarr, Jean E. Weare and Frances K. Waterman. The hospitality and assistance of Major and Mrs. Linwood S. Jackson during investigations in Kittery are also greatly appreciated.

One of the most important stages in the preparation of any piece of published writing has to do with the appearance and correctness of the typed manuscript. *A Shower of Stars* was fortunate in passing through the typewriter of Judith M. Haag. The author is also grateful to another fine craftswoman, Alice M. Fairweather, for her reading of the manuscript prior to final typing.

Line drawings are from various sources chosen for their authentic flavor. The portrayals of Minerva are by John Flaxman and were taken from rare volumes of his drawings printed in Paris *circa* 1823 and kindly made available from The Academy of the New Church Library, Bryn Athyn, Pennsylvania, by Mary Alice Carswell, Reference Librarian. Drawings pertaining to the Civil War are by Edwin Forbes and A. R. Waud, who followed the armies as artist-reporters. The "Rough Rider" cartoon appeared in a *Washington Times* of the Teddy Roosevelt era. Drawings of the original Medals of Honor, by Jules

Jacquemart, are from J. F. Loubat's *The Medallic History of The United States of America*. The good offices of Isa Barnett, Charles F. Fifer and Fred Carbone are also gratefully acknowledged.

Bibliography

Acts of Congress affecting the Medal of Honor (includes Joint Resolutions):

December 21, 1861: Authorized the Navy medal for "petty officers, seamen, landsmen and marines."

July 12, 1862 (JR): Authorized the Army medal for enlisted men.

March 3, 1863: Amended JR of July 12, 1862, to include officers and provide for past and future deeds of distinguished service in action.

May 2, 1896 (JR): Authorized new ribbon and a rosette to wear in lieu of the decoration.

March 3, 1901: Authorized awards to Navy and Marine Corps enlisted men for distinguished service in battle or heroism in line of profession.

April 23, 1904: Authorized new design for the Army medal.

February 27, 1907 (JR): Cancelled requirement that old medal must be turned in.

March 3, 1915: Authorized the medal for Navy, Marine Corps and Coast Guard officers for distinguished service in battle or heroism in line of profession.

April 27, 1916: Established the Army and Navy Medal of Honor Roll.

June 3, 1916: Directed investigation and review of the Medal of Honor list.

July 9, 1918: Clarified conditions of award for the Army medal and established other decorations.

February 4, 1919: Authorized a new Medal of Honor for persons in the naval service distinguishing themselves in combat and established other decorations.

August 7, 1942: Abolished the cross-type medal (naval service combat award) and restored the 1862 design, to be awarded to any person in the naval service for heroism in combat and line of profession.

July 25, 1963: Enlarged the authority to award Medals of Honor by specifying more conditions of conflict, and made the award requirements uniform for all the U.S. armed forces.

Biographical Dictionary of the American Congress, 1774–1961. Washington: U.S. Government Printing Office, 1961.

Biographical Review ... Leading Citizens of York County, Maine. Boston, 1896.

BROWNE, CHARLES FARRAR. *The Complete Works of Artemus Ward.* With a biographical sketch by Melville D. Landon. New York, 1898.

BRYANT, SETH E., Captain, 27th Maine and 32nd Maine. WAR JOURNAL. This journal, covering practically every day of the period September 9, 1862–July 17, 1863, was published in installments in a newspaper. The clippings were placed in a scrapbook by William W. Keays, veteran of the 27th, but Mr. Keays did not record the name of the paper or the date. The scrapbook is now in the possession of Mr. Keays' grandson, Alvin W. Curtiss of Melrose, Mass. It also includes REPORTS of 27th Maine reunions in the form of clippings from unidentified newspapers, with dates usually ascertainable from the text of the reports.

BURBANK, HORACE H., Private 27th Maine and Captain 32nd Maine. "My Prison Life," in *War Papers Read Before the Commandery of the State of Maine, Military Order of the Loyal Legion of the United States*, Vol. II. Portland, Maine, 1902.

CATTON, BRUCE. *A Stillness at Appomattox.* New York, 1954.

CHAMBERLAIN, JOSHUA L., Brevet Major General, U.S.V. *The Passing of the Armies.* New York, 1915.

COBB, CALVIN H., Vice Admiral, U.S.N. LETTERS:

To Gould Lincoln, April 18 and May 19, 1960. Private possession, Calvin H. Cobb, Jr., Washington, D.C.

To Charles L. Cobb, October 18, 1960. Private possession, Charles L. Cobb, Stafford Springs, Connecticut.

Congressional Record, July 6, 1914, and July 26, 1916.

DANNETT, SYLVIA G. L., and JONES, KATHERINE, M. *Our Women of the Sixties*. U.S. Civil War Centennial Commission. Washington, D.C., 1963.

DEUTRICH, MABEL E. *The Struggle for Supremacy: The Career of General Fred C. Ainsworth*. Washington, D.C., 1962.

Dictionary of American Biography. 22 vols., prepared under the auspices of the American Council of Learned Societies, New York, 1928–1958. Vols. I–III edited by Allen Johnson; IV–VII, by Allen Johnson and Dumas Malone; VIII–XX, by Dumas Malone; XXI, by Harris E. Starr; XXII, by Robert Livingston Schuyler and Edward T. James.

DIXON, JOSEPH H., Private, 27th Maine:
"Eliot in the Rebellion," *Old Eliot* (October–December, 1906), Vol. VII, No. 4. Historical Press: William Fogg House, Eliot, Maine.

LETTER to Martin Parry Tobey, January 29, 1863. Private possession, Walter B. Tobey, Eliot, Maine.

DOE, JOSEPH D., Sergeant, 27th Maine. DIARY, 1862–63. Private possession, Eleanor N. Clapp, Kennebunkport, Maine.

FOSTER, CHARLES W. "Origin and History of the Two Mottoes Used on Modern United States Coins," *The Numismatist* (December, 1930), p. 799.

GAYLEY, CHARLES MILLS. *The Classic Myths in English Literature and in Art*. Based originally on Bulfinch's *Age of Fable* (1855).

New York, 1939.

General Orders Affecting the Volunteer Force (1861–62–63). Washington: War Department, Adjutant General's Office, 1862-63-64.

GERRISH, REV. THEODORE, and HUTCHINSON, REV. JOHN S. *The Blue and the Gray*. Portland, Maine, 1883.

HAYES, CALVIN L., Sergeant Major 27th Maine and Adjutant, 32th Maine. STATEMENT concerning the 27th Maine and list of those who volunteered to extend their term of service. This was obtained by Frank M. Whitman who made a copy and sent it to Colonel F. C. Ainsworth, Chief of the Record and Pension Office, February 12, 1898. It is attached to Whitman's letter to Ainsworth of that date in the National Archives, Record Group 94, R & P 380505.

History of York County, Maine, With Illustrations and Biographical Sketches — Its Prominent Men and Pioneers. Philadelphia, 1880.

HOUSTON, HENRY C., Private, 32nd Maine. *The Thirty-Second Maine Regiment of Infantry Volunteers*. Portland, Maine, 1903.

Infantry Journal (July, 1944).

Instructions for Officers of the Adjutant General's Department and Others of Kindred Duties. Washington: Government Printing Office, 1864.

JOHNSON, REV. GEORGE H. *A Sermon Memorial to Christian Schussele. Delivered October 19, 1879*. Philadelphia, 1879. Possession of The Pennsylvania Academy of the Fine Arts.

KAUTZ, AUGUST U., Brigadier General, U.S.V. *The Company Clerk*. 12th ed.; Philadelphia, 1865.

LEGION OF VALOR OF THE UNITED STATES OF AMERICA, INC. *General Orders*, Vol. LXXV, No. 8. Arlington, Virginia, April 23, 1965.

LEONARD, E. J. and GOODMAN, J. C. *Buffalo Bill: King of the Old West*. New York, 1955.

LIBBY, GEORGE H., Private, 27th Maine. DIARY, 1863. Private possession, R. J. Libby, Fredonia, New York.

LOUBAT, J. F. *The Medallic History of The United States of America, 1776–1876*. With 170 etchings by Jules Jacquemart. New York, 1878. Vol. I, text; Vol. II, plates.

LYKES, RICHARD WAYNE. *Petersburg Battlefields*. National Park Service Historical Handbook. Washington, 1955.

MAINE ADJUTANT GENERAL'S ANNUAL REPORTS, 1861–66. Augusta, Maine. (Cited as MeAGR in the Notes.)

Maine Bugle, The (October, 1895).

MAINE CIVIL WAR CORRESPONDENCE. Incoming letters to the Governor and the Adjutant General affixed to pages bound in numbered volumes. In the office of the Adjutant General, State of Maine, Augusta, Maine:

Governor's Correspondence, 76 vols.

Adjutant General's Correspondence, 75 vols.

These original letters provide an interesting

summary of the political, military and human problems with which a Civil War governor had to deal — and of his importance in this conflict.

Medal of Honor Recipients — 1863–1963. Prepared for the Subcommittee on Veterans' Affairs of the Committee on Labor and Public Welfare, United States Senate. Washington: U.S. Government Printing Office, 1964. For the first time in a Government publication, information on all Medal of Honor recipients regardless of their arm of service. It includes names, citations, historical background, calendar of documents, bibliography, index and illustrations. 1058 pages. (Cited as MOHR in the Notes.)

Medal of Honor of the United States Army, The. Washington: U.S. Government Printing Office, 1948.

MOSBY, JOHN S., Colonel, C.S.A. *War Reminiscences and Stuart's Cavalry Campaigns.* Boston, 1887.

MULHOLLAND, ST. CLAIR A., Brevet Major General, U.S.V. *Military Order Congress Medal of Honor Legion of the United States.* Philadelphia, 1905.

NATIONAL ARCHIVES, Washington, D.C.:

Record Group 94, *Records of the Adjutant General's Office.*

Record Group 104, *Records of the Bureau of the Mint.*

Record Group 107, *Records of the Office of*

the Secretary of War

(The above cited as NA, RG 94, 104, 107, in the Notes.)

PAUL, ELBRIDGE R., Private, 27th Maine. LETTERS to his family, 1862–63. Private possession, Gladys Paul, Eliot, Maine.

PETERSON, MENDEL L. "The Navy Medal of Honor," *The Numismatist* (June, 1950).

POORE, BENJAMIN PERLEY. *Perley's Reminiscences of Sixty Years in the National Metropolis.* Philadelphia, 1886.

Portland Express (April 26, 1893): "A Sketch of the Military Career of Gen. Mark F. Wentworth."

Portland Press Herald (July 9 and 12, 1963), "Clearing House" columns.

Portsmouth (N.H.) *Daily Chronicle* (July 10–13, 1897).

Portsmouth (N.H.) *Journal of Literature and Politics* (July 30, 1864).

PULLEN, JOHN J. *The Twentieth Maine, A Volunteer Regiment in the Civil War.* Philadelphia, 1957.

RECORDS of the 27th Regiment Infantry, Maine Volunteers. Original records including enlistment rolls, descriptive rolls, muster-in rolls, muster-out rolls and monthly returns. In the Office of the Adjutant General, State of Maine, Augusta, Maine.

Report of a Board of Officers Appointed . . . to Examine and Report Upon Applications and Recommendations for Medals of Honor and Certificates of Merit. Washington: Government Printing Office, 1904. Further identified as a board appointed by Special Orders, No. 131, June 4, 1902, Headquarters of the Army, Adjutant General's Office.

Report of the Chief of the Record and Pension Office, War Department, to the Secretary of War, 1901. Washington: Government Printing Office, 1901. This is a compendious history of the Medal of Honor prepared under the direction of the bureau chief, Brigadier General F. C. Ainsworth. The same history also appeared in *Annual Reports* of the War Department for the fiscal year ending June 30, 1901 (Vol. I, Part 2: Reports of the Chiefs of Bureaus, pp. 1087–98), and it was reprinted in U.S. Senate Calendar No. 786, 58th Congress, 2nd session, Report No. 808, February 12, 1904.

Report of Medal of Honor Legion 16th Annual Convention and Banquet at Winsted, Connecticut, September 24 and 25, 1906.

Reports of the National Commission of Fine Arts. Washington: Government Printing Office, 1920 and 1921.

RODENBOUGH, THEOPHILUS F., Brevet Brigadier General, U.S.A., editor and compiler. *Uncle Sam's Medal of Honor.* New York, 1886.

SMITH, MARION JAQUES. *A History of Maine from Wilderness to Statehood.* Freeport, Maine, 1960.

STEELE, MATTHEW FORNEY, Major, 2nd

U.S. Cavalry, *American Campaigns*. Harrisburg, 1949. 2 vols.

STONE, JAMES M., Lieutenant Colonel, 27th Maine:

SPEECH read at the reunion of the 27th Maine in Kittery, August 27, 1889. Manuscript in possession of R. T. Cole, Kennebunk, Maine.

The History of the Twenty-Seventh Regiment Maine Volunteer Infantry. Portland, Maine, 1895.

SUTHERLAND, C. H. V. *Art in Coinage.* London, 1955.

SWINTON, WILLIAM. *Campaigns of the Army of the Potomac.* New York, 1866.

TOWNSEND, E. D., Brevet Major General, U.S.A. *Anecdotes of the Civil War in the United States.* New York, 1884.

TUCKER, CHARLES H., Corporal, 27th Maine. LETTERS to Martin Parry Tobey, 1861–63. Private possession, Walter B. Tobey, Eliot, Maine.

Under the Maltese Cross, Campaigns of the 155th Pennsylvania Regiment. Edited by Charles F. McKenna. Pittsburgh, 1910.

UPTON, EMORY, Brevet Major General, U.S.A. *The Military Policy of the United States.* Washington, 1904.

U.S. ARMY, *Official Army Register*, March, 1891.

U.S. ARMY REGULATIONS. Headquarters, Department of the Army, Washington.

AR 672–5–1, with changes through No. 3,

February 27, 1963.

AR 672–5–2, October 25, 1961.

U.S. SENATE:

Calendar No. 786, 58th Congress, 2nd session, Report No. 808. *Medals of Honor Etc.*, February 12, 1904.

Calendar No. 557, 63rd Congress, 2nd session, Report No. 639, *Army and Navy Medal of Honor Roll*, July 2, 1914.

Document No. 447, 64th Congress, 1st session: *Analysis of the Army Reorganization Bill*, May 26, 1916.

Document No. 58, 66th Congress, 1st session: *General Staff Corps and Medals of Honor*, July 23, 1919. This printed document includes reports, memoranda, etc., relating to the proceedings of the Medal of Honor Board in 1916–17.

U.S. WAR DEPARTMENT CIRCULARS:

1886. *Medals of Honor Awarded for Distinguished Service During the War of the Rebellion.* Compiled under the direction of Brigadier General Richard C. Drum, Adjutant General, U.S. Army, by Frederick H. Stafford of the Adjutant General's Office.

1897. *Medals of Honor Issued by the War Department* up to and including October 31, 1897. Washington: Government Printing Office.

1904. *Medals of Honor Issued by the War Department* up to and including September 1, 1904. Washington: Government Printing Office.

1904. Circular No. 36, August 22. Published the regulations for awards of the new Medal of Honor of the 1904 design.

WAINWRIGHT, NICHOLAS B. *Philadelphia in the Romantic Age of Lithography.* Philadelphia, 1958.

War of the Rebellion: A compilation of the official records of the Union and Confederate armies. Washington, 1880–1901. 70 vols. in 128 parts. (Cited as OR in the Notes.)

WARREN, JOSEPH F., Captain, 27th Maine. DIARY, 1863. Private possession, Margaret Soule, West Buxton, Maine.

WELLES, GIDEON. *Diary of Gideon Welles.* With an introduction by John T. Morse, Jr., Boston, 1911. 3 vols.

Notes

These abbreviations are used:

MeAGR: Maine Adjutant General, Annual Report. This is followed by the year of the report, in parentheses.

MOHR: *Medal of Honor Recipients — 1863–1963*. Prepared for the Subcommittee on Veterans' Affairs of the Committee on Labor and Public Welfare, U.S. Senate, 1964.

NA, RG 94: National Archives, Record Group No. 94, *Records of the Adjutant General's Office*. This is followed by the document file number.

NA, RG 104: National Archives, Record Group No. 104, *Records of the Bureau of the Mint*. Citations refer entirely to *Correspondence Pertaining to the Medal of Honor, 1861–62*.

NA, RG 107: National Archives, Record Group 107, *Records of the Office of the Secretary of War*. Particular series of documents are further identified in the citations.

OR: *War of the Rebellion*, 70 vols. in 128 parts.

If a writer has only one work listed in the Bibliography, the work is referred to in these notes by the name of the writer, the full title being omitted. Only numbers and years of U.S. Senate calendars and documents are given; full identification will be found in the Bibliography. Certain sources to which only passing reference is made are cited in full in the Notes and are not in the Bibliography.

Chapter 1: A Maine Mystery

Posthumous awards of the Medal of Honor: The author's examination and count of citations in MOHR show:

	Posthumous	Alive
World War II	212	219
Korean Conflict	94	37
	306	256

MOHR, pp. 101–306, indicates that fewer than 300 of the recipients were living at the time this publication was prepared.

Members of the 20th Maine who received Medals of Honor: Col. Joshua L. Chamberlain and Sergeant Andrew J. Tozier for gallantry at Little Round Top, July 2, 1863; 1st Lt. Albert E. Fernald for capturing a flag at Five Forks, April 1, 1865; and Capt. Walter G. Morrill for gallantry at Rappahannock Station, Nov. 7, 1863. The medal was issued for Chamberlain, Aug. 11, 1893; for Tozier, Aug. 13, 1898; for Fernald, May 10, 1865; and for Morrill, April 5, 1898.

Number of men in the armed forces since the start of the Civil War: *Statistical Abstract of the*

United States (1964), p. 263.

Number of awards on official Medal of Honor list for period 1863–1963: MOHR, p. 361.

Official accounts of the 27th Maine: A report signed by Mark F. Wentworth, April 5, 1864, in MeAGR (1863), p. 102; MeAGR (1866), p. 143.

Adjutant General John L. Hodsdon's "due meed of praise" statement: MeAGR (1862), p. 29.

Adjutant General's roster for the 27th Maine: MeAGR (1863), Appendix D, pp. 748-772.

Antiquity of Maine coast: *History of York County* . . . , pp. 276–277; Smith, pp. 32–40, 122–136. The five wars affecting Maine prior to the Revolution were King Philip's War and King William's War in the late 1600's and Queen Anne's War, King George's War and the French and Indian War in the 1700's.

Mark F. Wentworth: The author is indebted to Mrs. Jessie Hobbs Dunshee of Toms River, New Jersey, for her personal recollections of Gen. Wentworth and the Wentworth home in Kittery; other information is from *Biographical Review . . . Leading Citizens of York County, Maine*, pp. 597–599, and a story published in the *Portsmouth Daily Chronicle*, July 13, 1897, the day following Wentworth's death.

Disinterment of the early settler by the Indians: The story told by Mr. Tobey was that of Maj. Charles Frost, killed by Indians on July 4, 1697. See *Old Kittery and Her Families* (Everett S. Stackpole, Press of the Lewiston Journal

Company, Lewiston, Me., 1903), p. 168: "The night after Frost's burial the Indians opened his grave, took out the body, carried it to the top of Frost's Hill and suspended it upon a stake."

"Minerva Repulsing Discord": This title appears in Loubat, I, 368.

Chapter 2: The 27th Maine

Mark F. Wentworth, military background: *Portland Express*, April 26, 1893; MeAGR (1863), p. 748.

Kittery Artillery and Fort McClary: MeAGR (1861), Appendix A, p. 4; MeAGR (1862), pp. 18–19; Maine Civil War Correspondence (Governor's): I, 102; (Adjutant General's): I, 159, and II, 35.

Wentworth's efforts to obtain an infantry command: Maine Civil War Correspondence (Governor's): XXV, 6; XXVI, 75; (Adjutant General's): VII, 128; XVII, 132; XVIII, 45; XXVI, 174.

Charles H. Tucker's letters: Charlie was apparently a fun-loving youth who enjoyed life and even derived great satisfaction from the war. He wrote from camp on Sept. 21, 1862:

"Our food is vast different from that you get but we have good teeth, you know, and find no fault. We have beef hard bread tea and coffee. We have a dipper for our coffee a tin pan for our grub. We sit on the floor to eat. . . . I have only to say we all like first rate, and feel proud of being a soldier boy. Yes, we feel proud of leaving our friends and all to suffer the hardships of a campaign and to stand up and be shot perhaps for you and all others we leave behind. I hope the soldiers will not be forgotten by those left behind. . . . If we can help put down the rebellion and live under the stars and stripes and enjoy our liberty we are willing to do anything."

Condition of the militia in 1861: MeAGR (1861), pp. 5, 47, 50–52.

Volunteer regiments in Maine, 1862: MeAGR (1862), pp. 5–10.

Bounties for volunteer regiments and threat of special draft: Pullen, pp. 7–11; Upton, pp. 439–440.

Militia regiments in Maine, 1862: MeAGR (1862), p. 10 and Appendix D, pp. 678–868.

Bounties for militia: MeAGR (1862), p. 26 and Appendix A, p. 8; Bryant's journal, entry for Sept. 9, 1862; Dixon, "Eliot in the Rebellion," p. 159.

Reverend Henry F. Snow: Letter from Mrs. Addie B. Small of Cornish to E. C. Tobey, Sept. 2, 1963; MeAGR (1863), Appendix D., p. 765.

Election of militia officers: Under the law the governor of the state appointed the commissioned officers of a volunteer regiment; see act of Congress approved July 22, 1861, with attention to Sec. 4 and Sec. 10, the latter repealed by Sec. 3 of an act of Congress approved Aug. 6, 1861. See also Upton, pp. 250–251, 259–260. Under state laws the commissioned officers of a militia regiment were elected by members of the regiment; see *Revised Statutes of the State of Maine* (1857), Title One, Chap. 10, Sec. 36. See also Upton, p. 435. Accounts of militia elections for the 27th Maine are found in Bryant's journal, entries of Sept. 19 and 22, 1862, and Jan. 29, 1863. Officers of both volunteer and militia regiments received their commissions from the governor (Upton, p. 440).

Every man in the 27th a "volunteer": MeAGR (1862), pp. 11–12.

Reactions of the Maine Adjutant General to bounties, etc.: MeAGR (1862), p. 23 and Appendix D, pp. 678–868; MeAGR (1863), Appendix D, pp. 602–798.

Reactions of "volunteers" and men who had avoided draft: Bryant's journal, entry for Sept. 9, 1862.

Poem: This was "A Maine Girl's Greeting — Respectfully Inscribed to the Maine 27th," by Mrs. Moses Farmer of Salem, Mass. It was published in Augustin Caldwell, *Memories of Hannah Tobey Farmer, Wife of Moses Gerrish Farmer* (Boston, 1892), pp. 358–359.

References to Philadelphia hospitality: Bryant's journal, entry of Oct. 21, 1862; Rev. Theodore Gerrish, *Army Life. A Private's Reminiscences of the War* (Portland, Maine, 1882), p. 304.

Arming of 27th Maine: Bryant's journal, entries of Oct. 24, 1862, and Jan. 10, 1863.

Arrival on Lee's estate: Bryant's journal, entries of Oct. 26 and 27, 1862.

Fears for the safety of Washington: Steele, pp. 239–259, 276–277, 386. See also George Gordon Meade, *With Meade at Gettysburg* (Philadelphia, 1930), p. 23.

Troops in defenses of Washington: OR, Series 1, Vol. XXV, Part 2, pp. 30–32.

Mosby's comments on partisan warfare: Mosby, pp. 43–47.

From Mosby's "Children of the Mist" comments through the end of this chapter the story of the 27th Maine is constructed almost entirely from the journal of Capt. Seth E. Bryant; the diaries of Capt. Joseph F. Warren and Sgt. Joseph D. Doe; letters of Charles H. Tucker, Elbridge R. Paul and Joseph H. Dixon and front Lt. Col. James M. Stone's reunion speech — all cited in the Bibliography. Information on troop movements, geographical locations, distances, deaths, incidents of army life, the weather, etc., is found in one or another of these personal records. When he was on picket duty, Capt. Warren even recorded the nightly countersign. Sgt. Doe and Capt. Bryant made almost daily records of the weather. The few exceptions to these accounts written by members of 27th Maine are Mosby p. 82, describing his sending of a lock of hair to Lincoln; p. 127, his raid on Fairfax Court

House; pp. 69–77, the attack at Herndon Station; and pp. 87–97, the fight on the Little River Turnpike.

Chapter 3: Athena Americana

The soldier-behind-the-tree incident: Gerrish and Hutchinson, p. 299.

"Home or die": Joseph A. Dixon reported having heard a deserter say this (Dixon to Martin Parry Tobey, Jan. 29, 1863).

Impressions of Gideon Welles: Welles, Introduction, pp. xvii–xxi, and 67.

Welles' impressions of certain officers: Welles, pp. 44, 62.

The Purple Heart: MOHR, p. 15.

Medals a European tradition, Scott's reluctance to adopt, Scott's retirement: Townsend, pp. 164, 166, 263–267.

Authorization of the Navy Medal of Honor: Act of Congress approved Dec. 21, 1861, entitled "An Act to further promote the efficiency of the Navy."

Location and description of the Philadelphia Mint: Wainwright, p. 222.

James Pollock: *Dictionary of American Biography*, XV, 49–50.

"In God We Trust": Foster, p. 799.

Pollock's fast reply: Welles to Pollock asking for a design, Dec. 30, 1861; Pollock to Welles, Jan. 4, 1862, promising designs by next week; Welles to Pollock, Jan. 7, 1862, asking for a design in the shape of a cross with three ribbons, red, white and blue; Pollock to Welles, Jan. 11, 1862, acknowledging the request; and Pollock to Welles, Jan. 14, 1862, enclosing three designs. All of the foregoing are in NA, RG 104. Unsuccessful designs: The three designs sent to the Secretary of the Navy on Jan. 14, 1862, were accompanied by a memorandum in which the first of these designs was described as follows:

"*Obverse:* An ideal figure of America, partly copied from the statue in the Capitol — standing in a determined attitude. In her right hand she grasps the flag of the Union, and with her left, points to a scroll, resting on a column bearing the word 'Constitution,' beneath which are martial emblems. To the right of the figure, is an Eagle with expanded wings, holding in the dexter talon, a bundle of arrows, emblematic of war. Legend: Preserve, Protect and Defend the Constitution (borrowed from the inaugural oath)."

The reverse of this first medal was equally ordinary. The second medal which Pollock described at least had the merit of being simple: "A wreath of laurel surrounding an Eagle and Military and Naval Emblems" with a blank reverse. The third design was in the form of a cross; this was so cluttered, confused and vague in some of its symbolism that the memorandum had a great deal of explaining to do. For example:

"*Reverse:* In the center is the National Shield, emblematic of the Union, in front of which the *seahorse,* a characteristic myth of ancient art, symbolizes "liberty on the sea" (one of the most ancient emblems of Liberty being the horse without bridle). The accessories, consisting of the Anchor, boat-rudder, buoys, oar, boat-hook, trident and streamer, which last bears a descriptive title of the Medal & all intended to express the character of the service, which the medal is designed to distinguish and reward."

Secretary of the Navy Welles rejected all three designs. Three more which Pollock sent him on April 17 (NA, RG 104) fared no better. Pollock on April 17 (NA, RG, 104) also submitted a design to Secretary of War Stanton which was described as follows:

"*Obverse:* A seated figure representing the Goddess of American Liberty grasps in her left hand a standard bearing the flag of the Union, and with her right, is about to present to a Soldier, who is approaching her for that purpose, with a laurel wreath, emblematic of Victory. On the side of the pedestal, on which the Goddess is seated, are a cornucopia and a shield. On the latter is an Eagle with raised

344

wings, and bearing in his talons, a fasces. Beneath the soldier's feet, is a flag, the staff of which is broken. Note: I suggest the following as a suitable legend for the obverse of the medal: 'For Bravery in Defense of the Union. By a Grateful Country.' "

Stanton's reaction to this unfortunate design was apparently one of monumental indifference.

Goddess of Liberty on U.S. coins: Sutherland, pp. 189–190, Figs. 136 and 143.

John Jay quotation: *The Federalist Papers*, No. 2. "Thou, too, sail on . . .": From *The Building of the Ship* by Henry Wadsworth Longfellow, written in 1849.

Pollock's concept for the design: Pollock to Welles, Jan. 14, 1862, NA, RG 104.

Early U.S. medals: Loubat, I, Introduction, ix–x.

Medal ordered by Franklin: Loubat, I, 86, and II, Plate 14.

America portrayed as an Indian queen: Loubat, I, 14, and II, Plate 3; I, 28, and II, Plate 5; I, 40, and II, Plate 8; I, 57, and II, Plate 12; I, 115, and II, Plate 20.

Decline of classic imagery, trend to realism: Loubat, I, Introduction, xxiii–xxvi.

Wm. Wilson & Son, involvement in the design of the medal: NA, RG 94, AGO 8847-A (EB) 1882, includes a letter from the War Department to the Wilsons dated Jan. 20, 1862, declining an offer the firm had apparently made on the grounds that "arrangements have already been made to manufacture the 'Medals of Honor' which Congress authorized to be presented." This probably indicates a misdirected application on the part of the Wilsons, for the only medals authorized by Congress up to that time had been those for the Navy, not the War Department. After the legislation authorizing the Army medal had been introduced, Wm. Wilson & Son wrote to Secretary of War Stanton on Feb. 20, 1862 — NA, RG 94, AGO 8847-A (EB) 1882 — saying that they would like to submit a proposition and that they were preparing designs. Then, in a letter from Pollock to Welles, May 6, 1862, NA, RG 104, submitting two designs of which one was the winner, there is this statement: "If not approved, I have particularly to request that they be returned to my address. Those now submitted belong to private parties and will be called for at the Mint if not adopted." On Sept. 30, 1862, Pollock wrote to Welles introducing a Mr. Hinkle of the Wilson firm, who was carrying specimens of the medal to Welles, and in this letter (NA, RG 104) is the phrase, "Messrs. Wilson & Son, who furnished the design for the medal." A similar phrase, "of the firm of Messrs. Wm. Wilson & Son of this city, who furnished the designs for the medal," occurs in another letter from Pollock introducing Mr. Hinkle to Secretary of War Stanton, Oct. 7, 1862, NA, RG, 104.

Christian Schussele: *Dictionary of American Biography*, XVI, 470–471; Wainwright, pp. 65–69; Johnson, *A Sermon Memorial.* The Army book, *The Medal of Honor of the United States Army*, p. 6, credits Schussele with the design of the Medal of Honor. On Oct. 12, 1964, the Treasury Department, U.S. Mint Service, Philadelphia, sent the author copies of its file of correspondence bearing upon the Medal of Honor, mostly from the year 1862. Included was a copy of an "endorsement" of indeterminate nature, dated March 3, 1898, and apparently by the Superintendent of the Philadelphia Mint. On this is noted: "C. Schussle [*sic*], Designer; A. Paquet, Engraver." The author has not been able to find in the National Archives or elsewhere anything in addition which might be considered an original record documenting Schussele's having designed the medal, although he seems to have been an entirely logical person to have done so. Arriving in this country in 1848, Schussele settled in Philadelphia, a great publishing center where color lithography was beginning to flower. He worked with lithographers for a time and it is said that he also did designs for wood engravers. That Schussele embraced his new country with appreciation and affection is evident in his paintings; several are on patriotic and historical American themes. These include "Washington at Valley Forge," "Gen. Jackson Before Judge Hall," "McClellan at

Antietam" and "Home on Furlough." He became an instructor at The Pennsylvania Academy of the Fine Arts in 1868 and died in 1879. The firm of Wm. Wilson & Son went out of business years ago, leaving, so far as can be discovered, no records behind except the few letters and contracts which found their way into Government files.

Discussions of Athena (Minerva): Gayley, pp. 23, 59; Sutherland, P. 45.

Final transactions, Navy medal: The letters mentioned below are in NA, RG 104 1862 correspondence. Welles approved the Navy design in a letter to Pollock, May 9; then Pollock to Welles, May 13, said that the medals in gold would cost $30 to $35 each, in silver $2 to $2.50 each and in bronzed copper about 50¢ — also that the dies would be engraved by A. C. Paquet, assistant engraver of the Mint, and that would cost about $600. Acting Secretary of the Navy Fox wrote to Pollock, May 15, ordering as many of the medals in bronze as the Navy's appropriation of $1,000 would allow. Pollock to Welles, Sept. 30, and Welles to Pollock, Oct. 23, record the fact that Wm. Wilson & Son was assigned to manufacture or procure the attachments for the bronze star, including the ribbon — also the presentation case — and to assemble the complete decorations, all for $1.50 each. Pollock to Welles, Dec. 13, indicates that the cost of the medals was reduced to 35¢ each and the cost of the dies to $500, and that Welles received 175 medals in December for $823.75. Thus it seems clear that the bronze stars — which have since become known as the "Paquet stars" — were struck at the Mint and that the Mint and Wm. Wilson & Son cooperated to manufacture the complete decorations.

Edwin M. Stanton: *Dictionary of American Biography*, XVII, 517–521.

Final transactions, Army medal: Pollock to Stanton, July 14, 1862, NA, RG 104, said in part:

"I deem it proper to inform you that we are preparing a die for a medallic star for the Navy Department. The enclosed photograph will give you an idea of its form and size as well as emblematic devices. . . . The devices do not pertain to either arm of the service, but are emblematic of the struggle in which the nation is now engaged. The medal might therefore be adopted for the Army."

Early in October, a Mr. Hinkle of the firm of Wm. Wilson & Son went to Washington to show Gideon Welles the first specimens of the Navy medal (Pollock to Welles, Sept. 30, 1862, NA, RG 104). Hinkle was armed not only with a letter of introduction from Pollock (Pollock to Stanton, Oct. 7, 1862, NA, RG 104) but with a letter from Thomas A. Scott, first vice-president of the Pennsylvania Railroad (Scott to Stanton, Sept. 30, 1862, NA, RG 94, AGO

8847-A [EB] 1882). A man high in the councils of the mighty, whose assistant was a young fellow named Andrew Carnegie, Scott had been party to the scheme whereby Lincoln was secretly brought into Washington just before his first inaugural, with rail routings shifted, telegraph lines disconnected, the President arriving ahead of the time published by the newspapers and possible assassins thwarted. Scott had also been adviser to the War Department on matters pertaining to the operation of the railroads, so he was not without influence in Washington. (*Dictionary of American Biography*, III, 500–501, and XVI, 500–501.) In his letter to Stanton, Scott recommended the Messrs. Wilson as being "among the most reliable dealers in their line in the Union." The design presented to Stanton by Hinkle followed Pollock's idea for modifying the Navy medal with a different attachment. The bronze star of the Navy medal hung then, as today, from the arms of an anchor, with the ring of the anchor forming a natural attachment for the ribbon, a simple and beautifully appropriate arrangement. In place of the anchor suspension, Hinkle presented a sketch for a holder in the form of a wreath of oak and laurel leaves, with crossed cannon and a drum at the bottom of the wreath. This is described in Pollock to Stanton, Oct. 7, 1862, NA, RG 104, and the sketch is in NA, RG 94, AGO 8847-A (EB) 1882.

The eagle in the sketch resembled a sharp-eyed and somewhat furtive dove, but this is a flaw in its character that probably could have been corrected. However, Stanton would have none of it. He communicated with Senator Henry Wilson of Massachusetts, who had introduced the legislation providing for the Army medal, informing Wilson that he was dissatisfied with everything he had seen and asking if Wilson would undertake the selection and commissioning of an artist to get the decoration designed. Nothing came of this inquiry. Three weeks later the Wilson firm was back with another design which won War Department approval. Their proposal, Wm. Wilson & Son to the War Department, Oct. 30, 1862, NA, RG 94, AGO 8847-A (EB) 1882, read as follows:

"We propose to do the following work on the Medals for the War Department, at the rates annexed, it being understood that the medals are to be struck & furnished by the U.S. Mint from the dies prepared there for the Navy Department, from design furnished by us, and that the die for the attachment for the Army Medal is to be made at the Mint and the attachment holder struck there.

Filing, dressing up & polishing   25 cts. each
    medal

Engraving inscriptions on
    reverse of medal one and
    one half cents a letter.

Dressing up Eagle Military
    emblem holder, and
    attaching same to medal as
    per sample submitted   50 cts. each

Ornamental Ribbon with top
    clasp & pin as per
    specimen submitted   50 cts. each

Morocco case for each medal
    as per sample submitted   35 cts. each
                                1.60

Wm. Wilson & Son"

Assistant Secretary of War Watson to Pollock, Nov. 17, 1862, NA, RG 104, transmitted a copy of the contract entered into on that date with Wm. Wilson & Son and requested "such aid and facilities as they received from you in the preparation of the medals for the Navy Department." The contract signed by Stanton called for delivery by Jan. 15, 1863, of 2,000 Medals of Honor at $2 each. This date was not met, as explained by Pollock to Wm. Wilson & Son, Jan. 6, 1863, NA, RG 94, AGO 8847-A (EB) 1882:

"In consequence of the large amount of work in our Engraving Department incident to the preparation of coining dies for the New Year, it will be impossible to complete the work on the medals for the War Department by the 15th Inst. In addition to engraving the two dies for the attachment, there are in all six thousand separate pieces to be struck and bronzed for the 2000 medals and attachments. I think that the whole order can be completed by the 15th of February."

The Wilsons were able to assemble and ship 1,000 of the decorations by Feb. 13, 1863, according to their letter to the War Department of that date, NA, RG 94, AGO 8847-A (EB) 1882.

Chapter 4: Two Paces Forward

Defenses of Washington, June 30, 1863: Stone, Speech, MS p. 19.

Daniel E. Somes: *Biographical Dictionary of the American Congress*, p. 1631.

Stanton's letter to Somes: Stone, *History*, pp. 34–35.

Somes' visit to the 25th Maine: Libby's diary, entry of June 28, 1863

Col. Francis Fessenden: MeAGR (1864–65), I, 364–366.

Evils of short militia terms: Upton, pp. 4, 6, 10–12, 211–212, 244, 245, 443.

Service of other nine months' regiments: MeAGR (1863), p. 7.

Mutinies of the 2nd Maine: Pullen, pp. 77–80.

Somes' visit to the 27th Maine and initial reaction in the regiment: Bryant's journal, entries of June 29 and 30, 1863.

Dangers of death and imprisonment and concern about the hay crop: Stone, Speech, MS p. 21.

Wentworth's proposal to the regiment and order to take "two paces forward": *Portland Express*, April 26, 1893; Hayes' statement; Bryant's journal, entry of June 30, 1863.

Departure of nonvolunteers: Bryant's journal, entry of June 30, 1863. Maj. John D. Hill was one of the volunteers but was ordered to proceed home with the troops, according to Rand to the Secretary of War, Jan. 19, 1898, NA, RG 94, R & P 380505.

Promise of medals to Wentworth: Maine Civil War Correspondence (Governor's): LXXII, 87.

"We thought little of it . . .": Col. Ainsworth, Chief of the R & P Office, to Maj. Osgood, June 30, 1898, NA, RG 94, R & P 380505, quotes this statement as being in a letter from Rand to the War Department, Jan. 27, 1892.

General Orders No. 195: *General Orders Affecting the Volunteer Force*, p. 138.

About 50,000 men qualified under General Orders No. 195: The Adjutant General to Col. E. A. Parrott, July 9, 1909, NA, RG 94, AGO 1453594

Army forms, morning reports, descriptive book

and lists and muster rolls: Kautz, pp. 12–13, 30–33, 39, 78; *Instructions for Officers of the Adjutant General's Department and Others of Kindred Duties*, pp. 48, 49, 59, 77, 88, 89, with bound-in samples of most of the forms used. Houston, p. 82, mentions the anxiety with which new company clerks approached their first muster rolls.

Hodson's trouble with muster rolls: MeAGR (1864–65), II, Preface, v–vi.

Muster out of 27th Maine: Bryant's journal says they worked on the rolls at Portland from July 7 to July 17. The final record of the 27th, compiled from the muster-out rolls, is given in MeAGR (1863), Appendix D, pp. 748–772

Statements of number of men who remained: Warren's diary, entry for June 30, 1863; Maine Civil War Correspondence (Governor's): LXXII, 87; Hayes' statement; Stone, *History*, pp. 12, 21–30; Acting Secretary of War Meiklejohn to Rand, Jan. 15, 1898, NA, RG 94, R & P 380505

Letter from New England Relief Association: Maine Civil War Correspondence (Governor's): LV, 32.

Exchange of telegrams between Stanton and Gen. Paine: Dates given in text, NA, RG 107, *Telegrams Sent and Received by the Secretary of War.*

Medals authorized by General Orders No. 195 never manufactured: U.S. Senate Document No. 58 (1919), pp. 291–292.

Townsend's message to Potts: Sept. 29, 1864, NA, RG 94, R & P 380505.

Artemus Ward quotation: Browne, p. 431.

Complete muster-out roll used for ordering medals: U.S. Senate Document No. 58 (1919), p. 289.

Price of medal: Contract between the War Department and Wm. Wilson & Son, Aug. 1, 1864, for 8,000 additional medals at $2.50 each.

Chapter 5: They Never Failed to Understand

Bounties for reenlisted veterans: MeAGR (1863), Appendix A, p. 21. For an account of war inflation in Maine see R. H. Stanley and George O. Hall, *Eastern Maine in the Rebellion* (Bangor, Maine, 1887), pp. 184–189.

Wentworth's application for a new command: Maine Civil War Correspondence (Governor's): LVI, 139, 149, 170; (Adjutant General's): Vol. XL (pages unnumbered), letter from Wentworth, Aug. 4, 1863.

New regiments formed in 1863 and commanders: MeAGR (1863), pp. 38–42, and MeAGR (1864–65), I, 306–307, 364–365.

Authorization of the 32nd Maine: Houston, p. 12; MeAGR (1864–65), I, 545–549.

Commissioned officers: Houston, p. 35; MeAGR (1864–65), I, 509, and II, Appendix D, 768. Company officers who had formerly served in the 27th Maine included Capt. Seth

E. Bryant, Isaac P. Fall and Horace H. Burbank and Lts. John G. Whitten and William W. Pierce.

Youthfulness of soldiers: Houston, pp. 46, 47, 456; MeAGR (1864–65), II, Appendix D, 768–788.

Experiences at Camp Keyes: Houston, pp. 37–39.

Departure and trip south: Houston, pp. 56, 60–61; MeAGR (1864–65), I, 294–295.

Joining 2nd Brigade and first marching: Houston, pp. 67, 70, 72–80.

Firing incident at Bristoe Station: Houston, pp. 82–83.

Grant's drive toward Richmond: Swinton, pp. 402–497.

Long marches: MeAGR (1864–65), I, 295.

Proximity to battlefields of the peninsular campaign: Houston, p. 208.

Losses, unhealthy conditions, etc., in the vicinity of Cold Harbor: OR, Series I, Vol. XXXVI, Part 1, pp. 176, 180, 247–248; Houston, pp. 214–243.

Losses of the 32nd Maine by June 10; Maine Civil War Correspondence (Governor's): LXVI, 94. The present whereabouts of the diary which Calvin Hayes kept is unknown. However, Henry Houston had access to it while he was writing his history of the 32nd Maine, and an extracted entry for June 10 appears in Houston, p. 245. Houston notes the arrival of the four companies from Maine on p. 183.

Grant's move to Petersburg: Steele, pp. 512–519.

March of 35 miles: Houston, pp. 254–255, 258–260.

Events of June 15–19: Houston, pp. 256, 271–278; Steele, pp. 512–519; MeAGR (1864–65), I, 295. The attack on the morning of June 17 was upon enemy works near the Shand House.

Preparation and explosion of the mine and attack of the Ninth Corps: Swinton, pp. 518–524; Steele, pp. 520–522; Lykes, pp. 12–22; *Portsmouth Journal of Literature and Politics*, July 30, 1864; *Under the Maltese Cross*, pp. 311–314. One of the best accounts available is that in Catton, pp. 235–253.

Attack of the 32nd Maine and departure of Wentworth for home: *Portland Express*, April 26, 1893; Houston, pp. 346, 362–368, 421. Also recollections of Jessie Hobbs Dunshee as to the nature of Wentworth's wounds.

Extract from Hayes' diary, entry of July 31: Houston, p. 360.

Capt. Burbank's experience: Burbank, p. 11.

Experience of burial parties: Houston, p. 371.

The 32nd Maine after July 30, 1864: MeAGR (1864–65), I, 295–296.

"Honor roll": Army of the Potomac General Orders No. 10, March 7, 1865.

Houston's tribute to the 32nd Maine: Houston, p. 47.

Letter from Lt. Chase: Noted in Maine Civil War Correspondence (Governor's): LXIX, 20, in a letter from Wentworth to the Governor. This letter also expresses Wentworth's intention to return to the Army. The special order for his discharge appears in Governor's Correspondence, LXX, 3.

Wentworth's correspondence with Governor Cony: Maine Civil War Correspondence (Governor's): LXXII, 87. This is a letter from Wentworth to the Governor, Feb. 2, 1865, which refers and replies to a letter Wentworth had received from Cony dated Jan. 30, 1865.

Calvin Hayes' list of volunteers: Frank M. Whitman, past commander of the Medal of Honor Legion, to Col. Ainsworth, Chief of the R & P Office, Feb. 12, 1898, NA, RG 94, R & P 380505, has attached to it a statement and list which, Whitman wrote, he had obtained from a veteran of the 27th Maine. Whitman had lost the last page of the statement, which would have shown the signature of the veteran. However, the statement is from one who identifies himself as the former sergeant major of the 27th Maine and a fellow-townsman and lifelong friend of its colonel; this could be only Calvin Hayes. In the statement Hayes says the list is the one whereby the medals were distributed and that it was loaned to him by the colonel from his papers.

Storage of medals in Augusta and in Wentworth's stable: Erastus Moulton to Maj. Gen. Ainsworth, the Military Secretary, Aug. 22,

1904, NA, RG 94, R & P 380505. Moulton was a sergeant in the 27th Maine. In 1904 he was an officer of the regimental reunion association.

Chapter 6: Let Not Thy Left Hand Know . . .

Stanton's dismissal: *Dictionary of American Biography*, X, 81–90, and XVII, 517 and 521.

Stanton's ordering of 10,000 medals: A memorandum prepared for the Secretary of War by Maj. G. W. Davis, June 8, 1897, NA, RG 94, R & P 489258, says on p. 1, "On March 12, 1863, there were 2,000 purchased under contract from the Secretary of War from Wm. Wilson & Sons of Philadelphia, Pa., at cost of $2.00 each, and in the year 1865, 8,000 additional were bought from the same firm at a cost of $2.50 each." P. 18 of the same memorandum includes a summary up to that date (June 8, 1897) as follows:

Total number of medals manufactured	10,000
Issued and accounted for	2,394
Remaining on hand	7,606

The same memorandum, p. 17½, indicated that 2,291 had been issued through June 8, 1897; this means that 103 were disposed of in some way other than by issue. In 1904, when the design of the medal was changed, there must have been more than 7,000 of the old medals

360

still on hand. There appears to be no record of their disposition. However, U.S. War Department Circular No. 36, Aug. 22, 1904, said in part, "Medals and bowknots of the old design will be destroyed as soon as medals and rosettes of the new design shall have been issued to replace them." While this seems to have applied to the medals turned in by holders of the old decoration, it may also provide a clue to the fate of the 7,000 remaining in stock, or most of them.

Medals issued to President Lincoln's funeral guard: U.S. Senate Document No. 58 (1919), pp. 114, 133.

Dr. Mary E. Walker: Dannett and Jones, pp. 15–16; Poore, p. 457.

Awards during the Indian campaigns: *Report of the Chief of the Record and Pension Office*, p. 10.

Battle of the Little Big Horn awards and effect on policy: *Report of a Board of Officers . . . to Examine and Report Upon Applications . . .* , pp. 17–18.

Awards to Indians: MOHR, pp. 630, 634, 646, 649, 659, 665.

Buffalo Bill's Medal of Honor: Leonard and Goodman, pp. 213–215.

Awards to Asa B. Gardiner, Thomas C. Reed and others under General Orders No. 195: U.S. Senate Document No. 58 (1919), pp. 184, 290–292.

Estimate of 50,000 men qualified under General Orders No. 195: The Adjutant General to Col.

Parrott, July 9, 1909, NA, RG 94, AGO 1453594

Medals issued through 1884: These numbered 1,670 according to the *Report of the Chief of the Record and Pension Office*, p. 13, which shows a table of "Congressional Medals of Honor Tabulated by Calendar Years" to June 30, 1901.

Correspondence with Henry B. Osgood: *Official Army Register* (March, 1891), pp. 378–387; Capt. Osgood to the War Department, Dec. 29, 1891, and Assistant Adjutant General Breck to Osgood, Jan. 5, 1892, NA, RG 94, 19970–PRD–1891.

Fred C. Ainsworth: Although he was a mighty figure in the War Department around the turn of the century, General Ainsworth vanished into historical obscurity after his battle for power with Chief of Staff Leonard Wood and his retirement in 1912. His reappearance has been largely due to Mabel E. Deutrich, Director of the Archival Projects Division, Office of Military Archives at the National Archives in Washington, D.C., whose book *The Struggle for Supremacy* (Public Affairs Press of Washington, 1962) provided the first and only full-length portrait of the controversial soldier-archivist and administrator. Since Ainsworth, in keeping with his reputation for being a behind-the-scenes operator, left practically no personal papers behind, what Dr. Deutrich accomplished in producing her definitive biography is a remarkable work of scholarship giving evidence, in its thoroughness and precision, of her own experience as an archivist. *The Struggle for Supremacy* has provided almost the entire background for the discussions of Ainsworth in this and following chapters, aside from accounts of his dealings with the 27th Maine and the Medal of Honor, which are documented elsewhere in these Notes.

Record and Pension Office and the Medal of Honor: The functions of the R & P Office with respect to the medal are described in the *Report of the Chief of the Record and Pension Office*, p. 13. The first history of the Medal of Honor was prepared under Ainsworth's direction and is also included in this report.

Correspondence with Maine: Adjutant General Kelton to the Adjutant General, Maine, Jan. 16, 1892, and reply, Jan. 21, 1892, NA, RG 94, 19970–PRD–1891.

Correspondence with survivors of 27th Maine: U.S. Senate Document No. 58 (1919), p. 289, makes note of the Adjutant General, War Department, to Rand, Jan. 23, 1892, and Rand to Adjutant General in two letters (no dates) transmitting lists for Companies A and I. NA, RG 94, 19970–PRD–1891, includes Assistant Adjutant General Breck to Moses S. Hurd, Joseph F. Warren, David B. Fullerton, John M. Getchell, Dennis M. Shapleigh, A. O. Smart and Frank A. Hutchins, April 5, 1892, with replies from Hurd (Co. B), April 7; Warren (Co. C), April 12; Getchell (Co. E), April 20;

Shapleigh (Co. G), April 14.

Vote to publish regimental history: Reunion report in *Maine Bugle* (October, 1895).

Rand sends copy of history to the War Department in 1895: Mentioned in Rand to Secretary of War Alger, Dec. 30, 1897, NA, RG 94, R & P 380505.

Note on 27th Maine in circular: U.S. War Department Circular, Oct. 31, 1897.

Rand's 1897–98 correspondence with the War Department: Rand to Secretary of War Alger, Dec. 30, 1897, Acting Secretary of War Meiklejohn to Rand, Jan. 15, 1898, and Rand to the Secretary of War, Jan. 19, 1898; all in NA, RG 94, R & P 380505.

Further correspondence with Osgood: Osgood to the War Department, undated memorandum, evidently 1898, since the reply is Col. Ainsworth, Chief of the R & P Office, to Maj. Osgood, June 30, 1898, NA, RG 94, R & P 380505.

Hayes' statement and list: Attached to Frank Whitman's letter to Col. Ainsworth, Chief of the R & P Office, Feb. 12, 1898, NA, RG 94, R & P 380505. The jacket in which these documents are contained bears a notation: "Col. A. directs that this be filed with the papers of the 27th Maine Inf. without reply. Feb. 14, 1898."

Events at reunions of the 27th Maine: R. J. Libby to the author, Feb. 26, 1963, and March 8, 1963; Alvin W. Curtiss to the author, June 5, 1965.

Medals stored in Augusta and later in Wentworth's stable: Erastus Moulton to Maj. Gen. Ainsworth, the Military Secretary, Aug. 22, 1904, NA, RG 94, R & P 380505. Moulton was an officer in the 27th Maine reunion association and a former sergeant in the regiment.

Vice-Admiral Cobb's recollections: These were kindly made available by his brother Charles and his son Calvin H. Cobb, Jr., in the form of letters written by the Vice-Admiral to Gould Lincoln, April 18, 1960, and to Charles L. Cobb, Oct. 18, 1960.

Wentworth's death: *Portsmouth Daily Chronicle*, July 10 and 13, 1897.

Chapter 7: Wherein the Mouths of Lions Are Stopped

Frank M. Whitman: MOHR, p. 609; Mulholland, p. 395.

Gen. O. O. Howard: Mulholland, pp. 90–95.

Medals awarded through 1866; to 1890; in 1890's: *Report of the Chief of the Record and Pension Office*, pp. 10, 13. This report includes tabulations of awards by calendar years, by states and U.S. organizations and by grades, to June 30, 1901.

Civil War medals: MOHR, p. 361. Considerable reassurance as to the quality of Civil War awards in general may be had by reading the citations in MOHR, pp. 363–620, and the details of cases reviewed by the 1916–17 Medal of Honor Board as reported in U.S. Senate Document No. 58 (1919), pp. 289–478. The statement of the Medal of Honor Board referred to is also in this document, p. 112.

J. C. Julius Langbein: MOHR, p. 493; Legion of Valor, *General Orders*, p. 5.

"Flag awards": Rodenbough, pp. 98, 120, 134, 223, 228–229; MOHR, pp. 363–620; Chamberlain, p. 270.

Private Samuel E. Eddy: MOHR, p. 428.

27th Maine half the Army list in 1890: *Report of the Chief of the Record and Pension Office*, p. 13, indicates 1,705 medals awarded through 1889.

Whitman's 1891 correspondence: Whitman to the Adjutant General, Nov. 18, 1891, and Adjutant General Kelton to Whitman, Dec. 3, 1891; both in NA, RG 94, 19970–PRD–1891.

Effort to get appropriations for medals authorized under General Orders No. 195: Joint resolution introduced in the House of Representatives, Dec. 20, 1895, by Mr. Bingham (*Congressional Record* and *Journal of the House of Representatives*). See also House of Representatives Report No. 1742, 54th Congress, 1st session, May 12, 1896.

New ribbon and rosette for the medal: *Report of the Chief of the Record and Pension Office*, p. 15. *Joint Resolution of Congress*, May 2, 1896. Several of the medals now in the possession of families of the 27th Maine men have the 1896 ribbon.

Amendment of Army Regulations in 1897: *Report of the Chief of the Record and Pension Office*, p. 11.

Whitman's 1898 correspondence: Whitman to Col. Ainsworth, Chief of the R & P Office, Feb. 12, 1898, NA, RG 94, R & P 380505.

Imitation of the Medal of Honor by the G.A.R. and others: U.S. Senate Calendar No. 786 (1904), p. 2.

Authorization of the new medal: Act of Congress, April 23, 1904.

Protest from the Medal of Honor Legion: Typical is that of Horatio C. King, Judge Advocate General of the Medal of Honor Legion, to Secretary of War Taft, Sept. 2, 1904, NA, RG 94, R & P 380505. This document file contains similar letters from other officers of the Legion.

Merger of the Record and Pension Office and the Adjutant General's Office into the Military Secretary's Department: Ordered by another section of the same act of Congress which authorized the new medal, approved April 23, 1904. Later on, by the provisions of an Army appropriations act approved March 2, 1907, the department was named the Adjutant General's Department and Ainsworth became the Adjutant General. See also Deutrich, pp. 83–87.

(*Notice the dates of the correspondence in the following four notes as an instance of Ainsworth's ability to foresee and be prepared for actions af-*

fecting his department. All four are contained in NA, RG 94, R & P 380505.)

Request for opinion: "The New Medal of Honor — to whom shall new medals be issued to replace old medals?" a memorandum from Maj. Gen. Ainsworth, the Military Secretary, to Judge Advocate General Davis, Sept. 12, 1904.

Opinion: Transmitted to Ainsworth by Davis in a memorandum dated Sept. 20, 1904.

Letter from Roosevelt to the Secretary of War: Oct. 8, 1904.

Opinion transmitted to the Secretary of War: Oct. 11, 1904, in a memorandum for the Secretary of War from Ainsworth. This memorandum also had noted on it the concurrence of the Assistant Secretary of War to the Judge Advocate General's opinion. The concurrence of the Secretary of War is on record in several letters, including Taft to Gardner, House of Representatives, March 16, 1905.

Gen. George B. Davis: *Dictionary of American Biography*, V, 115.

The War Department continues to list 27th Maine men: U.S. War Department Circular, Sept. 1, 1904.

Protests by Whitman, 1904–05: Whitman to the Military Secretary, Dec. 27, 1904, and a supplementary letter, not dated, with reply from Ainsworth to Whitman, Jan. 4, 1905, NA, RG 94, R & P 380505.

Whitman's protest to the President: Gardner,

House of Representatives, to Theodore Roosevelt, Feb. 1, 1905; William Loeb, Jr., Secretary to the President, to Taft, Feb. 3, 1905; Taft to Gardner, March 6, 1906; all in NA, RG 94, R & P 380505.

Requirement for turn-in of old medals and subsequent repeal of this provision: U.S. War Department Circular No. 36, Aug. 22, 1904; *Report of the Medal of Honor Legion*, pp. 6–7; Joint Resolution of Congress, Feb. 27, 1907.

Number of surviving veterans: See BRYANT in the Bibliography. This was a report of a 1909 reunion.

Calvin Hayes' new medal and Vice-Admiral Cobb's inquiry to the War Department: Vice-Admiral Calvin H. Cobb to Gould Lincoln, April 18, 1960.

Requests from "volunteers" of other Civil War regiments for medals: Maj. Gen. Ainsworth, the Adjutant General, to George N. Southwick, House of Representatives, April 8, 1907, NA, RG 94, R & P 380505. Ainsworth to James M. Cox, March 25, 1909, and an Adjutant General (name illegible) to Col. Parrott, July 9, 1909, NA, RG 94, AGO 1453594.

The Certificate of Merit: On March 3, 1847, Congress empowered the President to grant this certificate to any private soldier for distinguished service. An act of Feb. 9, 1891, extended the award to all enlisted men including noncommissioned officers. The distinction between Medals of Honor and Certificates of Merit was set forth by the Commanding General of the Army in 1892 as follows:

"Medals of Honor should be awarded to officers or enlisted men for distinguished bravery in action, while certificates of merit should, under the law, be awarded for distinguished service whether in action or otherwise, of a valuable character to the United States, as, for example, extraordinary exertion in the preservation of human life, or in the preservation of public property, or rescuing public property from destruction by fire or otherwise, or any hazardous service by which the Government is saved loss in men or material. Simple heroism in battle, on the contrary, is fitly rewarded by a medal of honor, although such heroism may not have resulted in any benefit to the United States." (See *Report of a Board of Officers Appointed . . . to Examine and Report Upon Applications . . .* , p. 18.)

On Jan. 11, 1905, War Department General Orders No. 4 authorized a badge (medal) to be issued to each holder of the certificate still in service. The Certificate of Merit was abolished by the act of Congress of July 9, 1918, having to do with medals, but this act provided for a Distinguished Service Medal to be issued to holders of the certificate. Later, by an act of Congress approved March 5, 1934, such holders were authorized to exchange their Distinguished Service Medals for Distinguished Service Crosses. The Certificate of Merit had a long and honorable history. The medal which accompanied it for a time (1905–18) was of excellent design: Obverse, a Roman war eagle surrounded by the inscription VIRTUTIS ET AUDACIAE MONUMENTUM ET PRAEMIUM; reverse, FOR MERIT in an oak wreath joined at the bottom by a knot, all in a circle made up of the words UNITED STATES ARMY in the upper half and 13 stars in the lower half. The ribbon: vertical red, white and blue stripes.

Chapter 8: A Fast Shuffle on Capitol Hill

Ainsworth's retirement: Deutrich, pp. 111–122, 132.

Medal of Honor Legion and Sherwood Bill: MOHR, pp. 19–20; *Congressional Record*, July 6, 1914, pp. 11646–11649.

Army and Navy Medal of Honor Roll: Act of Congress, April 27, 1916. The Veterans Administration, Office of General Counsel, provides the following information:

"This Act was amended several times. Presently, sections 560–562, title 38, United States Code (as last amended by Public Law 88–651, October 13, 1964), provide for the Army, Navy, Air Force and Coast Guard Medal of Honor Roll, upon which is recorded, on written application to the Secretary of the Department concerned, the name of each surviving person who has served on active duty in the armed forces of the United States, who has attained the age of 40 years, and who has been awarded a Medal of Honor for distinguishing himself conspicuously by gallantry and intrepidity at the risk of his life above and beyond the call of duty while so serving. Persons whose names are entered on the Medal of Honor Roll who express a desire to receive a special pension are paid $100 a month for life by this agency based on a certificate of entitlement from the department concerned. That benefit is paid from the date of application for entry on the Roll. The law provides that the special pension shall be paid in addition to all other payments under laws of the United States."

Applications by 27th Maine veterans for Medal of Honor Roll: Papers in the possession of Mrs. Winnifred M. Dyer, Eliot, Maine, indicate that Joseph H. Dixon applied unsuccessfully for himself and six others.

Law calling for Medal of Honor investigation: Section 122 of act of Congress, approved June 3, 1916.

Story in the *Army and Navy Journal*: See June 17, 1916, issue.

Draft of defense act and later analysis by the General Staff: U.S. Senate Document No. 447 (1916), pp. 3, 17.

Members of the Medal of Honor Board: U.S. Senate Document No. 58 (1919), pp. 108–109.

General Nelson A. Miles: Mulholland, pp. 196–200; MOHR, p. 516; Legion of Valor, *General Orders*, p. 5.

Incident near the Washita River in 1874: Rodenbough, pp. 276–293; MOHR, pp. 641, 665, 668, 678.

The Board's attempt to secure a modification of Section 122: U.S. Senate Document No. 58 (1919), pp. 110–112, 117; *Congressional Record*, July 26, 1916, p. 11624.

Pertinent extracts from the report of the Medal of Honor Board: U.S. Senate Document No. 58 (1919), pp. 112–117.

Errors in transcribing and printing names and numbers: Comparison of enlistment rolls and other original records in the office of the Maine Adjutant General with the following — U.S. War Department circulars (see the Bibliography); MeAGR (1863), Appendix D, pp. 748–772; U.S. Senate Document No. 58 (1919), pp. 116, 127–132, 141–288; records of the Medal of Honor Board, NA, RG 94, AGO 2411162; and Stone, *History*, pp. 21–30.

George W. Mindil: U.S. War Department Circular of 1904 says that Mindil earned a medal for gallantry in action at Williamsburg, Va., May 5, 1862, while serving as a captain with Co. I, 61st Penna. Inf., and that he was awarded this medal on Oct. 25, 1893.

MOHR, p. 519, gives the citation for this deed, but states that the date of issue was Feb. 10, 1887. This date does not agree with U.S. Senate Document No. 58 (1919), pp. 290–292, which indicates that Feb. 10, 1887, was the date of issue of the medal later rescinded.

The Judge Advocate General's opinion following the report of the board: U.S. Senate Document No. 58 (1919), pp. 113–140.

Indians remaining on the list: MOHR, pp. 621, 624, 630, 634, 646, 648, 649, 652, 659, 665.

Death of Buffalo Bill: *Dictionary of American Biography*, IV, 260–261.

Dr. Mary Walker, still alive: *Dictionary of American Biography*, XIX, 352.

The Adjutant General's correspondence with survivors of the 27th Maine: Memorandum for the Adjutant General from M. A. Watson of the Adjutant General's Office, Feb. 10, 1917; the Adjutant General to the Commissioner of Pensions transmitting a list of 27th Maine veterans, Feb. 20, 1917; reply from the Commissioner of Pensions with notations on the list, March 15, 1917; all in NA, RG 94, AGO 2411162. The estimate of 300 survivors is from a reunion report of that year; see BRYANT in the Bibliography.

Vice-Admiral Calvin H. Cobb's investigation, comment, etc.: Admiral Cobb to Gould Lincoln, April 18 and May 19, 1960.

Chapter 9: "This Sole Remaining Seal of Honor"

Joshua Chamberlain, war and civilian service: *In Memoriam, Joshua Lawrence Chamberlain*, Military Order of the Loyal Legion, Commandery of the State of Maine, Portland, May 6, 1914; Pullen, pp. 98–128; MOHR, p. 401.

Chamberlain quotation: Chamberlain, p. 390.

New Army Medal of Honor legislation: Act of Congress, July 9, 1918.

Civil War applications: Secretary of War Root to W. B. Allison, Chairman, Committee on Appropriations, U.S. Senate, Feb. 15, 1901, NA, RG 94, R & P 92467–R.

Campaign or service medals: Initiated by General Orders No. 4, War Department, Jan. 11, 1905.

Richard E. Byrd, Jr., and Floyd Bennett: MOHR, pp. 361, 809.

Charles A. Lindbergh: MOHR, pp. 171, 361.

Adolphus W. Greely: MOHR, pp. 361, 811; *New York Times*, Oct. 21, p. 19.

William C. Mitchell: MOHR, pp. 13, 361, 965; *New York Times*, July 26, 1947, and March 28, 1948.

Unknown Soldiers: MOHR, pp. 25–26, 813–815.

Basis of Navy Medals of Honor awards: Acts of Congress of March 3, 1901, and March 3, 1915, authorized Medals of Honor for the Navy, Marine Corps and Coast Guard for heroism in battle or "line of profession." An act of Feb. 4, 1919, established a new Medal of Honor for persons in the naval service, to be awarded for combat action only; this was designed in the form of a cross. This same act of 1919 established Distinguished Service Medals and Navy Crosses. An act of Aug. 7, 1942, abolished the cross-type Medal of Honor and restored dual status to the old 1862 medal — that is to say, both combat and "line of profession." For noncombat Navy awards see MOHR, pp. 104, 138, 158, 180, 184, 204, 211, 809, 810, 811. For a "line of profession" award in World War II, see MOHR, pp. 864–865, the case of Owen Hammerberg who won the Medal of Honor for heroism in a diving operation at Pearl Harbor, Feb. 17, 1945. The words "in the line of his profession" are also used in the citation of Peter Tomich, MOHR, p. 946, although he was in a combat situation at Pearl Harbor, Dec. 7, 1941:

"Although realizing that the ship was capsizing, as a result of enemy bombing and torpedoing, Tomich remained at his post in the engineering plant of the U.S.S. Utah, until he saw that all boilers were secured and all fireroom personnel had left their stations, and by so doing lost his own life."

Number of medals awarded by different services: MOHR, p. 361, plus award to Army Capt. Roger H. C. Donlon in 1964 for gallantry in Vietnam. Evidently, in this MOHR tabulation, the Army total includes awards of the Army medal to Lindbergh, to Greely, to eight unknown soldiers (see MOHR, pp. 809–815) and to six members of the Marine Corps for acts in World War I; five of these Marines also received Navy Medals of Honor, which are included in the Marine Corps total. (See MOHR, pp. 780, 786, 787, 794, 795, 798.)

Awards for falling on grenades: MOHR, pp. 229–306, 816–965.

Daniel A. J. Sullivan: Ens. USS *Christabel*, May 21, 1918. (MOHR, pp. 798–799.)

Fred W. Stockham: Gunnery Sgt., 6th Regt., U.S. Marine Corps, in Bois-de-Belleau, France, June 13–14, 1918. (MOHR, p. 798).

Howard W. Gilmore: Cmdr., U.S. Navy, USS *Growler* in Southwest Pacific, Jan. 10–Feb. 7, 1943. (MOHR, p. 858.)

Herbert F. Christian: Pvt., 15th Inf., 3rd Inf. Div., near Valmontone, Italy, June 2–3, 1944. (MOHR, p. 834.)

Henry E. Erwin: S/Sgt., 52nd Bomb. Squad., 29th Bomb. Gp., 20th AF, over Koriyama, Japan, April 12, 1945. (MOHR, pp. 140–141.)

Samuel Woodfill: 1st Lt., 60th Inf., 5th Div., at Cunel, France, Oct. 12, 1918. (MOHR, p. 803.)

Clarence B. Craft: Pfc., 382nd Inf., 96th Inf. Div., on Hen Hill, Okinawa, May 31, 1945. (MOHR, pp. 127–128.)

Lewis L. Millett: Capt., 27th Inf., vicinity of Soam-Ni, Korea, Feb. 7, 1951. (MOHR, p. 274.)

Quote from a Civil War soldier: Rodenbough, *Uncle Sam's Medal of Honor*, p. 81; the soldier was Sgt. Charles H. Fasnacht of the 99th Penna., later a lieutenant. Citation in MOHR, p. 434.

Edward H. O'Hare: Lt., U.S. Navy, section leader of Fighting Squad. Three, USS *Lexington*, Southwest Pacific, Feb. 20, 1942. (MOHR, pp. 912–913.)

Charles E. Kelly: Cpl., 143rd Inf., 36th Inf. Div., near Altavilla, Italy, Sept. 13, 1943. (MOHR, pp. 165–166.) Method of arming mortar shells discussed in *Infantry Journal* (July, 1944), pp. 53–54. (Includes a reprint of an article in the Algiers edition of *The Stars and Stripes*, April 24, 1944)

Beaufort T. Anderson: T/Sgt., 381st Inf., 96th Inf. Div., on Okinawa, April 13, 1945. (MOHR, pp. 102–103.)

Lloyd L. Burke: 1st Lt., 5th Cav., 1st Cav. Div., near Chongdong, Korea, Oct. 28, 1951. (MOHR, p. 235.)

250, 150, 105 enemy deaths caused by Medal of Honor recipients: MOHR, pp. 265, 273, 898.

Bernard J. Ray: 1st Lt., 8th Inf., 4th Inf. Div., Hürtgen Forest near Schevenhutte, Germany, Nov. 17, 1944. (MOHR, pp. 925–926.)

Lloyd H. Hughes: 2nd Lt., 9th AF, Ploesti Raid, Rumania, Aug. 1, 1943. (MOHR, p. 872.)

William E. Barber: Capt., U.S. Marine Corps, 7th Marines, 1st Marine Div., in Chosin Reservoir area, Korea, Nov. 28–Dec. 2, 1950. (MOHR, pp. 230–231.)

Posthumous awards in Korean War: MOHR, pp. 229–306, 361.

Proposed medals for Eisenhower and Pershing: MOHR, p. 336.

Criticisms of medals: *Reports of the National Commission of Fine Arts: 1920 Report*, pp. 28, 32, and 1921 *Report*, p. 72.

Navy Medal of Honor, changes through the years: Mendel L. Peterson's article "The Navy Medal of Honor" in *The Numismatist* (June, 1950) provides an excellent brief account with illustrations.

Air Force design: *The Airman, Official Magazine of the U.S. Air Force* (Sept., 1965).

Two-thirds of medals have had old-style star: MOHR p. 361.

The Congressional Medal of Honor Grove: In addition to the regional areas mentioned, there will also be an area for recipients of unidentified origin and possibly one for the Philippines. Next to the archives building will be a large statue of George Washington kneeling in prayer. Aiding Freedoms Foundation in this project are several patriotic associations, including the Congressional Medal of Honor Society and the General Federation of Women's Clubs, which has conducted a nationwide campaign to raise part of the necessary funds. It is the intent to have the Policy Committee of the Grove permanently made up of current or former members of the Joint Chiefs of Staff. General Dwight D. Eisenhower is honorary chairman of Freedoms Foundation. Plans for the Grove and purchase of the land were initiated by Dr. Kenneth D. Wells, president of Freedoms Foundation. The land for the Medal of Honor Grove, which brings the total Freedoms Foundation area to 100 acres, was dedicated Oct. 1, 1964.